THE SOCRATIC PARADOX
AND ITS ENEMIES

THE
SOCRATIC
PARADOX
AND
ITS ENEMIES

ROSLYN WEISS

THE UNIVERSITY OF CHICAGO PRESS

Chicago and London

Roslyn Weiss is the Clara H. Stewardson Professor of Philosophy
at Lehigh University. She is the author of *Socrates Dissatisfied* (1998)
and *Virtue in the Cave* (2001).

The University of Chicago Press, Chicago 60637
The University of Chicago Press, Ltd., London
© 2006 by The University of Chicago
All rights reserved. Published 2006
Printed in the United States of America

15   14   13   12   11   10   08   07   06   1   2   3   4   5

ISBN: 0-226-89172-0 (cloth)

Library of Congress Cataloging-in-Publication Data

Weiss, Roslyn.
    The socratic paradox and its enemies / Roslyn Weiss.
        p.   cm.
    Includes bibliographical references and index.
    ISBN 0-226-89172-0 (cloth : alk. paper)
        1. Socrates 2. Plato. 3. Ethics. 4. Intentionality (Philosophy)
    5. Philosophy, Ancient I. Title.
    B317.W45 2006
    183′.2—dc22

                                          2005020954

♾ The paper used in this publication meets the minimum requirements
    of the American National Standard for Information Sciences—
Permanence of Paper for Printed Library Materials, ANSI Z39.48-1992.

For my S-D

The piecemeal engineer will . . . adopt the method of searching for, and fighting against, the greatest and most urgent evils of society, rather than searching for, and fighting for, its greatest ultimate good.

Karl Popper, *The Open Society and Its Enemies*

CONTENTS

ACKNOWLEDGMENTS

This book was made possible by a number of foundations and institutions. I acknowledge with gratitude a summer stipend from the National Endowment for the Humanities (2001), a Laurance S. Rockefeller Fellowship from Princeton University's Center for Human Values, where I spent the academic year 2002–3, a sabbatical leave granted by my home institution, Lehigh University, and the ongoing support provided by the Clara H. Stewardson Chair.

I wish to thank my colleagues in the Department of Philosophy at Lehigh University for the constructive criticism they offered on an early draft of the manuscript during our faculty seminar in the fall of 2003. Participants in the seminar included Robert Barnes, Gordon Bearn, Mark Bickhard, Robin Dillon, Barbara Frankel, Steven Goldman, Alexander Levine, and Michael Mendelson.

I had the privilege of presenting papers on various aspects of this book in the following venues: Conference of the Israel Society for the Promotion of Classical Studies, Hebrew University (2002), Ben-Gurion University (2002), Tel-Aviv University (2002), St. Francis College (2003), University of Louvain (2003), Bar-Ilan University (2004), Agnes Scott College (2004), University of Georgia (2004), and the Seventh International Symposium Platonicum, Würzburg (2004). I am most grateful for having had the opportunity to benefit from critical responses to my work in progress.

The following journals graciously granted permission to reprint revised versions of my published articles: *Ancient Philosophy* ("Hedonism in the *Protagoras* and the Sophist's Guarantee," vol. 10 [1990], pp. 17–39; "Killing, Confiscating, and Banishing at *Gorgias* 466–468," vol. 12 [1992], pp. 299–315); *Classical Quarterly* ("*Ho Agathos* as *Ho Dunatos* in Plato's *Hippias Minor*," vol. 31 [1981], pp. 287–304), by permission of Oxford University Press; and *Scripta Classica Israelica* ("Two Related Contradictions in *Laws* IX," vol. 22 [2003], pp. 43–65). Oxford University Press permitted publication of a revised version of parts of chapter 1 of my book *Virtue in the Cave: Moral Inquiry in Plato's "Meno"* (New York, 2001).

I wish to thank Professors Arlene Saxonhouse of the University of Michigan and John Ferrari of the University of California, Berkeley, for their careful reading of the manuscript and most helpful comments.

1

INTRODUCTION:
THE FIGHT FOR JUSTICE

The notorious Socratic paradox "no one does wrong willingly"[1] is not a re-
grettable curiosity of Socratic moral psychology.[2] It is, rather, Socrates'
weapon of choice for taking on the enemies of justice,[3] men who believe that
might makes right, that virtue is power, that for one person to succeed others
must fail,[4] that pleasure, wealth, and dominance are the genuine human goods

1. How one chooses to render *hekōn* or *boulomenos* when it appears in the Socratic paradox tends
to reflect how one understands the paradox. Some translate "deliberately" or "intentionally." Those
who use "willingly" or "voluntarily" may be suggesting that Plato's Socrates is metaphysically committed to something called a "will." Although I most frequently use "willingly," I do not mean to
burden it with any such metaphysical baggage. As I understand the paradox its sense is that in doing
wrong one fails to achieve the truly good life that all people want. I avoid "intentionally" and "deliberately" because, as the ensuing discussion makes clear, it is precisely those who do wrong
intentionally or deliberately who, in Socrates' view, do not act willingly.

2. All references to Socrates are to the Socrates who is a character in Plato's dialogues. That he
bears some resemblance to the historical Socrates is undeniable and important. Yet it is with the
character Socrates—with his conception of philosophy, with his arguments, with his tactics and
antics, with his beliefs, preoccupations, and questions—that this book is concerned.

3. Socrates need not regard the men he challenges as personal enemies. See *Rep.* 6.498d, where
Socrates says to Adeimantus: "Don't make trouble between Thrasymachus and me, now that we've
just become friends. Not that we were enemies before, of course."

4. Sophistic *aretē* is, as Adkins (1973, 4–5; see also 1960, 7) puts it, competitive rather than cooperative, a mark of distinction rather than parity.

and that moderation, justice, and piety are marks of the weak and stupid. As depicted in Plato's dialogues, these men come in all varieties: some are rude and offensive, others genteel and respectful, some are boastful, others diffident. But insofar as they are enemies of justice Socrates' aim with respect to all of them is the same: to expose the moral bankruptcy of their views in any way he can. His intent is not to harm but to benefit, to root out the decay before it rots not only the souls of these men but the very fabric of Athenian society.

Who Is Socrates?

Plato's Socrates is a fighter. His interest lies not in propagating novel views on human choice and decisionmaking, but in arousing, provoking, confronting, and combating those who are either complacent or overconfident in their moral beliefs.[5] Most of all, however, Socrates takes it as his task to challenge the beliefs of those who would stand in the way of justice. The images of himself that Socrates regards as particularly apt—the *Apology*'s gadfly (30a) and the *Meno*'s stingray (80a, c)—are adversarial ones.[6] Socrates often uses military metaphors to characterize his activities: he remains at the post where the god had stationed him, risking his life in the examination of himself and others (*Ap.* 28d–29a); he "fights for the just" (*Ap.* 32a1); he "will fight all-out, in word and deed," for the worth of searching for what is not yet known (*Meno* 86b–c); he "rallies the retreating and defeated [troops]" to combat misology (*Phaedo* 89a), and "fights back" to defeat the argument of Simmias and Cebes (89c). He believes that "we all must be lovers of victory in regard to knowing what is true and what is false concerning the things we are talking about" (*Gorg.* 505e).[7] Indeed, the term Socrates favors for his philosophical practice—*exetazein,* ex-

---

5. One advantage of not saddling Socrates with psychological innovations such as the intellectualized approach to virtue is that it frees Plato from the "developmentalist hypothesis," that is, from the view either that he changed his own mind or that he supplanted Socratic views with "Platonic" ones.

6. Even the *Theaetetus*'s midwife image is not unequivocally benign: Socrates' young men are said to bolt before their "delivery" is complete (150d–e), and at times to suffer severe labor pains. And Socrates is as apt to "deliver" them of false beliefs as of true.

7. See also *Rep.* 1.335e, 4.427e, 5.453a, 7.534c, 9.580a–c, 583a–b, 10.608b–c, 612b–d, 613b–614a, 621b–d; *Laws* 5.731a.

amination—is a military one signifying the review and mustering of troops.[8] Moreover, the elenchus, Socrates' unrelenting rapid-fire question-and-answer means of exchange, is polemical to its core.[9] The more sober characterizations of Socrates (such as Aristotle's, for example) include among the things for which he is noteworthy the introduction into philosophy of the search for definition and the use of inductive argument.[10] But such sober characterizations miss their mark. For although Aristotle is right to note that Socrates searches for definitions and uses inductive arguments, their strategic value is lost on him.[11] If Socrates searches for definitions he does so less because he is enamored of them than because his deceptively innocuous definitional questions

8. See Burnet 1924, 96; Goldman 2004, 3.

9. See Blundell 1992, 133: "Socrates does not just refute arguments, he refutes people." See also *Prot.* 333c: "though it may turn out that both I who question and you who answer are equally under scrutiny." That Socrates so frequently (*Crito* 49c11–d1; *La.* 193c; *Prot.* 331c; *Gorg.* 495a7–9, 500b; *Rep.* 1.346a, 350e5) demands of his interlocutor that he "say what you believe" (Vlastos 1983) signals Socrates' determination to examine not just beliefs but the people who hold them. It is important to recognize, however, that, strictly speaking, Socrates does not "refute" the views he examines. For, first, elenchus proceeds on premises that are provisional and may be withdrawn at any time and, second, Socrates' rhetorical ends require on occasion that he forgo logical rigor. But even when an interlocutor's view is not actually refuted, there is a sense in which the interlocutor himself is: he is shown to be unable to sustain his view without contradiction; he forfeits his warrant to hold it. As we shall see, Socrates' aims in argument vary with the interlocutor. When conversing with a pompous fool, Socrates might attempt to do no more than confound him. With more astute and more dangerous opponents, he might seek to uncover inconsistencies in their belief set, compelling them to relinquish—at least for the moment and in words—the more morally suspect of their beliefs. With interlocutors who conceal their true beliefs behind a façade of allegiance to conventional views, he might try, by way of argument, to expose their insincerity. Generally speaking, Socrates will elicit and then attack in whatever way is effective the views he finds morally repugnant. Note that *elenchein,* often translated simply as "refute," has a range of meaning that includes to test or examine or question as well as to disgrace, put to shame, dishonor, reprove, or reproach.

10. See Aristotle, *Met.* I.vi.987a32–b12 and XIII.iv.1078b17–30. These characterizations are not ones that Socrates can be found applying to himself in Plato's dialogues. According to Socrates, what he does is examine himself and others, and challenge anyone who claims to care for virtue and to have acquired it. He does not deny, however, that he talks frequently about cobblers, cooks, and the like (see *Gorg.* 491a–b). Although Aristotle says on occasion that it is the "Socrates in Plato" to whom he refers, perhaps implying that on other occasions it is the historical Socrates on whom he is reporting, it is likely that on all occasions the Socrates he refers to is the one he has learned about from Plato's writings.

11. Aristotle takes these practices to reflect Socrates' interest in identifying the starting point, the *archē,* of science.

loosen the tongues of his interlocutors who realize only too late in the process of venturing and then refining their definitions that they have displayed their ineptitude as thinkers and their shallowness as men. And if Socrates employs inductive arguments he does so less because he believes them to be sound than because they work: his interlocutors are for the most part easily seduced by their superficial plausibility. Moreover, arguments of this kind have, on occasion, the added benefit of exposing the interlocutors' pomposity: it is often over their objections and to their dismay that Socrates drags them into discourse about the likes of cobblers, weavers, cooks, and cleaners.

Socrates is a man on a mission. It is a mission that is divine in the sense that matters most, namely, that it serves the sacred purposes of seeking truth, promoting justice, and improving the lives of people. But he is not in the first instance a purveyor or teacher of innovative and idiosyncratic psychological notions. Professing to be no one's teacher (*Ap.* 19d, 33b), disavowing wisdom (*Ap.* 21b), claiming for himself only the "human" wisdom that is the recognition that one lacks wisdom (*Ap.* 23b),[12] Socrates practices a philosophy that is primarily therapeutic in intent: his overarching aim is to eradicate the false beliefs and puncture the bloated self-image of others.

The Paradoxes

If Socrates operates in what is essentially combat mode, his more startling views will be misconstrued unless they are interpreted as attacks on the views of others.[13] But surely, it will be said, Socrates believes that virtue is knowledge, that all the virtues are one, that no one does wrong willingly. Is he not an intellectualist about virtue, an egoist, a eudaimonist?[14] Does he not advo-

---

12. See *Lysis* 218a, where the philosopher is someone who *has* ignorance but nevertheless is not actually ignorant, that is, he has not become his ignorance. What distinguishes the person who has ignorance but is not quite ignorant from the person who actually *is* ignorant is that the former, but not the latter, is still able to see his own ignorance. Those whose ignorance has, as it were, seeped into their very identity are blind to their own ignorance and hence egregiously stupid and wicked.

13. See Villa (2001) who argues for a minimalist Socrates, the essence and sum of whose teachings is "don't do injustice." He calls Socrates' approach "negative" and "dissolvent."

14. A person is said to be a eudaimonist if but one consideration guides his choices: whether or not they will further his own happiness. One can also be a eudaimonist at the level of theory: one can hold the view that all rational pursuits are—and ought to be—directed toward the

cate remedial rather than retributive punishment? Does he not, at the very least, deny *akrasia*?[15]

To pose such questions, to ask what are the peculiar and idiosyncratic beliefs to which Socrates subscribes, is already to set off on the wrong foot. If there is to be any hope of discerning Socrates' intent, the question with which to begin is: what is it in the beliefs of others that provokes Socrates to take and often vigorously to defend in Plato's dialogues the extreme and jarring positions for which he has become known?[16] If Socrates is agonistic to the core, then what he says and how outrageously he says it cannot be properly appreciated apart from his targets and the dangers he thinks they pose. Socrates does not, after all, deliver lectures before large audiences in an attempt to convert as many people as possible to his distinctive platform; what he does is confront a series of interlocutors. It is what the individual interlocutor says or what he stands for that prompts the Socratic responses that have come frequently to be regarded as Socratic doctrine, that is, as a set of beliefs that originate, unprovoked, with him.

Once Socratic views come to be seen as Socrates' reactions against his opponents' views—in other words, as negations of those views—it will become possible to revisit the prevailing interpretations that make his paradoxes appear naïve and implausible. It will become possible to see Socrates' paradoxes—"no one does wrong willingly," "virtue is knowledge," and "all the virtues are one"—not as representing his own bizarre account of the inner workings of the human soul but instead as offering in each instance an alternative to, that is, a view that runs *para* (counter to), a particular contemporary *doxa* (belief or opinion). What will make Socrates' paradoxes paradoxical, then,

---

agent's own happiness. The only sense in which Socrates might be said to be a eudaimonist is insofar as he believes that all men wish to be happy and not wretched.

15. *Akrasia* is most frequently translated "weakness of will" or "incontinence," and signifies a lack of self-discipline. To deny *akrasia* is to hold that people always do what they think best, that they are never induced by strong desires or emotions to act in opposition to their self-interest as they see it.

16. Even without sophists on the scene, Socrates would surely have no dearth of work to do. There would still be Euthyphros and Critos and an array of immoral men in positions of authority who need to be defied. What I argue here, however, is (1) that the moral urgency of Socrates' mission is ratcheted up by the pervasive influence of sophists and rhetoricians on Athenian society, and (2) that their presence and their intellectual influence bear much of the responsibility for provoking the views that have come to be known as "Socratic paradoxes."

will not be that they are counterintuitive but rather that they oppose *doxai* that Socrates regards as moral hazards.

Are the Paradoxes Socratic?

Apart from the consideration that the views of an agonistic thinker are best interpreted as reactions against the views he combats, there are in addition several other reasons to doubt that Socrates subscribes to his paradoxes on their common interpretation.

First, Socrates' relentless and unwavering demand of people that they always do what is right, that they refrain from injustice no matter what (see *Crito* 49b; *Rep.* 1.335e), argues against his presumed belief that people cannot do other than what they regard as in their own best interest. Indeed, what Socrates says is that "in no way do we say that injustice ought to be done *willingly* (*hekontas*)" (*Crito* 49a4), suggesting that intentional injustice is precisely what most people regularly do, can certainly help doing, and ought not to do.[17]

Second, Socrates' selflessness as manifest not only in his neglect of his own affairs and the affairs of his family to the extent that he lives in dire poverty (*Ap.* 23b–c; 31b–c) but also in his spending his days "being a busybody in private," caring for others like a father or older brother all the while making himself hated, seems incompatible with any ordinary sense of egoism or eudaimonism.[18] No typical egoist or eudaimonist would be willing, as Socrates is, to live a just life while being thought to be unjust and suffering greatly as a consequence (*Gorg.* 508c–e; *Rep.* 2.361b–d). Whereas there can be little doubt that Socrates is about as "happy" as a human being can be, and that he chooses the path that alone, in his estimation, guarantees happiness, what strains credulity, in light of how Socrates lives, is that what motivates him is self-

17. One way to interpret "no one does wrong willingly" is as asserting that when one does wrong one is unaware that the wrongdoing is harmful to oneself. Such an interpretation, however, makes the exhortation not to do injustice willingly silly: what point is there in demanding of people that they refrain from doing injustice for as long as they think injustice harmful to themselves, when, on this interpretation of the paradox, that is precisely what everyone does anyway?

18. Vlastos (1991, 177) speaks of the "egocentricity which is endemic in Socratic eudaimonism, as in all eudaimonism." In Vlastos's view, Socrates associates with others for the sake of his own advancement toward truth; his self-absorption is relieved only by his divine service that requires of him that he tend to others. In my view, Socrates expects no benefit or at most only the most marginal benefit from his association with others. It is he who benefits them.

interest, that what drives him is a determination to achieve his own happiness.[19] It seems more appropriate to characterize Socrates as a *dikaiosunist*, if I may coin a term. His first and perhaps only consideration when acting is justice (*Ap.* 32a6–7; *Ap.* 33a1–3; *Crito* 48d1–5; *Gorg.* 522b9–c1). If Socrates is happy it is only because happiness is not in his view some separate (and higher) good that is achieved by living justly; for Socrates living justly is not, as it were, the price one pays for attaining happiness. Rather, to live justly, he thinks, simply is to live well, and to live unjustly to be wretched (*Crito* 47b; *Gorg.* 470e; *Meno* 73a–b; *Rep.* I. 353e10–354a4).[20] In Socrates' lexicon "happiness" is an adverb; it is the "well" in how one lives.

Third, when Socrates speaks approvingly of himself,[21] what he fairly boasts of is that *he* never does injustice intentionally (see *Ap.* 37a5–6; *Gorg.* 488a2–3).[22] Never doing wrong intentionally is for him a mark of distinction—not a

---

19. See *Laws* 5.731d–e, where it is said of one who loves himself excessively that he cannot see what is just and noble and cannot, therefore, benefit himself. Indeed, such love of self "is the cause of all men's wrongdoings on every occasion." Another way to put this point is that if one pursues one's own happiness, the true happiness that is justice is likely to elude one.

20. Socrates does say that if one wishes to be happy one must pursue and practice justice and temperance (*Gorg.* 507c–d), and that those who are happy are happy through possessing justice and temperance and those who are wretched are wretched through possessing wickedness (*kakia* [*Gorg.* 508b1–2]). Nevertheless, happiness need not be a state separate from the justness and temperance that guarantee it. See White 1990, 122: "virtue is not a means to the good that we are to pursue; it is that good itself"; also 126: "to possess goodness of soul is the same thing as to be happy"; and 127: Socrates does not intend "to convey that goodness is distinct from happiness and the cause of happiness." See also Allen 1984, 225.

21. Socrates thinks he is a good man. See *Ap.* 28a8–b1: "This has convicted many *other* good men, too"; *Ap.* 41d1: "nothing bad can happen to a good man"; *Gorg.* 521b5–6: "it would be a wicked man doing this to a good man."

22. In the *Gorgias* passage cited (though not at 509e5–6), Socrates uses the term *examartanein* for wrongdoing, a term that, along with its cognate *hamartanein*, is frequently rendered "to err," that is, to *go* wrong rather than to do wrong. Indeed, it is a common misconception that the Socratic paradox is "no one errs (*hamartanei*) willingly" (see, e.g., Penner 1997, 118; Kraut 1992, 535, where the relevant index entry reads, "involuntariness of error"; Saunders 1987, 24; Flew 1973, 24). In fact, however, the most frequent formulation of the paradox contains *adikein* rather than *hamartanein* or *examartanein*, and even when *hamartanein* or *examartanein* does appear, it is virtually always coupled with other terms (e.g., *aischron* and *adikon*) that remove all ambiguity. (In the *Gorgias* passage cited, *Gorg.* 488a2–3, Socrates' *mē orthōs prattō* ["I am acting incorrectly"] executes that purpose.) Only when these terms appear alone do they mean "go wrong" or "err." In the *Protagoras*, for example, where *examartanein* appears by itself at 357d4 and d5, it refers to a going wrong in the measuring of pleasure and pain, a failure due to ignorance. At *Rep.* 1.336e, where *hamartanein* appears alone, Socrates assures Thrasymachus that *errors* made previously in the discussion were unintentional. And at *Rep.* 9.589c6, where *hamartanei* appears alone, the reference is to someone

universal human trait. It is the just man, not every man, who scrupulously avoids injustice and wishes to harm no one (*Ap.* 28b5–9; *Gorg.* 460c3; *Rep.* 1.335d11; cf. Aristotle, *EN* IV.ix.1128b28–29: "but the decent man [*epieikēs*] never willingly does bad things").

No One Does Wrong Willingly

Of course, Socrates does say that no one does wrong willingly (*Gorg.* 509e5–6). And he says many other things that are rather close to it (including the notorious "denial of *akrasia*" at *Prot.* 358b–d). But before we can determine if these are views to which Socrates subscribes, and in what sense he does or does not subscribe to them, we need to ask both what they mean and what purpose they serve in context. Not every Socratic utterance is a Socratic view, and not every Socratic utterance that *is* a Socratic view means what it seems to mean.[23]

An adequate answer to the question of what Socrates means by his paradoxical utterances requires, then, nothing less than a full investigation of all the places within the Platonic corpus where these views are found. Such an investigation—especially with respect to the most puzzling of the paradoxes, "no one does wrong willingly"—occupies almost the whole of this book. Nevertheless, a partial answer may be suggested at the outset.

It is noteworthy that the Socratic paradox "no one does wrong willingly" is featured prominently in those dialogues in which the interlocutors are sophists, rhetoricians, or students of rhetoricians.[24] We find it most starkly in the *Gorgias*. It is hinted at (or seems to be hinted at) in the *Hippias Minor*. The *Protagoras* takes it down the distinctive path of the denial of *akrasia*. And the *Meno* argues for some form of it. (The paradox also appears briefly in the *Timaeus* and more centrally in the *Laws*. In the *Timaeus* the paradox does not seem to be aimed at anyone in particular. In the *Laws* it is aimed at the many and not at a specific individual but, then again, its advocate is not Socrates but

---

who disparages justice and needs to be persuaded because he does not willingly err—that is, he does not willingly suffer a lapse in understanding. None of these is a case, however, in which wrong*doing* is reduced to mere going wrong.

23. The paradoxes have a gnomic character, and it is a safe bet that they, like oracles, do not mean what they seem to mean.

24. It is not unlikely that the portrayals in the dialogues of prominent sophists and rhetoricians are Platonic caricatures and not faithful historical representations.

the Athenian stranger.) That the paradox makes its appearance for the most part just when Socrates confronts sophists and rhetoricians strongly suggests that it is not ab initio a Socratic view but that it arises as a pointed response to sophistic views. Notice also the conspicuous absence of Socratic paradoxes in the *Apology* and *Crito*, dialogues in which the character Socrates confronts is neither a sophist nor someone who has been influenced by sophists. Indeed, the passage in the *Apology* that is frequently cited as containing the "no one does wrong willingly" paradox (*Ap.* 25d–26a) actually contends not that no one does wrong willingly but that some do and others (Socrates among them) do not.[25] For the former, says Socrates, punishment is appropriate, but for the latter, instruction is. It is because Socrates corrupts the young unintentionally (that is, meaning them no harm but intending their benefit alone)—if indeed he corrupts them at all—that he deserves, as he maintains, not public punishment but private instruction.[26]

Furthermore, each occasion of the paradox's appearance is different from the others. This is hardly surprising so long as Socrates is seen to be wielding the paradox in the war he wages against a variety of opponents. Insofar as the belief he combats is different in each case, it is to be expected that he will use a different version of his paradox in each case.[27]

In seeking to understand the Socratic paradox, scholars have tended to look

25. Socrates uses "willingly" in this instance in its quite ordinary sense to mean intentionally.

26. Socrates' point here, at *Ap.* 25e6–26a1, is importantly different from a similar point he makes at *Ap.* 37a5–6 and *Gorg.* 488a2–3. Whereas in the latter two passages he asserts that he is a good man and therefore does not do injustice intentionally, in the first passage he claims that he is sufficiently streetwise to appreciate the foolhardiness of corrupting those with whom he associates. See *Prot.* 327b, where Protagoras observes that the reason everyone teaches everyone *aretē* is because they all recognize that bad men harm their associates. See also *Lysis* 214b–c: "We think that the closer one wicked man gets to another wicked man and the more he associates with him, the more he becomes hated by him, because he wrongs him; and it is, of course, impossible for wronger and wronged to be friends." Cf. *Laws* 5.728b–c: "the gravest of the so-called 'judicial penalties' for wrongdoing . . . is to become similar to men who are wicked. . . . He who grows similar in nature to such people must necessarily do and suffer what such men by their natures do and say to one another." If, Socrates thinks, he *had* foolishly corrupted others intentionally, it would have been appropriate to punish him, his foolishness notwithstanding. A foolish act, then, can be an intentional one and, when intentional, blameworthy.

27. I do not mean to suggest that Socrates' opponents differ radically from one another. As Socrates sees them, sophists and rhetoricians are more alike than they are different (see *Gorg.* 465c, 520a). And although some of these figures (the ones Adkins [1960, 232–35] calls "immoralists") are more outspokenly anticonventional than others, all sell the verbal skills that promise the same thing: power and political prominence.

to what is common to all the places where it appears rather than to what is distinctive in each. But such a procedure can only obfuscate the paradox's meaning if on each occasion the paradox reacts to a particular interlocutor within a unique context—to what he says, to his presumed expertise, to his hypocrisy, to his hubris. The views that history has irrevocably affixed to Socrates' name (perhaps taking its cue from the flat-footed interpretations of an Aristotle deliberately deaf to conversational nuance)[28] need to be examined again, afresh, in context, and the truth about them exposed. The infamous denial of *akrasia* is a case in point. Socrates denies *akrasia* only once—in the *Protagoras.* Nowhere else—not in the *Gorgias,* not in the *Hippias Minor,* not in the *Meno*—does he insist that it is impossible for a person to act against his or her better judgment; nowhere else, in other words, does he pretend that people are perfectly rational agents or even that they invariably choose what at the moment of decision seems best. Moreover, the denial of *akrasia* in the *Protagoras* relies on the hedonist identification of goodness and even of nobility with pleasure, a context that surely renders suspect Socrates' putative allegiance to it.[29] Socrates' assertion in the *Meno* that no one wants to be wretched, and his pronouncement in the *Gorgias* that people do bad and intermediate things for the sake of good ones, do not constitute denials of *akrasia.* Yet they are read as if they do.

What Socrates says to Polus is, in fact, not what he says to Protagoras; what he says to Hippias is not what he says to Gorgias; what he says to Meno is not what he says to Callicles—and with good reason: though afflicted with a common malady, each of these interlocutors exhibits unique symptoms and requires custom-tailored treatment. Each must be shown to be "ridiculous" (*katagelastos* [*Gorg.* 509a7]) in his own way. It is Protagoras who claims to teach

28. Aristotle is notorious for presenting the views of his predecessors in such a way that his own view appears more reasonable than theirs. It is a commonplace today for scholars to accuse Aristotle of distorting or at least interpreting uncharitably not only the pre-Socratics but also Plato, his older contemporary and teacher. Why, then, do these very scholars tend to trust his reports on Socrates? A noteworthy exception to this rule is Kahn 1996, 79–88.

29. It seems beyond doubt that Aristotle derives his belief that Socrates denies *akrasia* directly from the *Protagoras,* since he quotes Socrates' remark there that it would be strange if when knowledge was in a man something else could master it and "drag it about like a slave" (*EN* VII.ii. 1145b24–25; *Prot.* 352c1–2). See Grote 1875, II, 62n.: "We see from hence that when Aristotle comments upon *the doctrine of Sokrates,* what he here means is, the doctrine of the Platonic Sokrates in the *Protagoras*" (emphasis in original). Grote points out that Aristotle similarly relies on the *Protagoras* for his report (at *EN* IX.i. 1164a25) that Protagoras allowed students to assess their own fee.

aretē, so it is he who must be shown what distortions of the human personality and of *aretē* itself are required if he is to be its teacher. It is specifically in addressing Polus that Socrates promotes the idea that all bad and intermediate activities must aim at some benefit, because it is Polus who delights in the sheer power of being able to do as one pleases: for him, killing, confiscating, and banishing are in themselves most attractive ends. It is Callicles who must be reminded that no one does wrong willingly because it is Callicles who thinks that wrongdoing, when committed in service of increasing one's own pleasures, wins nature's approval. It is Meno who needs to consider that all people want the same thing: he is the snob who thinks *aretē* is a matter of having refined tastes and the power to satisfy them. And it is Hippias whom Socrates confronts with the notion that the intentional wrongdoer is the good man because it is Hippias who invests the deceitful doer of injustice with power and wisdom, regarding the truthful man as "simple" (*haplous*).

The Socratic Paradoxes and *Republic* 2

Although the views that are the targets of Socrates' most vehement challenges appear in several dialogues—the *Protagoras, Gorgias, Hippias Minor, Meno,* and *Rep.* 1—they all seem to converge on a single stretch of text: *Rep.* 2.357a–367e. Points of view that are glimpsed only dimly and obliquely in other dialogues—their proponents for the most part hold them either only implicitly or, even when explicitly, without articulating them fully—emerge with great clarity and transparency in *Rep.* 2.

The centerpiece of this early part of *Rep.* 2 is the view that "no one is willingly just" (*oudeis hekōn dikaios* [360c6]). It appears several times, each time with a slightly different emphasis. At 358c3–4 Glaucon says: "all those who practice [justice] do so unwillingly, as necessary but not good," stressing not only the distastefulness of doing justice but the constraint and compulsion without which no one would do it. At 359b6–7 he says that "even those who practice it do so unwillingly, from an incapacity to do injustice." Here it is the weakness and powerlessness of the man who acts justly that is emphasized. And at 366d1 Adeimantus remarks that no ordinary human being is willingly just; men disapprove of injustice, he contends, only because of cowardice, old age,[30] or some other weakness that renders them unable to engage in it success-

---

30. It is no doubt Cephalus that Adeimantus has in mind.

fully. The view that justice is no one's first choice, that no man who has access to the ring of Gyges with its invisible-making powers would conduct himself differently from any other man in that position—that, indeed, all men, both "just" and unjust, would, if they could, readily do injustice—is a view boldly expressed and forcefully defended in *Rep.* 2 first by Glaucon and then by Adeimantus. But it is also a view openly promoted by the more brazen of Socrates' interlocutors (Polus, Callicles, and Thrasymachus) and secretly subscribed to by the more conventional and less confrontational ones (Protagoras and Hippias).

Could there be a more compelling catalyst for Socrates' paradox that no one is willingly *un*just than the noxious notion that no one is willingly *just*? *Rep.* 2, by casting this objectionable view in a phrase that so closely mirrors the Socratic paradox, offers a viable and more judicious alternative to the prevailing supposition that what Socrates means to deny by way of his paradox is that people do indeed do wrong willingly. For why would Socrates (or anyone) wish to deny that people do wrong willingly? Does he think that no one who does wrong recognizes what he does as wrong? Does he believe that people who do wrong cannot help what they do? Does he excuse wrongdoing on the grounds that people are unable, after all, to act in opposition to what they take to further their own interests? On the prevailing understanding of the paradox, Socrates is committed to a whole host of peculiar psychological theses. The alternative view, however, spares him these psychological oddities, attributing to him instead a novel *moral* perspective, namely, that it is not injustice but justice that will satisfy the deepest human desire to live happily and well.

Rep. 2 also opens up alternative ways of conceiving the other two Socratic paradoxes—"virtue is knowledge" and "all the virtues are one." It is commonly assumed that "virtue is knowledge" is designed to oppose either (1) the manifestly reasonable idea that virtue involves the proper cultivation not only of the intellect but of the emotions and appetites as well,[31] or (2) the notion that virtue comes by nature or by habituation. Yet is it not most unlikely that Socrates, a man who puts care for the soul above all else (*Ap.* 29e2, 30b2), would care not at all for the disciplining of the emotions and appetites? On the

---

31. See, e.g., Grote 1875, I, 399–400, who criticizes Socrates for "the error of dwelling exclusively on the intellectual conditions of human conduct, and omitting to give proper attention to the emotional and volitional."

contrary, Socrates in the *Gorgias* decries appetites run amok and favors an ordered and "lawful" soul; he calls attention in the *Lysis* to the value of the restrictions that Lysis's parents place on their son; and he accords a place of prominence to the cardinal virtue of temperance in many dialogues, devoting the whole of the *Charmides* specifically to its definition. And although Socrates surely does not think that virtue is a matter of noble birth or that it requires nothing more than habituation, is it likely that he would endorse instead the idea that virtue is knowledge—in the sense that it is some sort of art or science? The notion that virtue is some sort of art or science is, in all the dialogues in which it appears, fraught with difficulties: what sort of skill is it? what exactly does its expert know? can it be taught? what, if anything, is it useful for? is the one who is proficient at it a man who does right or a man equally skilled at doing right and doing wrong? Indeed, it is not Socrates but his arch-rivals, the sophists, who famously regard virtue as a *technē*. [32] What *Rep.* 2 does is make it possible to see "virtue is knowledge" as neither advancing the idea that virtue requires nothing but a perfected intellect nor turning virtue into one *technē* among others, but rather as defying the odious view that it is the vicious who are wise and skilled (see *Rep.* 1.348e and *Rep.* 2.360e), and the virtuous who are dupes and fools. When "virtue is knowledge" is interpreted as promoting the idea that the virtuous are those who live well and flourish and not the simpletons who finish last, it is an idea that Socrates would roundly embrace. [33]

But why does Socrates hold that "all the virtues are one"? Whether read as the more minimal interentailment thesis, according to which anyone who has one of the virtues will of necessity have them all, or as the stronger identity thesis, according to which either (1) each of the parts of virtue is identical to every other part and to virtue itself, or (2) each of the parts of virtue is a unique manifestation of a single state of the soul, virtue, the paradox's cen-

32. The professionalization of *aretē* is a frequent target of Socratic attack; it is far from being a cornerstone of Socratic ethics. See Villa 2001, 304: "Socrates' 'human wisdom'—the recognition that human beings do not possess any craftlike knowledge when it comes to the 'most important things'—defines itself in contrast to the rhetorical stance of the 'moral expert'. . . . It is against the claims of such 'experts'—and the odd combination of hubris and complacency they represent—that Socrates directs the deflationary powers of the *elenchus*."

33. See *Gorg.* 491e, where Callicles says to Socrates: "By the temperate you mean the stupid ones?" to which Socrates replies: "How so? There is no one who would fail to recognize that this is not what I mean." See also *Rep.* 1.350c, where Socrates says to Thrasymachus: "Then the just man is like the wise and good, but the unjust man like the bad and ignorant (*amathei*)."

trality to the Socratic project remains something of an enigma. In *Rep.* 2, perhaps more vividly than elsewhere, the moral purchase of the view that "all the virtues are one" comes to light (though see chapters 2 and 4 for an extensive consideration of the unity of the virtues in the *Protagoras* and *Hippias Minor,* respectively). The paradox is here seen to oppose the notion, promoted in some sophistic circles, that certain virtues, specifically wisdom and courage, are characteristic of those who are superior and dominant, whereas others, specifically, justice, temperance, and piety, are to be found only among the most stupid (*anoētotatos* [*Rep.* 2.360d5]) and weak. For Socrates to affirm the unity of the virtues, that is, for him to assert that the virtues are a total package such that a person cannot have one of the virtues without having the others as well, is for him to deny that those who are wise and courageous are the wicked men who use their wisdom and courage in the service of the immoral ends of injustice, intemperance, and impiety, and to proclaim instead that those who are wise and courageous are in fact the very men who are just and temperate.[34]

Rep. 2 thus brings into focus the nexus of views that Socrates is determined to expose and oppose in his encounters with the select group of interlocutors who endorse them both in this dialogue and in others. His views that (1) the just and temperate life is the more desirable one, (2) those who live justly and temperately are therefore the smart ones, and (3) those who are intelligent and brave are none other than those who are just and temperate[35] are introduced and upheld in the face of—and in stark opposition to—the views endorsed and promulgated by his opponents. In all that he says, then, Socrates does indeed turn everything upside down, just as Callicles in the *Gorgias* says he does: "For if you are serious and these things you are saying happen to be true, wouldn't the life of us human beings have been turned upside down and

---

34. See *Gorg.* 491b, where Callicles regards the "superior" as not only intelligent but brave; 497e3–6, where Callicles maintains that the brave and wise are good; 507b, where Socrates argues against Callicles that the temperate are also just and pious—*and brave.* The famous Thrasymachus blush (*Rep.* 1.350d) comes just when he has been compelled to admit—with great discomfort and a profusion of sweat—that the just man has turned out to be good and clever, the unjust one ignorant and bad.

35. Hippias regards the truthful man as a simpleton (*haplous* [*HMi.* 365b]), and Thrasymachus regards the just man as naïve (*euēthēs* [*Rep.* 1.349b]). Glaucon calls the just man "simple and genteel" (*haploun kai gennaion* [*Rep.* 2.361b6–7]). For Thrasymachus, the *un*just man is both prudent and good (*phronimos* and *agathos* [*Rep.* 1.349d]), and for Hippias, the liar is the one who is able, prudent, knowledgeable, and wise (*dunatos, phronimos, epistēmōn,* and *sophos* [*HMi.* 366a]).

aren't we doing, as it would appear, all the opposite things to what we ought?" (*Gorg.* 481c).[36]

On the proposed agonistic reading of the Socratic paradoxes, it is the paradox "no one does wrong willingly" that occupies center stage. It displaces "virtue is knowledge" as the core paradox; it is the one that illuminates the other two. Whereas it had always been thought that "virtue is knowledge" is indispensable to the understanding of both "no one does wrong willingly" and "the unity of the virtues"—it is one's mastery of the *technē* of virtue or one's attainment of full knowledge of right and wrong that ensures that one will never do wrong and will be virtuous in *every* way—it is now "no one does wrong willingly" that holds the interpretive key to the others: since no one who does wrong lives the truly good life he wishes to live, it follows that no one who chooses to do wrong is wise, and that those who *are* wise put their courage to use to foster in themselves temperance and justice.

Socratic Reversals of Opposing Views

Since the Socratic view that no one is *un*just or commits *in*justice willingly reverses the sophistic view that no one is just or practices justice willingly, it is perhaps not surprising that the two views have much in common—if in reverse. When Glaucon and Adeimantus insist that no one is willingly just, they are moved in large measure by how much better life is for the unjust man than it is for the just.[37] Because of how undeniably rewarding life is for the unjust man in their view, Glaucon and Adeimantus think that no one who could live unjustly would choose to live justly, so that those who choose to live justly do so out of weakness, incapacity, or fear. To be sure, Glaucon and Adeimantus acknowledge that people do choose to live justly: their notion that no one is willingly just is not meant to deny that. Glaucon in fact believes that justice has

36. As Euben puts it, for Socrates, "being great becomes being good, courage becomes the willingness to suffer injustice rather than commit it, and the purpose of life is not to conquer Syracuse, avenge one's friends, build an empire, or leave monuments behind but to conquer tyrannical impulses [and] harm no one" (1990, 206).

37. Glaucon and Adeimantus profess to be playing devil's advocate, that is, to be speaking on behalf of those who favor the life of injustice over that of justice. They insist, moreover, that, for their own part, they prefer the life of justice. For convenience's sake, I treat the view they defend as theirs.

its origins in the carefully calculated determination by the powerless that it is in their best interests to forgo committing injustice for the sake of not suffering it (*Rep.* 1.358e–359b). And both Glaucon and Adeimantus recognize that not everyone who wishes to be unjust can be, and that those people who cannot be unjust do opt for justice. Furthermore, they note, many people who find justice distasteful still believe (however mistakenly) that good things— money, honor, good marriages, political office, the gods' favor, and so on— accrue to those who are just. (These people are mistaken because, as Glaucon and especially Adeimantus observe, good things accrue to those who seem just, and one needn't be just in order to seem just.) In saying, then, that no one is willingly just, Glaucon and Adeimantus make two claims: (1) that under ideal conditions—that is, when there is no risk in being unjust—everyone would choose injustice,[38] and (2) that under less-than-ideal conditions—that is, when there is great risk in being unjust—only those who are sufficiently courageous and intelligent would do so. Since Glaucon and Adeimantus believe that only superior men choose injustice in real life, their saying that no one is willingly just is not purely descriptive; it contains an implicit censure of those who choose justice. For Glaucon and Adeimantus, those who live justly forfeit their chance at a truly satisfying life. With every day that goes by they deprive themselves of true happiness, insipidly exchanging the joys of committing injustice for the paltry compensation of not suffering it.

When Socrates proclaims that "no one does wrong willingly," he, too, is spurred by the great disparity between the quality of the life of injustice and that of the life of justice. But for him it is the life of justice that is without question the far better one. Socrates no more wishes to deny that some men deliberately choose to be unjust than Glaucon and Adeimantus wish to deny that

---

38. Somewhat surprisingly, Glaucon and Adeimantus seem to acknowledge that there may be exceptions to the rule that no one wants to do right. Glaucon, for example, who uses the fable of the ring of Gyges (*Rep.* 2.359c–360d) to prove that *no one* would do right if he could get away with doing wrong, still notes that "*if* a man were to get hold of such license and were never willing to do any injustice and did not lay his hands on what belongs to others, he would seem most wretched to those who were aware of it, and most foolish, too" (*Rep.* 2.360d). And Adeimantus admits there might be someone "who from a divine nature cannot stand doing injustice or who has gained knowledge and keeps away from injustice" (*Rep.* 2.366c–d). And Thrasymachus recognizes that there are some people—albeit wretched ones—who are unwilling to do injustice (*Rep.* 1.344a). Interestingly, Cephalus recognizes that sometimes people are forced against their will (*akonta*) to lie and cheat when they do not have the money to discharge their obligations (*Rep.* 1.331b).

some men deliberately choose to be just. But, as Socrates sees it, it is justice rather than injustice that is the choice of superior men. It is men who live *unjustly*, he thinks, who sacrifice their chance at a genuinely fulfilling life; they exchange the joys of having a pure and untarnished soul for the meager compensations of wealth, power, and bodily pleasure.

The most widely accepted interpretation of Socrates' paradox "no one does wrong willingly" is that if only a person knew that justice was best for him, that it was the thing that would make him truly happy, he would surely choose it. But is this what Glaucon and Adeimantus mean when they say that no one is just or practices justice willingly? Do they mean that if people only knew how good injustice is they would surely choose it? And if this is not what they mean, might not the common interpretation of what Socrates means be mistaken?

It seems fairly clear that when Glaucon and Adeimantus assert that no one is just willingly they do not mean that if only a person knew how good injustice is he would surely choose it. For Glaucon and Adeimantus recognize that injustice is not an easy choice. Injustice as they see it is difficult and demanding because the injustice they—and Thrasymachus in *Rep.* 1—have in mind is injustice "in a big way" (*megala* [*Rep.* 1.344a1]), "the most perfect injustice" (*tēn teleōtatēn adikein* [*Rep.* 1.344a4]), injustice "on a sufficient scale" (*hikanōs* [*Rep.* 1.344c6]), "perfect injustice" (*telean adikian* [*Rep.* 1.348b9]), injustice done "perfectly" (*teleōs* [*Rep.* 1.348d5]), "the most perfect injustice" (*tēn teleōtatēn adikian* [*Rep.* 2.361a6]), done by the "consummately unjust man" (*tōi teleōs adikōi* [*Rep.* 2.368a5–6]), the man who is like "clever craftsmen" (*hoi deinoi dēmiourgoi* [*Rep.* 2.360e7]). Injustice of this magnitude requires courage and intelligence, the building of alliances,[39] the development of rhetorical skill, the use of force, and constant vigilance. This sort of injustice is not the momentary injustice of the cutpurse (*Rep.* 1.348d). For Glaucon and Adeimantus what makes full-blown injustice nevertheless well worth the effort is its enormous profitability.[40]

---

39. Ironically, it is precisely this kind of thoroughgoing injustice that, according to Socrates, *prevents* alliances. See *Rep.* 1.351c–352c; *Gorg.* 507e. In the *Republic* passage, Socrates argues that only if those who are unjust have at least a little justice in them and are not "thoroughly unjust" (*teleōs adikoi*) will they be able to accomplish anything together. In the *Gorgias,* Socrates warns against villainy "without end" (*anēnuton*) which renders a man "incapable of fellowship" and hence "incapable of friendship."

40. This is how Adeimantus puts the point: "'The trouble with that,' someone will say, 'is that it is hard to be evil and get away with it forever.' 'Well,' we shall say, 'nothing great was ever

In maintaining that no one does *wrong* willingly, Socrates for similar reasons does not mean that if people only knew how good justice is they would surely choose it. For even those who become convinced of justice's worth may find its demands daunting. Like perfect injustice, justice, too, is not an easy choice (especially for those who have a free hand to commit injustice [*Gorg.* 526a]), but one that requires both intelligence and fortitude. Like Glaucon and Adeimantus, then—but in reverse—Socrates believes that what makes justice worth the effort it requires is that only those who live justly live well.

Both Socrates (at *Rep.* 3.392c), on the one hand, and Glaucon and Adeimantus, on the other (at *Rep.* 2.358e, 359b, 362a), contend that there is a good by nature that is obscured by convention. Glaucon and Adeimantus think that what is good for people by nature is to dominate others, to appropriate and accumulate as much as possible and certainly more than their fair share, to commit murder and adultery and to take the property of others at will and with impunity, to help their friends and harm their enemies, to take and give in marriage whomever they wish, to bribe the gods, and to form associations that aid and abet their unfettered and unrestrained efforts in pursuit of their own advantage—all the while *appearing* to be just. Socrates thinks that what is good for people by nature is to have healthy and unencumbered souls, to be satisfied with little, and to be fair and just in their dealings with others, be they men or gods—even if they fail to appear to be just. Both Glaucon and Adeimantus, on the one hand, and Socrates, on the other, blame the false and distorted messages of society for dissuading people from pursuing their natural good. Glaucon and Adeimantus blame society for heaping praise on justice, when it is injustice that is profitable for those who can commit it with impunity. Socrates blames society for creating desires in people that far outstrip their needs and for causing them to believe that power, wealth, and reputation are more important than prudence, truth, and the best state of the soul. For Glaucon and Adeimantus, justice is a perversion of the life that is naturally satisfying: we hurt ourselves when we are just to others. For Socrates, wrong-

---

easy. But if we are going to be happy, we must follow where the trail of our argument leads us.'" Cf. Glaucon's argument at 2.360e–361b, 362b–c. Although, as Adeimantus says, speeches in both prose and poetry depict self-indulgence and injustice as sweet and easy to acquire (2.364a), it is difficult to sustain a life of self-indulgence and intemperance, a life in which one never runs out of resources and in which one is never caught and punished. It is difficult, too, to sustain all the while the appearance of justice.

doing is a perversion of the life that is naturally satisfying: we hurt ourselves when we are unjust to others.

For Glaucon and Adeimantus, then, only injustice can make one happy;[41] for Socrates only justice can. Glaucon and Adeimantus think one needs intelligence and courage in order to be thoroughly unjust; Socrates thinks one needs these very virtues in order to be thoroughly just. For Glaucon and Adeimantus intelligence and courage are the virtues that characterize the man who is unjust and intemperate; for Socrates they are the virtues that characterize the man who is just, temperate, and pious.

Despite the many similarities in the way Glaucon and Adeimantus think and the way Socrates does (though the former hold injustice in esteem and the latter justice), there is one great difference between them. When Glaucon and Adeimantus assert that no one is willingly just, they mean quite straightforwardly that people prefer injustice and would choose it if they could. For Socrates, however, that no one does wrong willingly does not mean that people prefer justice.[42] Socrates does not say—ever—that no one wants to do wrong or that everyone wants to do right. What Socrates means by saying that no one does wrong willingly is that whenever one chooses injustice over justice one fails to fulfill one's arguably most important wish—namely, the wish to live well and do well really. From Socrates' perspective, since people want (in a quite ordinary sense) to be happy, they can be said to be acting "unwillingly" when they act in ways that sabotage their happiness. Socrates need

41. See *Gorg.* 492c, where Callicles contends that wantonness, lack of discipline, and freedom are virtue and happiness, prompting Socrates to exclaim that Callicles is now saying what others are thinking but are unwilling to say.

42. Socrates' recognition that people want to be happy at the same time that they want things that may well not contribute to their happiness puts one in mind of the standard de dicto/de re distinction: when being happy consists in being just, a person might want to be happy de dicto but not de re. This analysis is satisfactory so long as it is not taken to entail that what is wanted de dicto but not de re is not really wanted after all. Or that what is wanted de re, when it conflicts with what is wanted de dicto, is not really wanted after all.

It is also not quite right to suggest (as Santas [1979, 187–88] does) that in Socrates' view what a person wants under one description ("what will make me happy" or "what is truly good for me") he does not want under another ("what is painful or unpleasant or too difficult"). To put the matter this way is potentially to make people want what they really do not want. If a person does not want to be just, it is not accurate to say that he wants to be just under the description "what will make me happy." What he wants is both to be happy and to be unjust. People's wants, like their beliefs, are not always in harmony.

not posit a special "rational will" or "true self" or subconscious desire whose object is what is truly good.[43] All he need say, and all he does say, is that since in wanting to be happy people want what is truly good, and since what is truly good is justice, it follows that when they act in ways that are unjust, in ways, that is, that are harmful to themselves—no matter how much they want the things that their unjust acts will bring and no matter how deliberate their actions—they act "unwillingly." It is here, if anywhere, that Socrates strains the limits of ordinary usage.

What is unique about the desire to be happy, what makes it different from other desires that are similarly opaque, is that it is both universal and inalienable: all people want to be happy and no one can want not to be.[44] Moreover, since the desire to be happy is not just any old desire but is the deepest, most fundamental, most overarching desire there is, people who fail to live justly, Socrates contends, undermine their most important wish. From Glaucon's and Adeimantus's perspective, however—and for that very same reason—it is those who fail to live *un*justly who do so.

Before moving on to the next section, we should take note of two other instances in which Socrates' views and the views of the proponents of injustice are interestingly parallel—though opposed. Consider, first, the following remarkable observation by Adeimantus at *Rep.* 2.366c–d:

> So, consequently, if someone can show that what we have said is false and if he has adequate knowledge that justice is best, he undoubtedly has great sympathy for the unjust and is not angry with them; he knows that except

43. For the view that Socrates does indeed attribute to people a rational will or true self whose object is the good, see, e.g., Cornford 1927, 306; Gould 1955, 47–55; Cushman 1958, 185, 194–95; Dodds 1959, 235–36; Adkins 1960, 305, 309. Note that when Aristotle says (*Met.* XII.vii. 1072a) that "what is desired is what appears beautiful; what is wanted (*boulēton*) primarily is what *is* beautiful," he expresses the difference between desiring and wanting without positing a special will whose object is "what is wanted."

44. Consider the example of Oedipus and Jocasta. Oedipus does not want to marry his own mother. But he does want to marry Jocasta, who, unbeknownst to him, is his own mother. What would Socrates say in this case? As I see it, Socrates would have no reason to deny either that Oedipus wants to marry Jocasta or that Oedipus really does not want to marry his own mother. When Oedipus finds out that Jocasta is his mother he might (1) no longer not want to marry his own mother, (2) no longer want to marry Jocasta, or (3) still want both not to marry his own mother and to marry Jocasta. In other words, he might change his mind about any of the things he wants—or not. In the case of someone who wants to be happy but does not wish to be just, however, there is only one thing that he can change his mind about (if he changes his mind at all) when he dis-

for someone who from a divine nature cannot stand doing injustice or who has gained knowledge and keeps away from injustice, no one else is willingly just; but because of a lack of courage, or old age, or some other weakness, men blame injustice because they are unable to do it.

According to Adeimantus in this passage, the man who understands that justice is best will regard the unjust with sympathy and without anger because he recognizes that *no one is willingly just.* Would Socrates not say just the opposite, that the man who understands that justice is best will regard the unjust with sympathy and without anger because he recognizes that *no one is willingly unjust?*[45] And indeed Socrates does say almost precisely that at *Gorg.* 469a–b, where he contends against Polus that the man who kills whomever he pleases *un*justly is wretched and pitiable—presumably because in committing injustice he cannot be doing what he wants. From Adeimantus's perspective the reason for withholding harsh judgment from the man who is unjust is that none but the most extraordinary human being could be expected to be just willingly; from Socrates' point of view the reason the man who is willfully unjust should be pitied is that he is utterly pathetic: he does not attain the thing he most urgently wants.

The second instance of parallel but opposed views involves the fable of the ring of Gyges in *Rep.* 2. What Glaucon seeks to show by way of the parable of the ring of Gyges is how much less justly human beings would behave if their bodies were invisible. Socrates reverses the message of Glaucon's myth by way of his own myth of the afterlife at the end of the *Gorgias:* what Socrates seeks to show by way of the *Gorgias* myth is how much more justly human beings would behave if their souls were visible.

Socrates' Beliefs

Once the Socratic paradoxes are viewed as reactions to positions taken by Socrates' opponents, it is possible to show that Socrates endorses neither the implausible doctrine that has come to be known as the denial of *akrasia* nor the

---

covers that justice is what makes people truly happy: he can decide that he wants to be just. What is nonnegotiable is his wish to be happy.

45. See *Ap.* 41d: "and I at least am not at all angry at those who voted to condemn me and at my accusers."

host of other odd ideas associated with it. In other words, it becomes possible to show that he is not an "intellectualist" about human choice; that he is neither a psychological nor an ethical egoist; that he is not a eudaimonist; that he does not believe that all wrongdoing is unintentional and therefore not culpable. It can be shown that in many respects his views concerning moral psychology are, in fact, quite ordinary: (1) people deliberately do wrong, believing (or even knowing) it to be wrong; (2) when people do wrong believing it to be wrong they are culpable; (3) people's desires and fears do at times cause them to choose what they believe (or know)—even at the very moment of choice—is not best for them; (4) people are able to do other than what seems to them best for themselves; (5) people are required and expected to do other than what seems to them best for themselves when what seems best for themselves does not coincide with what is right; and (6) people need not always and ought not always to aim at their own happiness as they perceive it. That Socrates harbors no strikingly peculiar views about how and why human beings choose to do wrong, and that he presumes no inability on the part of people to act against their own judgment of where their interests lie, does not mean that he subscribes to no distinctive *moral* position. Where Socrates departs idiosyncratically from the relatively unremarkable conception of human choice just sketched is in his genuinely innovative—indeed revolutionary—belief that when people, out of desire or fear, fail to choose what is (even in their own estimation) best for themselves and, in addition, when they deliberately do injustice, they bring on themselves a condition of wretchedness that no one could possibly want.[46]

Socrates believes that there is a genuinely good condition for human beings to be in, a state in which their soul has attained an optimal fitness and orderliness. Such a condition is most beneficial to people and, qua beneficial, desirable. Moreover, insofar as people may be presumed to want what is truly good and desirable ("No one is satisfied with possessing what only seems good: here all reject the appearance and seek (zētousin) the reality" [Rep. 6.505d5–9]), they may be presumed to fail to "do what they want" when they fail to achieve

---

46. That no one wants to be wretched, that we all want to live well, do well, and fare well (*Meno* 78a; *Euthyd.* 278e, 282a), and that we all therefore "want" what is really good for us does not preclude our regularly doing things that we ourselves think are not best for us. People are simply not (except in the *Protagoras*) all that rational.

such a condition.[47] This condition is justice, which is brought about by one's refraining from injustice and which, once in place, works to keep one from committing injustice. When, therefore, people do commit injustice—in particular, when they commit injustice intentionally, that is, in full recognition that what they are doing is unjust—they put themselves or their souls in a state that is undesirable for them, a state that makes it impossible for them to live as they want.

Socrates, as we said, is well aware that people regularly deliberately choose to commit injustice. If he were not, it would be difficult to understand why he considers some people—and not others—wicked.[48] Wicked men, he thinks, though surely misguided about their true interests, are not *only* misguided. For there are other people, similarly misguided, who, despite thinking like the wicked that injustice pays, nevertheless refrain from doing wrong. It is wicked people who recklessly and ruthlessly, without any regard for others, pursue their own interests; their injustice is not limited to those occasions when they fail to recognize that what they are doing is wrong.[49] These people, unjust precisely because their wrongdoing is intentional, are those for whom punishment is appropriate.[50] There is only one kind of ignorance that exculpates: the mistaken belief that one's action is not going to harm another. For

47. The point Socrates makes in this passage from the *Republic* is that whereas people are content to appear just and noble, no one wants merely to appear to have good things. As the passage continues (*Rep.* 6.505d11–e1), Socrates says that "this [the reality, not the semblance, of what is good] is what every soul pursues (*diōkei*) and it is this for the sake of which it does everything." We must be clear that Socrates does not mean that each and every choice that a person makes is consciously directed at the good or made with the good in mind. Note the rather conspicuous shift from the concreteness of the good things men want to the abstraction of the soul's pursuit of "the good." The good is every soul's ultimate goal—not every man's proximate one.

48. When Socrates says at *Gorg.* 521d (see also 511b, 521b) that if someone unjustly prosecutes him it will be a base man who is his prosecutor, he obliquely characterizes Meletus as a base man, a man who intends him harm. And he regards tyrants as the quintessential base men.

49. Segvic (2000, 22) thinks that, according to Socrates, "wrongdoers do not aim at something they recognize as wrong or bad; rather, they are misguided and ignorant about the nature of their action and its goal." On Segvic's view, it would be difficult to explain why Socrates regards wrong doers as wicked and blameworthy.

50. Some wrongdoers could, I suppose, believe that what they are doing is not wrong—as, for example, when they harm their enemies. If people who do wrong actually believe that what they are doing is not wrong (as opposed to believing that doing wrong is itself right), perhaps they have never examined their beliefs or have never had their beliefs examined. To subject one's beliefs to critical scrutiny is a requirement of Socratic ethics; sometimes that is the only check there is on

Socrates, failure to recognize either that unjust actions are harmful to oneself or that actions harmful to others are unjust is no excuse.

Punishment is therefore reserved for those who deliberately do wrong. The so-called therapeutic model of punishment ascribed to Socrates and thought to confirm that Socrates thinks all wrongdoing is involuntary is in fact fully consistent with, and even arguably requires, that wrongdoing be deliberate: only those whose wrongdoing is deliberate stand to benefit from therapy because only they have damaged souls in need of repair. Socrates regards those who commit injustice by mistake as innocent: their souls are unblemished and they need no punishment—therapeutic or otherwise. That he sees punishment as curative in no way suggests that he regards the perpetrator of the injustice whose soul requires healing as someone who could not help but do wrong.

To be sure, people who deliberately commit injustice are, Socrates thinks, to be pitied (*Gorg.* 469b; *Laws* 5.731c7–8), for it is they whose lives are miserable. They harm their souls, their very selves.[51] But to be pitied is not to be pardoned. Those who deliberately commit injustice are culpable: they could have and should have refrained from injustice.[52] The ideal way for people to live is justly. Those who live justly even for crass reasons—dread of punishment, habit, fear of the gods—are still better off (whether they know it or not and whether they think so or not) than those who are unjust, because the souls of those who are just for any reason are still in a better condition than are the souls of those who are unjust. Tyrants are the most wretched of men regardless of whether they or anyone else so perceives them.

The Urgency of the Paradox

Ordinary people are confused. On the one hand, they think that justice is a good thing, a virtue. Although they do not regard it as advantageous, they

---

patently false belief. The more crudely self-serving a belief is, the more one ought to be suspicious of it and the more one ought to be willing to test it or to have it tested.

51. Socrates ranks the soul above the body, and so deems its welfare far more important to a person's living well than that of the body. See *Crito* 47–48; *Gorg.* 511–512; *Rep.* 10.618d–619a. Interlocutors who champion injustice frequently forfeit their case as soon as they concede to Socrates that the soul has greater worth than the body.

52. Note what Socrates says of his accusers and of those who voted to convict him (*Ap.* 41d8–e1): "they supposed they would harm me. For this they are worthy of blame."

nevertheless see in it a noble and beautiful thing. On the other hand, however, they care most about pleasure and ease.[53] If they could lead lives of comfort and enjoyment with only the barest minimum of pain and fear, that would surely be their preference.[54] They are essentially hedonists, though not in the radical sense limned in the *Protagoras* where they are accused of assimilating good to pleasure. For even if, as Socrates indicates in the *Phaedo* (68d–69a), ordinary people are temperate and courageous (and probably also just and pious) for the sake of attaining greater pleasure or avoiding greater pain in the long run, there is nevertheless no reason to suppose that they are therefore unable to recognize any good other than pleasure, any evil other than pain.

It is true, of course, that when ordinary people must make a choice between what is beneficial and what they crave, they often choose what they crave. Similarly, when ordinary people must make a choice between what is just or noble and what is pleasant, they often choose what is pleasant. Moreover, when they do choose the just it is likely to be, precisely as the sophists say, because of fear of punishment or of public humiliation—because, in other words, they are powerless to do what is unjust and get away with it. But whatever they choose, ordinary people are well aware of having made a choice and they are able to form a judgment as to whether it was the morally right one: they know not only when they have been imprudent; they know, too, when they have been unjust.

Sophists and rhetoricians compound the difficulty ordinary people face in trying to make the "right" choice. They turn intemperance and overindulgence—which are really nothing but manifestations of psychological weakness—into virtues. Indeed, they seek to strip temperance and justice of the

53. See Aristotle, *EN* II.iii. 1104b30–33: "There are three things that inspire choice and three that inspire flight, namely: the noble, the useful (*sumpheron*), and the pleasant, and their opposites, the base, the harmful, and the painful." Aristotle seems to undermine his own point, however, when he goes on to say that the noble and useful appear pleasant (1105a1) and attract for that reason.

54. See Aristophanes' *Clouds,* where Unjust Logic says: "For consider, lad, all that moderation involves, and how many pleasures you're going to be deprived of: boys, women, relishes, cottabus, drinking, boisterous laughter. Yet what is living worth to you if you're deprived of these things?" (ll. 1071–74, trans. West and West [1984]). If set beside the speech of Unjust Logic, how hollow would Socrates' insistence ring that it is the unexamined life or the life in which one lacks a healthy soul that is not worth living. See *Ap.* 38a; *Crito* 47e, 53c; *Gorg.* 512a; *Rep.* 4.445a–b. For other things in Plato that are said to make life not worth living, see *Menex.* 246d; *Symp.* 211d, 216a; *Rep.* 3.407a–b; *Statesman* 299e; *Laws* 11.926b.

beauty and nobility that ordinary people see in them, charging that it is not by nature that temperance and justice are beautiful and intemperance and injustice ugly, but by opinions and conventions born of the impotence of ordinary men (see *Gorg.* 482e–484c, 492a–c; *Rep.* 2.363e–364a). The more extreme among them, like Thrasymachus, put injustice in the class of virtue and wisdom and, though perhaps not going so far as to call justice a vice, regard it as naïveté, as "genteel simplicity" (see *Rep.* 1.348c, 349b; but cf. 348e). Moreover, they enflame the already too potent passions that most people have to contend with by teaching that a life without a steady stream of bodily pleasure is a life without value. Without such constant "influx" one might as well be, as Callicles and others of his ilk unhelpfully maintain, a stone or corpse (*Gorg.* 494b).[55]

Socrates' gripe with the sophists, then, is not simply that they fail to make good on their guarantee to improve their students. What troubles him is that they effectively foil any possibility of their students' becoming better. If anything, they make their young associates worse. With the promise of success and distinction, they lure young men away from traditional moral instruction but do nothing to mold their characters, to strengthen their moral fiber, or to encourage them to question or to examine their unreflectively adopted ends. On the contrary, the sophists glorify pleasure, power, honor, wealth, and reputation, feeding their clients a steady diet of spiritual poison. Moreover, sophists like Callicles eliminate *to kalon* (the beautiful or noble) as a category distinct from advantage,[56] thereby taking from people their only non–crudely self-serving reason to do right.

In addition, the sophists sever virtue from the individual virtues that are traditionally thought to compose it.[57] They teach "virtue" but not justice or temperance. Protagoras is just plain lying when he claims in the *Protagoras* to teach justice, temperance, piety, and the rest of *andros aretē* (manly virtue)

55. It might be said that the sophists turn the *akratēs,* the person who cannot resist the pleasures he believes he should resist, into an *akolastos* who, believing his every indulgence in pleasure to be a good thing, feels no regret and is beyond cure. As Aristotle might put it, they turn the merely "half wicked" into the more fully wicked (*EN* VII.x. 1152a17–18).

56. Socrates, too, thinks that everything beautiful or noble is advantageous but he does not think that nobility reduces to advantage. Also, of course, what the sophists intend by "advantage" is advantage to the body, whereas what Socrates intends is advantage to the soul.

57. One reason that Socrates comes back time and again to the relationship between virtue and its parts is that not everyone sees the individual *aretai* (especially justice and temperance) as being essentially related, or even related at all, to what they call *aretē.*

(325a2, 329c5). And when he insists that courage comes by nature and nurture and not by knowledge or *technē,* he admits in effect that he does not teach courage either. Yet, how can sophists teach virtue if they teach neither justice nor temperance nor courage? It is because the virtue they teach has nothing to do with justice or temperance or courage. The virtue they transmit is power: the ability to get what one wants and rise to the top.

Not only, then, do sophists not teach the virtues of justice and temperance and actually denigrate those who *are* just and temperate, but they have the temerity to call what they do teach "virtue." In the face of their corruptive influence, Socrates has no alternative but to fight.[58] He must reassure people that only justice can give them the happiness they really want. He must make the case that those who have power, wealth, an abundance of pleasure in all forms, and no fear of comeuppance are not happy if they are unjust. And he must show that those who are unjust cannot but be wretched. The Socratic paradox, then, takes on a formidable opponent—the pervasive belief that justice is something that nobody really wants and hence something that only the weak and incompetent and unintelligent practice. And when justice is threatened, Socrates must step forward. As he says in the *Republic:* "I cannot *not* help out. For I am afraid that it might be impious to be here when justice is spoken badly of and give up and not bring help while I am still breathing and can take a stand" (2.368b).

58. I have argued (see Weiss 2000) that for Socrates winning is everything, because with the stakes so high he cannot afford to fail. When Protagoras and Callicles accuse Socrates of being a lover of victory (see *Prot.* 360e3 and *Gorg.* 515b), he deflects the accusation by insisting that it is not love of victory that motivates him. See also *HMi.* 373b, where Hippias complains that Socrates is always troublesome (*tarapei*) in argument and does wrong (*kakourgounti*), and *Rep.* 1.341a, where Thrasymachus charges Socrates with "playing the sycophant" (*sukophantein*) in the argument.

2

THE *PROTAGORAS*: "OUR SALVATION IN LIFE"

The *Protagoras* is Plato's protracted reductio ad absurdum of one man's pretensions to be the premier teacher of virtue—of virtue as a whole, and in all its parts.[1] It is the slow and systematic unmasking of a professional con man, who, for all his carefully cultivated gentility and civility, is sorely lacking in character. As we shall see, Protagoras is both dishonest and cowardly. He plays it safe, putting expediency before all other considerations.

The *Protagoras,* as much perhaps as the *Laches,*[2] is a dialogue about courage.[3] Yet the particular aim of the *Protagoras* in looking into the nature of courage is to discredit its protagonist who lacks the very courage he esteems. Like the other famous and well-paid sophists assembled in the house of Callias, Protagoras peers at the world from the morally stunted perspective of narrow

---

1. Protagoras is confronted as a representative of the sophistic profession—indeed, as the paradigmatic sophist. The question Socrates poses to Hippocrates concerns not what Protagoras is and what he teaches, but what sophists are and what they teach. Nevertheless, each sophist is different. The *Protagoras* is concerned with the dangers of sophistry specifically as it is practiced by Protagoras—as Plato depicts him.

2. The two dialogues contain remarkably similar arguments for the coincidence of courage and wisdom. See *Lach.* 192–193; *Prot.* 350–351.

3. See *Prot.* 353b1–3: "I think this will help us to find out about courage, how it is related to the other parts of virtue."

self-interest. What sort of virtue, what sort of courage, could such a man possibly teach?

To think well of the character Protagoras, or to think that Plato does, is to miss the humiliation and defeat that he is made to suffer in the dialogue—and not only at its end—at Socrates' hand. It is to fail to detect the mockery behind the false flattery that Socrates lavishes on his famous interlocutor. It is to disregard the cautionary warning that Socrates issues to Hippocrates at the dialogue's inception, his withering portrait of the sophist as a hawker of snake oil for the soul from which any man of sense would prudently recoil. It is to mistake the Great Speech for a great speech, when it is actually a performance riddled with the kinds of inconsistency that are the inevitable by-product of disingenuousness and deceit.

Socrates' famous paradox "no one does wrong willingly" is featured prominently in the *Protagoras,* appearing in it twice: once in Socrates' analysis of Simonides' poem at 345d–e, and again at 358b–d in connection with the infamous Socratic denial of *akrasia.* On both occasions Protagoras is the paradox's target—and this is so for at least the following five reasons: first, Protagoras preys on impressionable young men eager to make a name for themselves on the political stage, deceptively appropriating the term *aretē* to name what he teaches; second, Protagoras himself is neither a virtuous man nor a man who cares for virtue; third, he egregiously misrepresents in his speech the content of his instruction; fourth, he is paradigmatic of the self-interested calculator of pleasure and pain; and fifth, he attempts to isolate courage from the other virtues or parts of virtue,[4] seeing in it a mark of distinction and regarding the other virtues as common.

Advance Warning

The warnings about sophistic education begin in the earliest stage of the dialogue. From Socrates' conversation with Hippocrates we learn that the sophist is known for being a clever speaker himself (310e6–7) and making others clever speakers (312d5–7); one supposes that clever speaking is the skill that Hippocrates hopes to acquire by associating with Protagoras. It is significant that Hippocrates never thinks to apply the term *aretē* to what he will learn

---

4. Protagoras initially sets wisdom, too, apart from the other virtues, but Socrates brings wisdom and temperance together at 332a–333b.

from Protagoras. Indeed, we discover that there is some measure of ignominy attached to being a sophist (Hippocrates blushes at the very mention of it [312a]; even Callias's doorman expresses contempt for sophists [314c–d]), so that Hippocrates wishes to learn from Protagoras only *epi paideiāi* and certainly not *epi technēi* (312b2–4)—that is, he wishes to learn from him as a layman (*idiōtēs*) would (312b4) and not in order to become an expert (*dēmiourgos*) (312b3). We see, too, that Protagoras has no readily specifiable area of expertise, no technical knowledge of any kind (312e5–6). And we are alerted, finally, to the danger inherent in placing one's soul in the sophist's untrustworthy hands (313a1–3): like a salesman, the sophist is inclined to praise his wares regardless of their worth (313d5–7)—if he even knows their worth (313d7–e1); moreover, he is occupationally prone to deception (313c8–9). Yet if, as Socrates maintains, it is entirely on the condition of the soul, on whether it becomes good or bad, that one's doing well or ill depends (313a7–8), then one is well advised to be wary of the sophist.[5]

Satisfaction Guaranteed

Before Protagoras begins his speech he makes a cogent if perfunctory case for why a young man like Hippocrates, who wishes to make a name for himself in the city (*ellogimos genesthai en tēi polei* [316c1]), would have reason or incentive to abandon his former associates and pay for the privilege of associating with Protagoras instead. Although Protagoras is somewhat evasive, he is still, at this early stage, candid enough to acknowledge that what he does is persuade the best young people to abandon their friends and relatives in order to achieve their own personal advancement (*hōs beltious esomenous* [316c9]), teaching them exclusively the subjects they wish to learn (318d–e). He makes it clear that if Hippocrates becomes his pupil, he will, indeed, get just what he wants: instead of getting what he already gets from his current associates or being taught the same subjects he is taught in school (as he might were he to associate with other sophists),[6] he will become, Protagoras says, a *dunatōtatos*

---

5. Cf. *Crito* 48b and *Gorg.* 470e, where living well or being happy depends solely on whether one is good, just, and noble.

6. Other sophists, like Hippias, do not limit themselves to teaching *aretē* exclusively but teach many other subjects and skills, like arithmetic, astronomy, geometry, music, and poetry (318e). In the *Hippias Minor*, Hippias is caricatured as a kind of jack of all trades.

(319a1), a powerful presence, in the public arena. Even though Protagoras studiously avoids the potentially damaging admission that what he teaches is skill at speaking, he nevertheless is forthright enough to affirm—indeed he boasts—that what his students will learn from him will be *un*like what they have already learned or might learn elsewhere. Even this limited nod to truth, however, does not survive the Great Speech. It is with that speech that the flagrant deception begins.

The Great Speech

Since the plain truth concerning Protagoras is that he teaches young men skills that are competitive rather than cooperative, skills that are designed to distinguish an elite from among the multitude, to build the reputations of a select handful of men at the expense of the rest, and, as a consequence, to concentrate wealth and power in the hands of the few, he can hardly afford to be completely honest and forthcoming when Socrates compels him to defend his practice and profession in democratic Athens.[7] Protagoras's speech represents his eloquent, but also labored, effort to conceal what he actually teaches without at the same time reducing to naught his own value as a teacher of *aretē*.

Scholars have engaged in vigorous and vehement debate about the origins of the Protagorean speech (is it Protagoras's or is it a Platonic invention?); about its merits (is it brilliant or is it hopelessly confused?); about Plato's take on it (would Plato not agree with, for example, much of what Protagoras says about punishment?);[8] about how effectively it answers Socrates' arguments concerning Athenian political practice and the Athenian approach to the transmission of personal *aretē* (does it assimilate political expertise to personal *aretē*? does it mistake a merely necessary condition for political participation for a sufficient condition for political proficiency?); and about how seriously Protagoras himself takes his myth and what follows from it (surely he does not

7. As M. Frede (1992, xii–xiii) explains: "Democracy rests on the assumption that the affairs of a city are not the subject of some special expertise, but that every citizen is competent to judge them. To claim that a special expertise or art is needed for these matters comes dangerously close to claiming that the people are not fit to rule, for they do not have this expertise."

8. See O'Brien 1967, 143; Jowett 1892, I, 123; Stewart 1960, 214; Randall 1970, 88; Shorey 1909. C. C. W. Taylor (1991, 96) points out the affinities between Protagoras's and Plato's accounts of punishment: according to both, punishment's aims are reformation and deterrence (see *Gorg.* 476–479; *Laws* 5.753d–e, 9.854–856, 862d–863a).

take it literally, but does he not perhaps subscribe to it on some other level?). In all these scholarly deliberations, however, the most critical question is neglected: does Protagoras say in his entire speech anything true about what he actually does?

Many scholars consider the speech to be a great one. It is, they think, both subtly nuanced and well crafted, a veritable tour de force of oratory.[9] Indeed, that the question of whether Protagoras represents at all accurately what he teaches is largely neglected by Plato scholars in favor of questions concerning the origins of the speech and the soundness of its argument is a measure of its stunning strategic success. The speech dazzles. Protagoras is the consummate speaker, able to lure young people away from family and friends in every city through which he passes, "charming them with a voice like Orpheus's—and they follow spellbound" (315b1). Even Socrates is captivated at first: "I stayed gazing at him, quite spellbound for a long time" (328d4–5). Socrates, however, soon recovers. For he judges the speech by the yardstick of truth. That Protagoras so artfully avoids or conceals the truth is not from Socrates' perspective a credit to him. The virtue of an orator, as Socrates says in the *Apology*, "is to speak the truth" (*Ap.* 18a).

The Great Speech is prompted by Socrates' two stated reasons for doubting the teachability of virtue (*Prot.* 319b–320b): first, that the sensible Athenians, when deliberating in the Assembly, seek advice from experts whenever they confront a technical matter, but when the question at hand concerns management of the polis, they seek equally the advice of anyone; and second, that the wisest and best Athenians are unable to transmit to others, even to their own sons, the virtue that is theirs. In response to Socrates' points, Protagoras first invents a myth.[10] By telling a story about Zeus and Hermes, Protagoras attempts to blur the critical distinction between two rather different ideas: that everyone must share in a sense of shame (*aidōs*) and right (*dikē*) if there are to be civilized communities at all, and that *aidōs* and *dikē* are a *technē* allotted to all. By turning basic civic *aretē* into a *technē,* the myth makes *aretē* teachable and paves the way for sophists to be its teachers. Yet sophists do not

9. See, e.g., Guthrie 1956, 31; Grote 1875, II, 45, 47; Jowett 1892, I, 116; Weingartner 1973, 57; Shorey 1933, 124. Among those who disparage the speech are Schleiermacher, Ast, and Hermann (cited by Grote 1875, II, 47, n1); Gomperz 1905, 310.

10. Adam and Adam (1905, xxi–xxiii) regard the myth as Protagoras's own composition, included either in his *Peri politeias* or in his *Peri tēs en archē katastaseōs,* noting that myth was coming into favor in the literary circles of the day.

actually teach *aidōs* and *dikē*—or, as Protagoras later calls them, justice (*dikaiosunē*), temperance (*sōphrosunē*), and piety (*to hosion* or *hosiotēs*)—at all.[11] It is hardly in order to become superlatively just and temperate that young men eagerly lavish on Protagoras all the money they can lay their hands on.[12]

According to the myth, people at first, thanks to Prometheus, acquired the skills necessary for existence in small groups, but they did not, until Zeus dispatched Hermes, possess the skills necessary for living politically, in communities composed of members not all related by blood.[13] The skills of *aidōs* and *dikē* enabled human beings to combat beasts without combating each other. These skills, the myth maintains, were not, however, distributed as the others were: these were distributed to all. For unlike other skills, the skills of *aidōs* and *dikē* are the necessary (and, as Protagoras implies, also sufficient) conditions for participation in political life.

What does it mean, in the context of Protagoras's speech, that *aidōs* and *dikē* (322c4) or *dikaiosunē* and *sōphrosunē* (323a1–2) were distributed to all? Does their universal distribution disqualify them as genuine *technai* on the grounds that it is in the nature of *technai* to be distributed more sparingly? As the speech continues into its logos component, it becomes clear that, from the perspective of the speech, there is no qualitative difference between the political *technē* or *aretē* and the other *technai;* political *technē* or *aretē* is just one *technē* among other *technai*. All *technai* require natural talent and instruction if they are to be fully mastered; the only difference between the political *technē* and others is how widely they are taught. The demythicized sense of universal distribution is universal instruction: because people appreciate the critical importance to society of justice and temperance, everyone teaches these

---

11. In order successfully to "help others to become noble and good" (328b2–3), Protagoras would have to nurture his pupils individually over time. See *Gorg.* 455a: "for he [a rhetorician] would not be able to teach so large a mob such great matters [the just and unjust] in a short time."

12. Sophistic education, the education that is paid for, is regularly contrasted in Plato with the kind of moral education that everyone provides to everyone for free. See *Meno* 91c–92e, where Anytus sharply condemns paid sophistic education, insisting that virtue can be learned from any Athenian gentleman with whom one takes the trouble to associate. See also *Gorg.* 520c–e, where Socrates argues that it is shameful for a man to take money for advising people on how they might be better themselves and how they might manage their households better. At *Meno* 94c–d Socrates says of Thucydides that since he willingly spent money to have his sons taught everything, he surely would have, if only virtue were teachable, had them instructed also in virtue, since moral improvement costs nothing.

13. On this point, see C. C. W. Taylor 1991, 81, 84–85.

things to everyone. As is the case with every *technē,* those who have a greater measure of natural talent in *aretē* turn out "better" than those who do not.[14] But, since all are taught *aretē,* and taught it constantly, all learn *aretē* and, in comparison to those raised in lawless societies, are therefore *dēmiourgoi,* experts, in justice.[15] The other *technai,* being less important to society and not needing to be possessed universally in order for the society to survive, are taught by some to some, and are hence acquired only by some. Here, too, it is those favored with natural talent who will be more skilled than those not so favored.

Political skill is assimilated by Protagoras in the myth to the cooperative excellences, *dikaiosunē* and *sōphrosunē,* that are required for common living. Nothing but natural talent accounts for the excellence that distinguishes some from others. Everyone teaches everyone—not in order to make some stand out over others but, on the contrary, because "we benefit . . . from one another's *dikaiosunē* and *aretē*" (327b1–2). *Aretē* is, then, in the Great Speech, someone else's good; it benefits in the first instance not oneself but one's associates; and it is, in turn, one's associates' *aretē* that is of benefit to oneself.[16] If Protagoras, as he says, indeed does what everyone else does—though somewhat better—then, on his account, he neither teaches his students what they wish to learn (since he does nothing to help them to distinguish themselves in the public arena) nor has he grounds for persuading them "to abandon their association with others, relatives and foreigners, young and old alike, and to associate, instead, with him" (316c7–9).

One telling irony of the speech is that through it Protagoras assures a young man who has no desire to be a *dēmiourgos* in sophistry (312b3), someone who wishes to learn from Protagoras only *epi paideiāi* (312b3–4), as a layman would (312b4), that he is already, by virtue of the ongoing ubiquitous instruction in *aretē* to which he is subjected daily, a *dēmiourgos* in the very *aretē* that Protagoras

---

14. It is hardly a coincidence that Protagoras identifies not only natural talent but wealth as well (326c3–6) as factors that contribute to a student's being especially successful at *aretē.* Socrates had mentioned to him that Hippocrates has both (316b9–10).

15. To be a *dēmiourgos* is to be an expert at some *technē* and no mere layman. Those who study *epi technē* do so in order to be *dēmiourgoi* (312b3). It is the *dēmiourgos* who is consulted on technical matters (319c2–4; 322d8). And in *technai* generally, one *dēmiourgos* suffices for many laymen (322c7).

16. As Socrates sees it, if by teaching *aretē* to others we first and foremost benefit ourselves, that in itself ought to be sufficient reason not to charge a fee for our instruction.

teaches (327c7). For as Protagoras says, anyone who is instructed all the time is ipso facto a *dēmiourgos;* a layman, he thinks, is someone who understands nothing at all. In a society in which everyone teaches everyone flute-playing, Protagoras observes, *all* would be capable (*hikanoi*) at flute-playing when compared with laymen who understand (*epaïontas*) nothing of it at all (327c2).

Protagoras's answer to Socrates, then, is that the Athenians rightly listen to everyone on political matters, not because, as Socrates thinks, political *aretē* is *not* a *technē* so that there are no experts to consult and all are laymen, but rather because in the case of political *aretē* there are no laymen: everyone, says Protagoras, is a *dēmiourgos* by virtue of having been raised in a civilized society.[17] Instead, then, of advancing the cause of the professional—that is, the sophistic—teaching of *aretē,* or, indeed, of sustaining any form of teaching of *aretē,* the speech confirms Socrates' idea, suggested by his browsing-cattle metaphor at 320a, that *aretē* is picked up "automatically."[18]

There can be no doubt that Protagoras, were he unafraid to speak the truth

17. As C. C. W. Taylor (1991, 83) rightly points out, however, "if everything above mere oral and intellectual imbecillity is counted as excellence, then the concept is so diluted as virtually to vanish."

18. Whereas for Protagoras, young men's passive absorption of society's lessons counts as a form of being taught, for Socrates this model of "spontaneous" (*automatou*) or chance picking-up of virtue is a model of how *aretē* fails to be taught. See Gomperz 1905, II, 312. At *Meno* 92e Socrates makes the same point, contrasting the *teaching* of virtue with its spontaneous (*apo tou automatou*) absorption. Note as well the *Protagoras*'s use of *perituchōsin* (to happen on [320a3]) and the *Meno*'s related *entuchēi* (to fall in with [92e4]).

Nussbaum (1986, 104) thinks that Protagoras, according to his own account, would teach virtue the way a Greek instructor teaches Greek: "Even if all adults are competent native speakers and teach the language to their children, there is still room for an expert who can take people 'a little further along the road'—presumably by making the speaker more explicitly and reflectively aware of the structures of his practice and the interconnections of its different elements. Even so, an expert ethical teacher can make the already well-trained young person more aware of the nature and interrelationships of his ethical commitments." But, first, Protagoras makes no claim to expertise of *this* kind with respect to *aretē.* Second, he thinks (or, at any rate, he says) that street instruction alone makes one an expert (*dēmiourgos*) at justice; indeed, if this were not the case, why would ordinary Athenians be qualified to offer their opinions on political matters? (Note that in the *Protagoras,* the *dēmiourgos* is consistently contrasted with the layman; the ordinary Athenian is, therefore, no lay practitioner but an expert. See 312b and 327c and note 15.) Third, Protagoras is deliberately vague about what he does. And that is because, fourth, he does not do what he says he does, namely, teach what others teach—only somewhat better; what he teaches has nothing whatever to do with enhancing the cooperative *aretai* young men otherwise acquire by a kind of effortless osmosis. By his own admission, Protagoras lures young people away from their other associates and what they teach.

about himself and his profession, would say that the Athenians are foolish to consult everyone on political matters: not all men are *dēmiourgoi* in political *technē;* political *technē* is something at which only a few are skilled and at which most are laymen—that is, they understand nothing at all. Political *technē,* he would say, consists primarily of the ability to speak well; and speaking well is both what Protagoras himself is proficient at and what he is able to teach others. Lacking the courage, however, to speak the truth, and having been put by Socrates in a position where it would require courage to speak the truth, Protagoras tells a story that removes the distinction between individual political success, on the one hand, and basic civility, on the other, making political *technē* the province of the many—indeed of all—rather than of the few.[19]

Protagoras is unwilling to describe openly, accurately, and frankly what it is that he does. The cost of honesty is, to be sure, fairly high: it might deprive him of his flourishing enterprise, his reputation, and possibly even his life. These are goods whose loss Protagoras is not prepared to risk. He prefers instead to cede the very ground on which his claim to teach *aretē* rests.

Protagoras is nothing if not cautious. That "caution is in order" (316c) is just about the very first thing Protagoras says to Socrates. And note the surprising way in which he explains, at 317b–c, why he, unlike the great "sophists" of the past who disguised their true profession,[20] openly admits to being a sophist. Rather than brag (as one might expect) that, unlike his predecessors, he speaks the truth regardless of the risk, he says: "I consider this admission to be a better *precaution* than denial. . . . I have given thought to *other precautions* as well, so as to avoid suffering any ill from admitting that I am a sophist." When he finds that the risk to him of debating with Socrates on Socrates' terms is too great, he avoids it: "Socrates, I have had verbal contests with many people, and if I had done what you tell me to do, and had conversed according to the demands of my opponent, I should have seemed superior to no one, nor would Protagoras have been a name among the Greeks" (335a). He does what he must and says what he must to keep himself safe: "It seems to me to be *safer* to respond not

---

19. As Gomperz (1905, II, 312) puts it: "It is clear as daylight that this argument leaves practically no room for teachers of morality and their work. Naturally Protagoras does not accept a conclusion so disastrous for a professional teacher of virtue."

20. Protagoras regards as sophists such men of renown as Homer, Hesiod, Simonides, Orpheus, Musaeus, Iccus of Tarentum, Herodicus of Selymbria, Agathocles, Pythoclides of Ceos, and many others (316d). These men, however, were poets, prophets, physical trainers, and musicians.

merely with my present answer in mind but from the point of view of my life overall" (351d). Indeed, his concern for his own safety is reflected in the very fact that, although he has nothing but contempt for the many (he says such things as that they notice nothing themselves but only follow their leaders, that he would be ashamed to agree to things that many people agree to, that the many often say what is not correct or whatever occurs to them [see 317a–b, 333c1–2, 352e3–4, 353a7–8, 359c6–7]), he addresses at considerable length and with ostensible seriousness Socrates' first question concerning the many's practice of permitting all citizens to speak on political matters. As a guest in democratic Athens, he knows better than openly to disparage the many.[21]

We have seen thus far that Protagoras is a man who hawks his wares without regard for their merit, and that, as a risk-averse calculator of his own self-interest, he panders to Athenian democratic sensibilities rather than tell the truth about his own profession. He is certainly a skillful speaker but, like the accusers at Socrates' trial who "speak so persuasively" (*Ap.* 17a) yet say "little or nothing true" (*Ap.* 17b), Protagoras speaks persuasively but says scarcely anything true.

The virtue that Protagoras describes in his speech and that he pretends to teach just a bit better than everyone else, the virtue that all have and that all must have if there are to be civilized societies, the virtue at which everyone in a civilized society is of necessity a veritable *dēmiourgos* consists of two or at most three parts. The parts of this virtue that Protagoras lists in his speech are *aidōs* and *dikē,* which are initially replaced by the pair *dikaiosunē* and *sōphrosunē,* and eventually by the triumvirate *dikaiosunē, sōphrosunē,* and *to hosion.*[22] Protagoras also concentrates these three virtues into a single unit (*kai sullēbdēn hen auto prosagoreuō* [325a1; also 329c5]), which he calls alternately "manly virtue" (*andros aretēn* [325a2]) and "virtue" (*aretēn* [329c6]). Note that Protagoras does not once mention wisdom or courage. Throughout his speech, the whole of

---

21. C. C. W. Taylor (1991, 83) thinks that Protagoras, being a "subjectivist," actually believes what he says, namely, that the Athenians are right to believe that all should be consulted on matters of public policy. But the truth of the matter is that Protagoras, like Meletus in the *Apology* and Gorgias in the *Gorgias* (460a), is forced by Socrates into a position where he cannot say what he thinks for fear of giving offense. See M. Frede 1992, xix: Protagoras "hesitates to speak his mind and to develop his view in a direction which inevitably would bring him into conflict, not only with the people of Athens, but also with traditionalists among the upper class."

22. *To hosion* is mentioned first along with *dikaiosunē* and *sōphrosunē* at 325a1. It appears again at 325d4, where *kalon* and *aischron* also appear. When Protagoras wishes to use just one term, he uses *dikaiosunē* (323b6).

virtue, indeed the whole of manly virtue, consists of *dikaiosunē, sōphrosunē,* and *hosiotēs* alone. Yet surely it is courage and wisdom if anything—and not justice, temperance, and piety—that he thinks are the components of *andros aretē.* That Protagoras here applies to the common and pedestrian virtues of justice, temperance, and piety—indeed to the virtues that every man, *woman, and child* must share in (325a6)—the term *andros aretē* is but another sign of his disingenuousness. Protagoras omits wisdom and courage, the virtues that distinguish extraordinary men from ordinary ones, in order to be able to justify the Athenian practice of according to all men a voice in public deliberations about matters of justice.

The Unity of the Virtues: Justice, Holiness, Temperance, and Wisdom

Socrates, having heard Protagoras's long and magnificent Great Speech, is left with but one small and seemingly quite peripheral question to ask.[23] Although the question Socrates asks is ostensibly meant to elicit an answer from Protagoras that will somehow lay permanently to rest all Socrates' doubts about the teachability of virtue, its real purpose is to get Protagoras to talk about the parts of virtue he had up to now neglected: wisdom and courage. What Socrates asks is how virtue is related to its parts and how the parts of virtue are related to each other.

It is instructive to see how the two hitherto unmentioned virtues, wisdom and courage, make their debut. When Protagoras is asked by Socrates if a person who has one part of virtue must necessarily have all the others, he exclaims: "By no means, since many are courageous but unjust, and many again are just but not wise" (329e5–6). Protagoras's immediate impulse, we see, is to set courage and wisdom apart from justice. In so doing, he reveals what is for him the gaping chasm that exists between the virtues of the superior minority and those of the inferior multitude. We note, too, that Protagoras assumes an easy compatibility between *in*justice and courage.

Socrates now begins the long and arduous process of getting Protagoras to acknowledge a connection or similarity between, on the one hand, the virtues wisdom and courage that he had up to now suppressed and, on the other hand,

---

23. At *Euthyphro* 13a, there also remains one "small point" that Socrates says is not clear: what is meant by *therapeia* (care). Here, too, it is no small point.

the virtues justice, temperance, and holiness that were featured prominently in his speech.

Socrates starts by suggesting a likeness between the two virtues or parts of virtue—justice and holiness—that Protagoras is least likely to regard as being worlds apart. After all, Protagoras had mentioned both of these among the virtues that all people must have, and must even be *dēmiourgoi* in, if there are to be civilized societies; and both are virtues of the undistinguished. Nevertheless, now that Protagoras has asserted that the virtues are different from one another both in themselves and in their functions, he balks (*duscherōs* . . . *echein* [332a2]) at Socrates' suggestion that justice and holiness might be the same. He rather rashly insists, in a stark reversal of his declaration at 329e5–6 that the parts of virtue differ from one another, that everything resembles everything to some degree—even black and white, hard and soft, and the parts of a face. It is no mean accomplishment, then, when Socrates does finally succeed in securing Protagoras's admission that justice and holiness are related more significantly than are black and white, hard and soft, and the parts of a face, and hence that there is resemblance (if not identity) between justice and holiness. They were shown to be, as Socrates says at the end of the next argument (333b5–6), *schedon ti tauton,* "nearly the same."[24]

Socrates next goes on to attempt to bring wisdom into line with temperance. The argument he uses begins by identifying folly as the opposite of both, and continues: if each thing has but one opposite, and folly is the opposite of both wisdom and temperance, it follows that wisdom and temperance must be the same. Protagoras assents, albeit grudgingly (*mal' akontōs* [333b4]), to Socrates' conclusion. This argument is surely less substantive than verbal, playing as it does on the linguistic opposition between *aphrosunē* (folly) and *sōphrosunē* (temperance), and contending that if acting foolishly is a sign of lack of temperance, then the source of intemperance, like the source of foolishness, is folly. Nevertheless, for Socrates to have elicited Protagoras's assent even just to the idea that to act temperately is to act wisely constitutes a criti-

---

24. For further discussion of this argument, see Weiss 1985a. I argue that Protagoras is brought to agree that there is greater likeness between justice and holiness than between, say, white and black, because whereas he is unwilling to say of justice that it is unholy or not holy, or of holiness that it is unjust or not just, he would have no comparable reluctance in the case of white and black or the parts of a face. It may not be clear what it would mean to say that a nose is un-mouth or not-mouth, but it nevertheless seems all right to say so.

cal victory: it merges the temperance that is for Protagoras a virtue of the common man with the wisdom that is for him a virtue of the distinguished.

Socrates turns now to the relationship between justice and temperance: can one who acts unjustly be temperate, in the sense of showing good sense, *sōphronein,* in his injustice? Since (1) Protagoras had earlier claimed that one could be both just and not wise (329e5–6), and (2) temperance has now been shown to be wisdom, what could be more natural than for Socrates to ask at this juncture if someone can be temperate but unjust, in order to conclude that one cannot be wise (substituting "wise" for "temperate") but unjust, just but not wise?

Although this third argument does not get very far before being cut short by a Protagorean tirade, it gets far enough for the reader to discern the direction in which it was headed. Socrates begins by eliciting from Protagoras the reluctant admission that he sees no conflict between acting unjustly, on the one hand, and the kind of temperate and sensible behavior (*sōphronein*),[25] good thinking (*eu phronein*), and taking good counsel (*eu bouleuesthai*) that issue in doing well (*eu prattousin*), on the other (333d4–8).[26] It is evident that had Socrates been permitted to pursue his argument to its end, he would have attempted first to persuade Protagoras that it is not in fact possible for someone to be temperate but unjust, next to establish some resemblance between temperance and justice, and finally to narrow the gap between justice and wisdom. His strategy, as best one can guess from what little of the argument we have, would have been to derive the conclusion that it is impossible to be both temperate and unjust as follows: (1) temperance, as *sōphronein, eu phronein,* or

25. Socrates plays on the etymological relation between temperance (*sōphrosunē*), on the one hand, and *sōphronein* and *eu phronein,* sensible acting and sensible thinking, on the other, as well as on Protagoras's acquiescence in Socrates' previous conclusion that temperance is wisdom.

26. Protagoras begins by assigning such a belief to the many, saying that he would be ashamed to profess it (333c1–3). For Callicles in the *Gorgias,* prudence is distinct from temperance, the former being a virtue of the superior (489e2–9), the latter a vice of the inferior. For him, the former involves the careful advancement of one's self-interest; the latter, the restraint of appetite. The question whether injustice is compatible with prudence, wisdom, ability, skill, or power is raised not only in the *Protagoras* and *Gorgias* but also in the *Hippias Minor* and in *Rep.* 1 and 2. In *Rep.* 1 (348d), Socrates asks Thrasymachus if he calls injustice a tendency toward vice (*kakoētheian*), to which Thrasymachus replies that he does not; rather, he calls it good counsel (*euboulia*). Socrates then goes on to ask if the unjust are good (*agathoi*) as well as prudent (*phronimoi*), to which Thrasymachus replies that they are—so long as they do injustice perfectly. The parallels to our *Protagoras* passage are striking.

eu bouleuesthai, issues in good things;[27] (2) good things are beneficial for human beings and bad things are harmful for them; (3) doing injustice issues in bad things, that is, in things that are harmful to human beings; hence, (4) it is impossible to be both temperate and unjust. Propositions (1) and (2) appear in the text. It is proposition (3), however, the one that is not in the text, that is the pivotal one. If temperance is to be incompatible with injustice, injustice will have to be shown to yield bad things, things harmful and detrimental for human beings, rather than the things good for human beings that temperance is presumed to yield. Once proposition (3) is established it is but a short step to (4)—and from there (now that temperance and wisdom have been shown to be the same) an even shorter step to (5): it is impossible to be both wise and unjust.

Alas, the argument is aborted as Protagoras attacks proposition (2) with inordinate relish: may not good things be beneficial, he demands, even if they are not beneficial for men? Unleashing a veritable torrent of words, Protagoras not only does violence to the conversational pattern that had thus far governed his exchange with Socrates, but he refuses to continue unless the rules adopted henceforth are his. Socrates meets Protagoras halfway, consenting to be answerer rather than questioner, but Protagoras exploits the situation: the "question" he poses concerning the interpretation of poetry has the effect of enabling him, and compelling Socrates, to make a long speech. Although it may seem that Socrates has been defeated, the game is not over yet. What Socrates will do, as we shall see, is use the poetry-interpreting exercise as the occasion for making the very point he would have made in his temperance/justice argument had he not been so rudely interrupted.

Poetic Justice

Protagoras takes his turn first, trying to impress his audience by revealing a contradiction in a poem by the great Simonides.[28] According to Protagoras, Simonides, although he initially contends that it is hard to become good, nevertheless goes on subsequently to dispute Pittacus, who similarly main-

27. Recall that in the previous argument, Protagoras agrees that to act correctly and beneficially (*orthōs te kai ōphelimōs*) is to be acting temperately (332a6–7).

28. Protagoras (at 316d) includes Simonides among those who were really sophists but disguised their sophistry with other *technai*—in this case, poetry.

tains that it is hard to be good. Protagoras takes no stand of his own on the question of whether it is hard to become good, being content to find a flaw in Simonides, but Socrates not only defends Simonides against the charge of inconsistency—he notes that becoming good and being good are hardly the same thing—but lauds the point he takes (or pretends to take) Simonides to be making, namely, that whereas it is difficult to become good it is not only difficult but actually impossible to stay that way.

Despite the zeal with which he takes his turn at interpreting Simonides, Socrates makes it clear that he has little use for the activity of poetry interpretation, regarding it as something people engage in when they are unable to sustain an intelligent conversation with one another (347c–348a). Indeed, what his rather frivolous interpretation seems to prove, if anything, is the general worthlessness of the occupation. Neither Protagoras's ability to catch a poet in a contradiction nor, for that matter, Socrates' ability to free him from it seems to signal any sort of genuine excellence in the interpreter; moreover, no truth of any importance concerning how one ought to live emerges from the discussion.

What scholars find particularly noteworthy in the poetry-interpreting section of the *Protagoras* is that Socrates inserts into his interpretation of the poem a variation on his famous paradox "no one does wrong willingly." According to Socrates' interpretation of Simonides' poem, when the poet declares that he praises and loves "all who do no shameful thing (*aischron*) willingly," he must be understood to be saying instead that he willingly praises and loves all who do nothing shameful, since, after all, Simonides was not so uneducated as to believe that anyone willingly does bad things (*kaka*). Indeed, no wise man, Socrates says, thinks that anyone willingly errs (*examartanein*) or willingly does shameful and bad things (*ergazesthai aischra te kai kaka*) (345d–e).

Does Socrates exploit his foray into poetry interpretation solely for the purpose of affirming his paradox? Is his introduction of the paradox at this juncture, as many commentators believe, nothing more than an anticipation of what will come much later, at 358b–d? Or should we perhaps see in Socrates' iteration of his paradox in the Simonides interlude not only a foretaste of what is to come later but an important connection to what has gone before?

Recall the argument that broke off midstream. Protagoras, unhappy with the trajectory of the argument concerning temperance and justice, stopped the flow of the argument with a disquisition on the relativity of advantage: things that are advantageous in one context or for one kind of being or entity are disadvantageous in another context or for another kind of being or entity. In speculating on where the argument would have gone were it not for this interruption, I suggested that Socrates would have argued, against Protagoras, that people cannot exhibit temperance—that is, they cannot act sensibly, think well, or take good counsel—if they act unjustly, since acting unjustly brings people not good things, things that are beneficial, but bad things, things that are harmful. If, moreover, it is not possible to be temperate but unjust, it is not possible, either—since temperance and wisdom are the same—to be wise but unjust.

For Socrates to say now that Simonides surely does not believe—since no wise man believes—that anyone does shameful and bad things willingly is for him to make, somewhat belatedly, the very same point. It is to say that since wise men recognize that in doing wrong one brings on oneself bad things, harmful things, things that no one could want, wise men could never believe, as Protagoras evidently does, that those who do wrong act sensibly and prudently, taking good counsel. On the contrary, wise men know that those who do shameful things fail to do what they want.

Note that Socrates, in interpreting the Simonides poem, does not maintain that wrongdoing is never deliberate, that it is "unwilling" in the sense that it is done under constraint. For, on Socrates' interpretation, when Simonides praises unwillingly (that is, under constraint) those who wrong him—his parents or city—forcing himself to do so despite his anger, it is surely parents or city who freely and intentionally wrong him, who wrong him quite deliberately and voluntarily, that he must force himself to praise. Indeed, Socrates reads Simonides as confessing, in effect, that on occasion he has had to praise even a tyrant or someone else of that ilk against his will (346b–c). The tyrant, of course, is the quintessential wicked man whose distinguishing feature is the purposeful committing of injustice.

What Simonides and other wise men understand, then, which the unwise Protagoras does not, is not that all wrongdoing is done under compulsion but that it is committed unwillingly: it invariably brings people the bad and harmful things they do not want and fails to bring them the good and beneficial things they want. The truly wise therefore avoid injustice; it is the unjust who are not wise.

The Unity of the Virtues: Courage

If, indeed, in interpreting Simonides' poem Socrates surreptitiously completes the earlier aborted argument for the relationship between two of the parts of virtue—justice and wisdom—it is hardly surprising that the conversation resumes with a reassessment of Protagoras's stance on the question of the relationship among the parts of *aretē*. Protagoras now maintains (349d) that four of the virtues are reasonably close to one another, but courage is utterly distinct from all the rest. As proof for this position Protagoras cites what he regards as a fact: "you will find many people who are extremely unjust, impious, intemperate, and ignorant, and yet exceptionally courageous" (349d6–8).

Since Protagoras so decisively isolates courage from all the other virtues, Socrates shrewdly proposes to him a conception of courage that takes it in a quite different direction: perhaps, Socrates ventures, courage is a kind of confidence. Protagoras readily confirms that in his view the courageous are indeed confident (*tharraleoi*), "going toward the things that most men are afraid to go toward" (349e3). But no sooner does Protagoras characterize the courageous as confident than Socrates proceeds to coax courage back to its place among the virtues, making the case that courage is wisdom. Recall that it was the elite virtues of both courage and wisdom that were conspicuously excluded from the Great Speech and were thus initially set apart from the common virtues of justice, temperance, and holiness. Wisdom, however, has by now been tainted: it was assimilated to temperance at 332a–333b. Protagoras will strive mightily to keep courage from being similarly tainted. He will therefore strenuously resist Socrates' conclusion that courage is wisdom.

Socrates' argument runs as follows: since (1) the courageous are confident, (2) courage is noble; yet confidence without knowledge of danger-related *technai* is ignoble madness, and (3) those who are most proficient (knowledgeable) in these danger-related skills are most confident and hence most courageous, it follows that (4) courage is wisdom.

Protagoras protests. He accuses Socrates of failing to remember that his position is limited to the view that (all) the courageous are confident, and he claims not to have been asked whether (all) the confident are courageous. Had he been asked, he says, he would have said that they are not. He acknowledges that Socrates did show that one's confidence increases as one's knowledge does, since one who has knowledge is indeed more confident than one who does not.

But Protagoras challenges the legitimacy of Socrates' concluding, on the basis of the premises he has just cited, that courage is wisdom. It is, he says, as if Socrates had asked, first, if the strong are powerful and, next, if those who know how to wrestle are more powerful than those who do not and become still more powerful with increased learning, and had concluded solely on the grounds of an affirmative response to these questions that wisdom is strength.

Let us pause for a moment and ask who is the one with the poor memory. Did Socrates not in fact ask Protagoras whether all the confident are courageous? He did (350b4). And did Protagoras not answer that they are not? He did (350b5–6). It is Protagoras, then, who fails to remember. But is it not true, as Protagoras avers, that Socrates drew his conclusion that courage is wisdom just from the propositions that "all the courageous are confident," and "one's confidence increases as one's knowledge does"? It is not. For Socrates' argument contained, besides these two premises labeled above as (1) and (3), respectively, a third premiss as well, the one labeled (2), namely, "one who is confident without knowledge is not courageous (but mad)—because such confidence is ignoble" (350b5–6). Indeed, this premiss was not even Socrates' own contribution but was actually volunteered by Protagoras (350b5–6), the very man who had declared just a moment earlier that a man can be most courageous yet most ignorant (349d7–8). Since Protagoras's strength/power argument contains nothing that corresponds to premiss (2), it fails to replicate faithfully the full version of Socrates' argument concerning courage and confidence. In other words, Protagoras's question "Are the strong powerful?" corresponds to Socrates' premiss (1): the courageous are confident. His "Are the strong more powerful when they know how to wrestle than when they do not?" corresponds to the original premiss (3): the courageous are more confident when they have knowledge of danger-related skills than when they do not. But Protagoras never poses the following question that would have corresponded to Socrates' premiss (2): Since strength is noble, and since nothing is noble without knowledge, is it not the case that power without knowledge is not strength but madness? What Socrates had argued in his courage/confidence argument was: (a) if, on the one hand, when knowledge is present, the more knowledge the courageous have, the more confident they are, and (b) if, on the other hand, when knowledge is absent the confident are not courageous but mad (since courage is noble and nothing can be noble apart from knowledge), it follows that (c) the kind of confidence that increases when knowledge is present is courage and (d) the kind of confidence that persists when knowledge is absent is madness. *That* is why courage must be wisdom.[29] Had Protagoras accurately reproduced the steps in Socrates' argument concerning courage and confidence in his own argument concerning strength and power, he would have had no choice but to conclude in the case of strength precisely what Socrates concluded in the case of courage, namely, that it is wisdom.

However illegitimate Protagoras's resistance to Socrates' conclusion is, it is lucky for him that he refused to concede the argument. For had he accepted that courage is wisdom, Socrates could easily have proceeded to discredit him and other sophists as teachers of at least one part of virtue—courage—insofar as they are not themselves masters of, and are certainly unequipped to teach, such danger-related skills as diving, riding on horseback, and fighting with a shield. Protagoras's luck does not hold for very long, however, since Socrates' resources have by no means been exhausted. Socrates immediately tries another tack.

Socrates' new point of departure is the Protagorean pronouncement that just as power derives from knowledge (*epistēmē*) as well as from madness (*mania*) and passion (*thumos*), but strength from nature and the proper nurture of the body (*eutrophias tōn sōmatōn*), so confidence derives from skill (*technē*) as well as from madness and passion, and courage from nature and the proper nurture of the soul (*eutrophias tōn psuchōn*).

Note that this proclamation egregiously undermines Protagoras's own position. For by assigning to strength and courage sources distinct from the sources of power and confidence, Protagoras forfeits his right to hold that the strong are powerful or the courageous confident. Moreover, by removing courage from the realm of *technē*, consigning it instead to the realm of nature and nurture, Protagoras in effect places courage wholly beyond his reach: he cannot affect a person's nature and he is hardly a nurturer of souls.[30] In Protagoras we have a man who not only considers himself to be noble and good but boldly and openly proclaims himself a teacher of *aretē*, deeming it fully appropriate to charge a fee for his services (348e–349a; see also 349e–350a). Yet

29. For a fuller discussion of this argument, see Weiss 1985b.

30. See Stokes 1986, 372: "Protagoras cannot afford to allow too large a place for natural endowment in the growth of goodness, since that would correspondingly reduce the importance of his and others' teaching."

he teaches neither justice, temperance, and holiness, on the one hand, nor, as it seems, courage, on the other.

Less shocking, perhaps, than Protagoras's unwitting banishment of courage from his professional purview, but of great importance nonetheless, is what his association of courage with nature and nurture reveals about his attitude toward the many. Protagoras's disdain for the many, manifest throughout the dialogue in a number of undeniably disparaging remarks he makes about them (317a–b, 333c1–2, 352e3–4, 353a7–8, 359c6–7), announces itself here even more loudly and clearly. For here Protagoras recognizes that there are some, the courageous, whom nature herself has favored. Unlike the universally taught and learned—and therefore common and plebeian—*aretē* that Protagoras describes in his speech, courage, the virtue that is neither wisdom nor skill, is neither taught nor learned. As Protagoras sees it, courage is the virtue of the few, the virtue of the best, a natural endowment to be appropriately nurtured.

The disparity among (1) what Protagoras actually teaches, (2) the *aretē* that he says he teaches, and (3) what he takes real *aretē* to be is alarming. If Hippocrates is right, then what Protagoras actually teaches is skill at speaking. Nevertheless, an ever-cautious, self-protective Protagoras insists that he teaches *aretē*, the kind of *aretē* required for civilized life, the kind of *aretē* that everyone teaches everyone but that he teaches a bit better than everyone else. Yet real *aretē*, courage, belongs, he thinks, to those who are superior by nature. If it is courage that truly is, for Protagoras, real *aretē*, manly *aretē*, then real *aretē*, manly *aretē*, is not something he can teach.

Protagoras, qua teacher of *aretē*, is surely not entitled to his view of courage. As a man who professes to teach *aretē*, he is not at liberty to relegate courage, which he recognizes as a part of *aretē*, to the realms of nature and nurture. And Socrates will not allow it. In taking up the argument anew, Socrates will identify for Protagoras the only kind of virtue—indeed, the only kind of courage—that he has warrant to profess to teach.

Hedonism, *Akrasia*, and *Technē*

As the dialogue continues, it takes on the task of identifying the only sort of *aretē* and, eventually, the only sort of courage that sophists can teach. Yet the *technē* that emerges as the one sophists can teach is one that measures and weighs pleasures and pains. It is hardly likely, however, that Socrates regards a *technē* of pleasure as the gateway to virtue. Nor is it at all thinkable that the sophists, who alone are fit to teach such a *technē,* would for that reason qualify for him as *the* legitimate teachers of *aretē.*

From 351b–358d Socrates carefully assembles all the ingredients he needs for his sophistic roast: a common ground for the sophists and the many to share,[31] so that the sophists will have a guaranteed market for their product; an identity for their product; the elimination of any possibility that something might interfere with the efficacy of this product; the sophists' agreement that the product identified is indeed theirs; and the sufficiency of this product for virtue. Socrates' work proceeds in stages.

In the first stage (351b–c), Socrates lays the foundation for the emergence of hedonism as the common ground that Protagoras and the many share.[32] Socrates airs his suspicion that Protagoras, despite his frequent disparagement of the many,[33] subscribes to a hedonism not very different from theirs. Protagoras's agreeing that "a man who lives his life pleasantly to the end lives well"

---

31. The exaggerated form of hedonism that will provide this common ground is likely not one that the many actually subscribe to. See the section "The Urgency of the Paradox" in chapter 1.

32. Among those who regard the *Protagoras*'s hedonism as a nonironic expression of Socrates' point of view are Gosling and Taylor (1982, 45–68); Grote (1875, II, 87–89); Hackforth (1968, 38–42); Crombie (1962, I, 240); Irwin (1977, 103–8, 308–9, n13); Nussbaum (1986, 89–121). Those who doubt that the hedonism in the *Protagoras* is Socratic include A. E. Taylor (1937, 260); Vlastos (1969 and 1985a); Sullivan (1961); Santas (1979, 198–99, 318–19, n8); Zeyl (1980); Kraut (1984, 266); Manuwald (1975); D. Frede (1986); Kahn (1996, 239). The view that pleasure is the good is surely anomalous in Plato. In the *Apology* and *Crito* pleasure does not appear among the ends worthy of human care and commitment. The *Gorgias* fiercely opposes pleasure and the life spent in its pursuit. In the *Republic* Socrates is utterly dismayed when Glaucon ventures that the good might be pleasure (6.509a). Many have tried to reconcile the *Protagoras*'s hedonism with the rest of the Platonic corpus—Grote (1875, 121–22); Gosling and Taylor (1982, 45–68); Nussbaum (1986, 89–121); some even advance the view that hedonism represents the culmination of the Socratic ethical enterprise—Irwin (1997, 103–8); Nussbaum (1986, 110). Some contend that the *Protagoras* contains an enlightened hedonism (see Goodell [1921]; Gosling and Taylor [1982]; Rudebusch [1989 and 1999]). The hedonism in the *Protagoras* is, in my view, of the crudest sort (as it is in the *Gorgias*—see chapter 3, note 87); see Weiss 1989; see also Vlastos 1985a, 18, n57. Note that Socrates uses the identical expressions in the two dialogues to formulate the hedonist view. See note 36. Zeyl argues that Socrates uses hedonistic premises because he wants to show that *even* on hedonistic premises virtue is knowledge. In my view, Socrates uses hedonistic premises because he wants to show that *only* on hedonistic premises is virtue knowledge.

33. See 317a–b, 333c1–2, 352e3–4, 353a7–8, 353b1–3, 359c6–7.

constitutes, as far as Socrates is concerned, an endorsement of hedonism. Indeed, precisely this formulation appears later (at 355a, discussed just below in connection with stage 3) as one of three that Socrates uses to express the hedonist view. Although Protagoras attempts to take exception to Socrates' various formulations of hedonism, his objection is the same as the many's: he recognizes some pleasures that are not good, some pains that are not bad, and neutral things that are neither bad nor good (351d4–7; cf. 351c4, where the many's would-be objection is found).[34] As Socrates will contend, however, it is not by any standard other than pleasure and pain that the many—and Protagoras—judge pleasures and pains good and bad. Protagoras, it is true, does venture a second reservation. To Socrates' question "So, then, to live pleasantly is good, and unpleasantly, bad?" (351b7–c1), Protagoras hedges: "If, at any rate, he lived taking pleasure in *noble* things" (351c1–2). Protagoras is not prepared to endorse hedonism outright, and he is well aware that an unqualified affirmative answer to Socrates' question would indeed be tantamount to such an endorsement. Socrates, however, just ignores Protagoras's qualification, treating "noble" as no different from "good": is not a pleasant thing good qua pleasant, he asks, so long as it does not lead to pain? (351c). (In stage 5 Socrates twice explicitly assimilates the noble to the good—as pleasant [358b; repeated at 358e–360a]. Protagoras raises no objection on either occasion.) Although Protagoras dodges Socrates' further probing of his stand and, instead of answering, suggests that an investigation be undertaken into the question of whether "pleasant and good are the same" (351e5–7), Socrates takes Protagoras's view on the relationship between pleasure and good as having been already disclosed (352a6–8), and proceeds to "uncover" Protagoras's view on knowledge. As far as Socrates is concerned, then, Protagoras's hedonist credentials are firmly established.

In the second stage (352a–e), Socrates works to secure Protagoras's opposition to the notion endorsed by the many that knowledge can be overcome by pleasure, for unless knowledge is invulnerable to pleasure there will remain one intractable obstacle to the effectiveness of a sophistic *technē.* Does Protagoras agree with the many, Socrates asks, that knowledge is not a powerful thing, that it is no leader or ruler of people, and that people are ruled, even

---

34. That Protagoras expresses the reservation that some pleasures are bad and some painful things good is, by his own admission, just his way of playing it safe (*asphalesteron* [351d3]). He answers, he says, taking into account how what he says will affect the rest of his life (351d3–4).

when knowledge is present in them, by passion, pleasure, pain, love, or fear? Does he believe, as they do, that these things often drag knowledge around as if it were a slave? Or does Protagoras perhaps disagree with the many, thinking that knowledge is a noble thing, quite able to rule a person, so that someone who recognized good and bad would not be compelled by any of these other things to act contrary to the dictates of knowledge; his intelligence (*phronēsis*) would suffice to save (*boēthein*) him?

In posing these questions, Socrates counts on two things: first, that Protagoras, a teacher by profession, will be in no position to disparage knowledge and wisdom and, second, that Protagoras would never of his own accord agree with the many. Socrates is not disappointed. Protagoras declares that it would be shameful for him "above all people" to pronounce wisdom (*sophia*) and knowledge anything but the most powerful of human things (352c–d).[35] And when Socrates reviews for Protagoras once again the belief of the many that most people, even if they know what is best and are able to do it, are nevertheless unwilling (*ouk ethelein*) to do it because they are overcome by pleasure or pain or are ruled by one of the other things Socrates has just enumerated, Protagoras, as expected, has nothing but scorn for their view: "I think the many say many other things incorrectly, too" (352e3–4).

Taking advantage of this rare opportunity to stand together with Protagoras in opposition to the many, or at least to pretend to do so, Socrates invites Protagoras to help him persuade and teach the many about the true nature of the experience that they call "being overcome by pleasure," since the many incorrectly cite being overcome by pleasure as the reason people fail to do what they know to be best (352e5–353a3). Socrates' purpose in dealing with the many's erroneous view, as he informs Protagoras, is that it will reveal something about courage and its relationship to the other parts of virtue.

Before addressing the many's purportedly mistaken belief that people are frequently overcome by pleasure, Socrates and Protagoras teach them that when they speak of being overcome by pleasant things like food, drink, or sex,

---

35. As Zeyl (1980, 267, n31) correctly notes, Protagoras's acceptance of knowledge's power is "hardly consistent with his own non-cognitive view of virtue," that is, with the "little more than social conditioning" that is at the core of the teaching Protagoras describes in the Great Speech. Protagoras's problem, as Socrates well knows and exploits, is that, regardless of what he said in his Great Speech, as a *teacher* of virtue he cannot afford to deny the power of knowledge. And even in the Great Speech, virtue is characterized as a *technē*.

and of indulging in these things while realizing (*gignōskontes*) all along that what they are doing is bad (*ponēra* [353c7]), they mean nothing more by something's being "bad" than that it leads to later pain in the form of disease and poverty. Similarly, when they speak of painful things (exercise, military training, medical procedures, etc.) as being good, they mean nothing more than that they lead to pleasant things, such as health, bodily fitness, preservation of cities, power over others, and wealth, as well as to relief from pain. The many, then, pursue pleasure as good and avoid pain as bad; they are unable to say that the good is anything other than pleasure or the bad anything other than pain; it suffices for them to live life pleasantly without pain; and the good and the bad are what result in pleasure and pain, respectively.

Protagoras readily agrees with Socrates that the many can point to nothing other than pleasant consequences as an explanation for why they call something painful good, and to nothing other than painful consequences as an explanation for why they call something pleasant bad. Is it, however, only the many who have no standard for good and bad other than pleasure and pain, or does Protagoras lack such a distinct standard as well? Does Protagoras's unwavering acquiescence in Socrates' diagnosis of the many's confusion reflect only his belief that the many are hedonists, or does it confirm his own inability to produce a standard for good other than pleasure? Although Socrates allows Protagoras to side with him against the many for now, sparing him for the moment the embarrassment of being seen to share the beliefs of the many, Socrates will soon (358a–b) confront all three sophists present—Hippias, Prodicus, and Protagoras—directly, securing their full assent to the hedonist position heretofore attributed explicitly only to the many.

In stage 3 (352e5–357e2), Socrates seeks to redescribe what the many identify as the cause of their failing to do what is best even when they know what is best—namely, that they are "overcome by pleasure" (352e5–353a2). Socrates gives the many a final opportunity to say, if they are able, that "the good is anything other than pleasure or the bad anything other than pain" (355a1–2). Interestingly, Socrates treats the following three formulations as equivalent expressions of the hedonist thesis: (1) that the good is nothing other than pleasure and the bad nothing other than pain, (2) that "it is enough for you to live life pleasantly and without pain" (355a2–3)—which is the way Socrates first presented the hedonist platform to Protagoras at 351b6—and (3) that the good and bad are nothing but that which *results* in pleasure and pain, respectively (355a3–5).[36] The many, not being present, raise no objections to any of these formulations. Neither, however, does Protagoras.

With hedonism now agreed on, Socrates can proceed to demonstrate the absurdity of the many's view that pleasure can overcome knowledge, causing a person to choose what he knows is not best, and can suggest in its place an alternative account of what the many wrongly describe as "being overcome by pleasure." Note, however, that in bringing to light the absurdity of the many's view Socrates does not do anything to establish the rightness of what is presumably his and Protagoras's view that knowledge and wisdom are powerful. On the contrary, in his refutation of the many's view Socrates saps knowledge of its power to overcome anything. This is his argument:

1. Good = pleasure. (355b5–c1)
2. *A* knows *x* is bad but does *x* anyway because overcome by pleasure. (355c1–4; the many's assumption)
3. *A* knows *x* is bad but does *x* anyway because overcome by good. (355c7; 2, 1, substituting "good" for "pleasure")
4. The only way it would not be absurd to say that "*A* knows *x* is bad but does *x* anyway because overcome by good" is if the goods in *x* were worth its bads.
5. For the goods in something to be worth its bads the goods would have to be larger/more than its bads. (355d8–e1)
6. If the goods in *x* were worth its bads, then *x* would be the right choice.
7. *x* is not the right choice. (ex hypothesi; also, 355d5–6: if *x* were the right choice *A* would not be said to have erred [*exēmartanen*])
8. The goods in *x* are not worth its bads. (6, 7)
9. The goods in *x* are smaller/less than its bads. (5, 8)
10. It *is* absurd to say that "*A* knows *x* is bad but does *x* anyway because overcome by good." (4, 8)
∴ 11. Although *A* takes greater bads for lesser goods, it is incorrect to say that he is overcome. (355e2–3; 10)

---

36. Cf. *Gorg.* 494d: "And if a pleasant life, a happy one, too?"; see also 494e–495a: "or is it the man who claims, just like that, that those who enjoy themselves, however they may be doing so, are happy, and does not discriminate between good kinds of pleasures and bad? Tell me now too whether you say that the pleasant and the good are the same or whether there is some pleasure that is not good." See *Gorg.* 492d6–7, 494d7, and 494e9–495a4 for additional parallel formulations of hedonism.

The many think that a person who has knowledge can nevertheless be overcome by pleasure, since at least on occasion knowledge is weaker than pleasure. But, Socrates argues, this way of explaining why people choose the worse of two options is absurd given hedonism. For, if good = pleasure, how can we say that a person knows that *x* is bad yet still chooses *x* because overcome by pleasure, that is, by good? How can good cause someone to choose bad?[37] Since, given hedonism, the goods/bads or the pleasures/pains—whichever set of terms we use—that compete with one another for ascendancy in the heart of the agent who is about to act, are commensurate with one another, the only way that goods could overcome someone, causing him to choose bad, is if they were "worth" the bads, were greater or more than the bads. But, if the agent chooses an option in which the goods exceed the bads, the choice he makes is the *right* one. On the argument's assumption, however, that the choice he makes is the wrong one, the goods have to be unworthy to prevail over the bads, that is, they have to be less or smaller than the bads. But in that case, how can the agent be overcome by them? The person indeed makes the poor choice of taking (*lambanein* [355e3]) greater bad for lesser good; but he is surely not overcome.

Socrates next substitutes "pleasure" for "good" and argues substantially the same way (355e–356a):

1'. Good = pleasure. (355b5–c1)
2'. *A* knows *x* is bad but does *x* anyway because overcome by pleasure. (the many's assumption)

---

37. The absurdity arises as soon as the substitution of "good" for "pleasure" is made at premiss (3) in the first argument and "painful" for "bad" at (3') in the second. What is absurd (*geloion* [355d1]) is that someone would knowingly do what is bad because overcome by good (355d1–3), or knowingly do what is painful because overcome by pleasure (355e6–356a1)—when the goods or pleasures are clearly (*dēlon* [356a1]) smaller/fewer than the bads or pains. Some other views are as follows: Vlastos (1969) thinks the absurdity occurs at *Prot.* 356c3 and identifies it as that a man does what he cannot do, namely, knowingly choose the lesser pleasure; Gulley (1971) locates it in the second argument when the substitution of "painful" for "bad" is made; Gallop (1964) sees it at 357d–e, the absurdity being, he thinks, the contradiction that a man knows what he does not know, namely, that something is most pleasant/good or painful/bad. Woolf (2002, 238) argues that Socrates is not charging the many with saying something absurd but with doing something absurd, that is, with taking less pleasure/good for more pain/bad, and this despite their presumed commitment to hedonistic principles. Yet, what Socrates sets out to show is that with the substitution of the terms "pleasure" for "good" and "pain" for "bad" the many's description of what they do becomes absurd.

3′. *A* knows *x* is painful but does *x* anyway because overcome by pleasure. (355e6–356a1; 2′, 1′, substituting "painful" for "bad")

4′. The only way it would not be absurd to say that "*A* knows *x* is painful but does *x* anyway because overcome by pleasure" is if the pleasures in *x* were worth its pains.

5′. For the pleasures in something to be worth its pains the pleasures would have to be larger/more than its pains. (356a1–5)

6′. If the pleasures in *x* were worth its pains, then *x* would be the right choice.

7′. *x* is not the right choice. (ex hypothesi)

8′. The pleasures in *x* are not worth its pains. (6′, 7′)

9′. The pleasures in *x* are smaller/less than its pains. (5′, 8′)

10′. It *is* absurd to say that "*A* knows *x* is painful but does *x* anyway because overcome by pleasure." (4′, 8′)

∴11′. Although *A* takes greater pains for lesser pleasures, it is incorrect to say that he is overcome. (10′)

Here, too, *A* is not overcome by pleasure but nevertheless takes greater pains for lesser pleasures. He certainly errs, but how could he be overcome by the pleasures in *x* if they are smaller or fewer than its pains?

Socrates does flag a possible objection to his argument: that it might be the nearness of a pleasure that accounts for a person's choosing a smaller one when he might choose a larger (356a5–7).[38] In such a case, presumably, even with the hedonist identification of pleasure with good, pain with bad, in place,

---

38. Several commentators (e.g., Penner [1997, 23–24]; Devereux [1995, 391–92]; Brickhouse and Smith [1994, 94, and 2002, 7]) treat Socrates' response to the putative objector at 356a as if it were his general analysis of why people take lesser or smaller pleasure/good when they might take greater or larger. Because of this misstep these scholars misunderstand the analysis Socrates does offer. Their interpretation of Socrates' analysis of wrong choice is as follows: At t_1 (the time prior to the decision), *A* believes that *x* is the most pleasant/best option. At t_2 (the moment of decision), *A* believes—because of the nearness of a new pleasure, *y*—that not *x* but *y* is most pleasant/best. At t_3 (the time following the choice of *y*) *A* regrets his choice of *y*. Socrates' actual analysis, however, ends before the imagined objector enters the scene. Socrates contends that, given hedonism, the only plausible explanation for *A*'s choosing *x* is that he mistakenly thinks that *x* contains more/greater pleasures or goods than it does pains or bads. There is in Socrates' analysis no t_1 and t_2, no new pleasure *y*, and no change of heart on *A*'s part between t_1 and t_2 because of *y*. There is, however, a t_3; there is regret (*metamelein* [356d6]). The regret comes not because the desire *A* had at t_1 for *x* once again asserts itself now that the distortion caused by the bigger-appearing-because-nearer pleasure *y* at t_2 has been corrected. It comes, rather, simply because *A* now sees that, con-

"being overcome" might still explain why someone makes the wrong choice. (The nearness phenomenon surfaced earlier as well when, in describing how the many experience being overcome, Socrates singled out their vulnerability to near [*parachrēma*] pleasures [355b2–3].) Socrates deflects the objection, however, by contending that so long as the difference between a present/near pleasure or pain and a future/distant pleasure or pain is a difference of pleasure and pain, their nearness or remoteness should pose no problem for the expert (*agathos* [356b1]) at weighing: he will discount any illusion—produced by nearness or remoteness—of increased or diminished quantity of pleasure or pain, and will determine accurately whether the pleasures exceed the pains or vice versa. In other words, the expert chooses correctly; the nonexpert errs. Neither is "overcome."

In the exchange that follows (356c–357e), Socrates goes on to explain that when we err in choosing pleasures and pains (goods and bads), we err because we lack knowledge. Since the choice to be preferred remains the one in which the pleasures exceed the pains, and the choice to be rejected the one in which the pains outweigh the pleasures (356a3-c1),[39] our doing well (*eu prattein*) depends on our choosing greater pleasures and lesser pains—whether near or distant. And since our making the better choice depends on our mastery of the hedonic calculus, itself a kind of knowledge, it is this calculus that constitutes "our salvation in life" (*sōtēria tou biou*). The cause of our making the wrong choice, Socrates continues, is the lack of this knowledge.[40]

---

trary to what he had originally thought, *x* contained less/fewer pleasures or goods than pains or bads.

39. The verbals *lēptea* and *praktea* at *Prot.* 356b–c are best rendered "should be taken" and "should be done" rather than "must be taken" and "must be done." Insofar as Socrates maintains that our doing well (*eu prattein*) depends on our choosing greater pleasures and lesser pains, his point is surely not that we cannot help but make this choice but that this is the choice we ought to make. Gallop (1964, 128) supports this reading. The contrary view is held by Santas (1979, 30–31) and by Gulley (1971). Since, however, as Socrates argues, given hedonism the reason one fails to make the better choice is not that one is overcome but that one is ignorant, it follows that those who are skilled at the measuring art (are not ignorant) will invariably choose, as they should, greater pleasures and lesser pains.

40. Dyson (1976) and C. C. W. Taylor (1991) note difficulties in the calculus itself. Taylor wonders how one can literally weigh "prospective or hypothetical objects, i.e. possible actions and the consequences which would ensue if these possible actions were actually performed," as well as how one can quantify pleasure or enjoyment in precise units (195–98). Dyson contends that measuring can only take place after the fact; the many unknowns and contingencies prevent accurate measuring before the fact (40). It is interesting that in the *Gorgias* (464e–465a) Socrates maintains

Let us summarize the results of Socrates' argument in stage 3: (1) given hedonism, it is absurd to speak of one's knowing what is best yet doing otherwise because one is "overcome by pleasure"; (2) given hedonism, the correct explanation for one's choosing the less good—that is, the less pleasant—option when one is able to choose the better—that is, the more pleasant—option is that one errs; (3) the hedonic calculus prevents error; (4) one who makes mistakes in choosing lacks knowledge in the form of the hedonic calculus.

Before proceeding to stage 4, let us step back for a moment and evaluate the argument of stage 3. Is it true that if pleasure is the only good then it is absurd to say that passion, pleasure, pain, love, or fear might overcome one's knowledge of the best choice? In other words, given the hedonist assumption that there is nothing good other than pleasure and nothing bad other than pain, does it follow that it is impossible for one's knowledge that option x is best (most pleasant) to be overcome by passion, pleasure, pain, love, or fear?

The many, we know, understand passion, pleasure, pain, love, and fear as irrational forces that drive them to act against their determination of what is best. And Socrates knows this as well: at 355a8–b1, Socrates, in presenting the many's view, speaks of their experience of "being driven and dazed" (*agomenos kai ekplēttomenos*) by pleasures, and notes the effect on the many of the immediacy of the pleasures (*dia tas parachrēma hēdonas*), by which they are overcome (*hēttōmenos*) (355b2–3). Nevertheless, Socrates, surely quite deliberately, not only proceeds to suppress all reference to passion, love, and fear, limiting himself to just pleasure and pain, but also turns the pleasure and pain that were understood by the many to be irrational forces that *oppose* self-interested calculation into measurable components of particular options.[41] Moreover, Socrates is determined not to give the attraction of immediate pleasure its due, initially just completely ignoring it, and eventually, when he finally does ad-

---

that whereas one who possesses a genuine *technē* knows what is best, pleasure can only be guessed at. Socrates seems, then, at least in the *Gorgias,* to deny the very possibility of a *technē* of pleasure.

41. Stocks (1913) is to be credited with recognizing that the goods and bads are in the choice and not in the agent (as Adam and Adam [1905, 184] maintain). The *en humin* in the phrase *ouk axion ontōn nikan en humin tōn agathōn ta kaka* (355d3–4) does not signify that the bads are in the choice and the goods "in you," but rather that the bads and the goods belong to the choice and "you" is the seat of the rivalry. As Socrates says at 345c, a pleasure is thought (by the many) to be bad if the bad to which it leads outweighs *its* pleasure.

dress it, distorting it by assimilating it to a false impression concerning the size of the pleasure. Pressing too hard the analogy between pleasure and perception, Socrates contends that just as visible things appear larger than they are the closer they are, so will pleasures appear larger than they are the nearer they are; and just as someone who wants the truly larger visible thing would do well to discount the nearness factor, so would someone who wants the truly larger pleasure do well to discount the nearness factor. The truth, however, is that the many do not find an immediate pleasure more attractive because it seems bigger to them; they find it more attractive because it is available to them *now*.[42] The only way Socrates can deny people's susceptibility to the thrill of instant gratification and to the many other irrational desires and fears that might interfere with their pursuit of maximum pleasure or their overall interest in living pleasantly is by resorting to verbal hocus-pocus.

The argument in which Socrates substitutes "pleasure" for "good" and "good" for "pleasure," "pain" for "bad" and "bad" for "pain," is just so much logical sleight of hand. According to Socrates' argument, a person who knowingly takes lesser pleasure for greater pain cannot now be said to have been overcome by pleasure because the number or size of pleasures in the choice is smaller than that of its pains: how could anyone be *overcome* by *smaller* pleasures? Of course, what Socrates is trading on in accusing the many of absurdity is how counterintuitive it seems for someone to be "overcome" by something "smaller." Yet, whereas it is perhaps obvious that something larger cannot be overcome by something that is smaller than *it,* what Socrates tries to persuade us of here is that *A* cannot be overcome by pleasures that are smaller *than the pains in x.*

Socrates knows exactly what he is doing. He understands perfectly, as he shows, the many's situation as they experience it (352b–c). And when he initially takes exception to their account of their experience it is not because of the absurdity of being overcome but only because their view demeans knowledge. But Socrates eventually resorts to mocking the many's position, importing for that purpose an insolent fellow who bursts out laughing at its sheer ridiculousness. Is it, however, really ridiculous to think that people who value pleasure above all else or who value only pleasure might in full awareness choose a smaller immediate pleasure because it is near or simply because they

42. See *De Anima* III.x.433b7–10, where Aristotle notes that whereas thought bids us hold back because of the future, "desire is influenced by what is just at hand."

desire it more, or might choose a greater pain in order to avoid a lesser imminent or more frightening one?

What drives Socrates to reduce irrational forces to quantifiable amounts of pleasures and pains, goods and bads, is his recognition that so long as people believe they can be overcome they will have little use for the hedonic calculus. And, in fact, the calculus is not worth very much either if people will not use it because desire for an immediate pleasure overcomes them, or if they use it to measure the pleasure and pain in their options but are overtaken by desire or fear before they can implement its results. But, more than that, Socrates knows that so long as it makes sense to speak of people's being overcome, courage will never turn out to be as worthless and as silly as he is about to make it.

Let us turn now to stage 4. Here (357e3–358a4) Socrates begins by recapitulating the preceding three stages, reminding the sophists who are present that his and Protagoras's initial disagreement with the many concerned the many's having maintained that pleasure and other things are stronger than knowledge, while Protagoras and Socrates maintained that, on the contrary, knowledge is stronger than pleasure and everything else. What is strikingly absent from the current summary is any reaffirmation of knowledge's power to overcome pleasure and other things. Socrates claims that he and Protagoras have now shown that the experience of being overcome by pleasure is ignorance.[43] Had Protagoras and Socrates proposed that diagnosis straightaway, Socrates says, the many would have laughed, but if they laugh now they will be laughing at themselves. For they have agreed that those who make mistakes with regard to pleasure and pain, good and bad, lack knowledge in the form of measurement.[44] And an erroneous act that one performs because one lacks knowledge is done from ignorance.

---

43. Not "results from ignorance," as Guthrie (1956) translates. There is no longer any overcoming; there is no struggle between knowledge, on the one side, and pleasure, pain, passion, love, and fear on the other. Knowledge is but the instrument of pleasure maximization.

44. Socrates, having identified "our salvation in life" as a *technē* or *epistēmē* of measurement (357b4), goes on to say that "what exactly this art, this knowledge is, we shall inquire into later" (357b5–6). Some scholars take this latter remark as a hint that the actual art that Socrates regards as the answer to all life's problems has not been identified and will not be identified in the *Protagoras*. There is, however, another possibility. Socrates might be suggesting that the nature of the hedonic measuring art has up to now been left rather vague—not that it has not been identified— and that to specify precisely how such an art would work might well be an impossible task. See note 40.

According to Socrates, the many who make wrong choices lack the measuring art, which, if they but had it, would ensure that they make only right choices. Knowledge as the measuring art, however, does not conquer all; indeed, it does not *conquer* anything. Knowledge as the measuring art does not even rival pleasure and pain.[45] If anything, it is the faithful servant of pleasure.[46] Ironically, what threatens pleasure's dominance is no longer knowledge but ignorance.

Having identified this "greatest ignorance" (357e2), namely, the lack of the measuring art,[47] as the cause of people's failure to make the right choice, Socrates, to the utter delight of the assembled sophists, names them as the only source from which the salvific *technē* of measuring pleasure and pain can be acquired. He recommends to all who had previously thought that the skills needed for public and private success were not teachable that they seek out the sophists and happily spend all their money on sophistic instruction. For it is as a consequence of people's having withheld their money from the sophists that they do badly in public and in private. Hippias, Prodicus, and Protagoras all vigorously applaud Socrates' "answer" to the many: they think it "marvelously true" (*huperphuōs alēthē* [358a4]).

In the fifth stage (358a5–d4), Socrates removes the final barrier to the foolproof reliability of the hedonic calculus. In order for the sophistic *technē* to be able to deliver on its exaggerated promise to be "our salvation in life," it is imperative that the people who have it both use it and implement its determinations. If it were possible for people to know what is best (that is, most pleasant) but still choose otherwise, then knowing what is best would be no guarantee of success. The many's resistance to instruction in *aretē* is grounded in their experience that even when they know what is best they often fail to do it. The argument of stage 3 removed a serious obstacle to people's always and necessarily choosing greater pleasure over lesser pleasure when they could

45. Santas (1971, 295) shows how language of value-estimate displaces that of strength.

46. Cf. *Gorg.* 491e8–492a2, where Callicles says: "the man who will live rightly must let his own desires be as great as possible and not chasten them, and he must be sufficient to serve (*hupēretein*) them through courage *and intelligence*." As Ferrari (1990, 124) astutely notes: "even if those people were fully adept at the art of measurement he [Socrates] describes . . . they would not, after all, truly be able to 'save their lives'. . . . For the life governed by such measurement is enslaved to the body."

47. How different from this is "the greatest ignorance" identified in *Laws* 3.689a1. There the greatest ignorance is to hate, not love, what one's judgment pronounces to be noble or good, and to love and enjoy what one judges to be vile and wicked.

and when they knew which was which: it purportedly showed that, given hedonism, no one could be "overcome" by pleasure, so that if people do nevertheless sometimes take greater bad for lesser good it is because they do not compute correctly the size or amount of the goods and bads or pleasures and pains in the options before them.[48] In stage 5, the argument is taken a step further. Here it is insisted that human nature itself prevents people from choosing less pleasure when they might choose more. If pleasure and good are the same, Socrates maintains, then it is simply, "so it seems" (*hōs eoiken* [358d1]), "not in human nature" for a man to choose what he believes to be worse (less pleasant) when he might choose what he believes to be better (more pleasant). Having discounted in stage 3 the possibility that a person might be "overcome" by pleasure, Socrates is able to state categorically in stage 5 that no one who is able to choose more pleasure (or good) chooses less.

In both stages 3 and 5 Socrates ties his conclusion to hedonism.[49] Indeed, he had said when he first established the hedonist leanings of the many that "on this [namely, that a thing cannot be good for any reason other than pleasure or bad for any reason other than pain] all the arguments depend" (354e7–8). In stage 3, it is on the premiss that pleasure and good are the same that the conclusion that it is impossible to be overcome by pleasure is founded. And in stage 5, it is only after Socrates secures the assent of the sophists to the proposition that "the pleasant is good, the painful bad" (358a5–6), it is only after he assimilates noble to good and beneficial—and thus to pleasant (358b3–5)—that he ventures to deny *akrasia*.

The denial of *akrasia* is unique to the *Protagoras,* tied as it is to hedonistic premises.[50] Nowhere else in Plato do we find a declaration of the psychologi-

---

48. As Wolz (1967, 213) reasonably asks: "why should young men pay a high fee for the acquisition of a kind of knowledge which cannot withstand the onrush of a blind impulse?"

49. Socrates frequently blames the conclusions he reaches on the interlocutor's premises. It is therefore counterproductive to try to read the account of *akrasia* in the *Protagoras* apart from hedonism. The denial of *akrasia* turns on the acceptance of hedonistic premises, so that it is bound to be misinterpreted when presented "in a way that should be of interest to hedonists and non-hedonists alike" (Segvic 2000, 39). See Santas 1971, 273–74: "The complete dependence on hedonism in which Socrates places his argument against the explanation 'overcome (or driven or dazed by) pleasure' indicates clearly not only that this explanation is to be reconstituted along hedonistic lines but also that the alleged absurdity is to be found in a conjunction of the explanation and hedonism, not simply in the explanation." See also Kahn 1996, 239.

50. That is why Aristotle is obliged to quote the *Protagoras* when criticizing Socrates' denial of *akrasia* (*EN* VII.ii. 1145b24–25).

cal impossibility of a person's making choices that contradict his better judgment. Whereas other dialogues, as we shall see, consider what people want and why they choose what they choose, none asserts that it is not in human nature to act against what one *knows or believes* to be the better option.[51]

Note that Socrates advances no argument in stage 5 for the impossibility of *akrasia*. He alludes briefly to the earlier discrediting of "being overcome" as an explanation for one's making the wrong choice—"To give into oneself is nothing other than ignorance, and to control oneself is nothing other than wisdom" (358c13)—thereby discounting what he assumes is the only objection that might be raised against his new assertion.[52] As long as the possibility of being overcome is not a viable one, Socrates can simply proclaim the impossibility of what might be called "irrational conduct." He says, and all those present agree, that if the pleasant is the good, then no one who knows or believes that there is something better he might do that he is able to do[53] will continue to do what is worse. "No one goes willingly toward the bad or toward

51. The expression "knows or believes" (*oute eidōs oute oiomenos* [358b7]) is no accident. Knowledge is no longer a powerful force within a person, a force capable of overcoming competing forces. Once everyone wants pleasure, and once pleasure is not a force competing with one's judgment, one will act in accordance with knowledge if one has it; if not, one will do what one *thinks* best.

52. A second such allusion is found at 359d6.

53. Santas (1971, 295–98) takes the notion of something's being "possible to do" (*dunata; exon* [358e1]) to signify that the agent is psychologically able to do it. Since, he argues, a person who is "overcome" is not psychologically able to do other than what he does, if a person does choose the worse of two options, he might do so for one of only two reasons: either because he thought it the better option or, if not, then because he was overcome and so was unable to do otherwise. What cannot happen, according to Santas's reading, is that a person who is psychologically able to do otherwise will knowingly choose the worse of the available options. It is clear, however, that Socrates does not think that being overcome renders a person psychologically unable to do otherwise. At 355a–b Socrates describes the many's position, which he shows to be absurd, as follows: "you say that frequently a man, knowing the bad to be bad, nevertheless does that very thing, when it is possible for him not to do it (*exon mē prattein*), having been driven and overwhelmed by pleasure." Here a person, though "driven and overwhelmed by pleasure," is still said to be *able* not to do what he is driven to do. See also 352d–e: "most people are unwilling to do what is best, even though they know what it is and it is possible for them to do it (*exon autois* [352d7]). And when I have asked them the reason for this, they say that those who act that way do so because they are overcome by pleasure or pain." (Similarly at 355d2, where the expression used is *ou deon auton* [its not being necessary to do it].) In the *Hippias Minor* at 366c, Socrates explains that by "if he is able" he means if he "is not prevented by disease or other such things." As Austin says (1961, 146) (quoted by Santas): "We often succumb to temptation with calm and even with finesse."

what he believes to be bad; neither is it in human nature, so it seems, to want to go toward what one believes to be bad instead of to the good. And when one is forced to choose one of two bad things, no one will choose the greater if he is able to choose the lesser" (358c6–d4). Whatever chance there might have been for someone to choose pleasure over good, or, for that matter, good over pleasure, is absolutely precluded when good and pleasant are the same.

Stage 5 leaves no loose ends. Socrates here puts to rest Protagoras's earlier tentative attempt to qualify his assent to the proposition that to live pleasantly is good and unpleasantly bad. Protagoras had ventured that this is only so if the pleasant life's pleasures are themselves noble (351c1–2). At 358b4–5, however, Socrates secures the agreement of all the sophists to the proposition that every action leading toward living painlessly and pleasantly is noble and beneficial.[54] The noble, like the good, derives its character from its role in the advancement of pleasure.

Scholars generally read the denial of *akrasia* as if it were unrelated to hedonism. On their view, Socrates actually thinks that only belief governs action. As Penner (1990, 29) puts it: there are no "irrational executive desires."[55] Penner consequently contends that Socrates denies the possibility of (1) synchronic belief-*akrasia,* that is, choosing against what one at the moment of choice thinks is best; (2) synchronic knowledge-*akrasia,* that is, choosing against what one at the moment of choice *knows* is best; and, because he thinks Socrates invests knowledge with strength, (3) diachronic knowledge-*akrasia,* choosing against what one in the time preceding the moment of choice *knows* is best. At most, according to Penner, Socrates accepts the possibility of diachronic belief-*akrasia:* choosing against what one (merely) believes throughout most of the context of the choice—though not at the moment of choice itself—is best. Because belief is less powerful than knowledge, pleasure can have the effect, for the moment, of dislodging an otherwise settled belief.

The alternative to this general approach is, as we have seen, to understand Socrates to be denying, *only given hedonism,* the possibility of acting contrary to one's beliefs. It is only once competing forces and competing goods have

54. In conversing with Polus in the *Gorgias* Socrates offers a definition of *to kalon* in terms of pleasure or benefit or both (474d). As I argue in chapter 3, however, this definition is designed to confuse Polus; it is not to be regarded as Socrates' preferred definition.

55. For classic discussions of the alleged Socratic denial of *akrasia,* see also Davidson 1980; Watson 1977. Devereux (1995, 392) argues, like Penner, that desire can cause a standing true belief to be momentarily "clouded," so that one ends up acting on a temporary false one.

been eliminated and people have been transformed into one-dimensional pleasure maximizers that *akrasia* is precluded. The many's description of what happens to them is absurd, Socrates says, when the four terms—pleasure, pain, good, and bad—are reduced to just two. Were it not for hedonism, then, Socrates would recognize both diachronic belief-*akrasia* and synchronic belief-*akrasia* as possible. And were it not for hedonism, he would recognize, too, the possibility of diachronic and synchronic knowledge-*akrasia*. For the truth is that in souls dominated by passions and appetites, knowledge is not reliably effective. The many are indeed right to think that a person can have knowledge (*epistēmē*) and intelligence (*phronēsis*) in him and recognize (*gignōskei*) the good and the bad yet fail to do as knowledge bids, choosing otherwise because overcome. In many people knowledge does fail to rule the soul; in such people knowledge is "dragged around like a slave" (352c1). If knowledge becomes for Socrates in the later books of the *Republic* so exalted that the philosophers who achieve it are rendered invulnerable to excessive desire and passion, it is not, at any rate, this knowledge about which Socrates asks Protagoras to reveal his view as it compares with that of the many.[56]

Taken in its hedonistic context, then, what are the implications of the denial of *akrasia?* What does it mean to say that no one ever chooses what he regards as the worse of two choices? It means that people are all the same. It is not that there are some who succumb to temptation and others who overcome it, some who rule themselves and others who are out of control, some who choose the just and right even when it strikes them as painful and others who avoid pain at all costs. No; nature herself has made everyone the same. All pursue what they believe to be most pleasant. No one has or can have any other standard. People differ only in their level of skill.

Courage under Hedonism

As Socrates told Protagoras quite early on, the reason he is investigating so assiduously the experience the many call "being overcome by pleasure" is that

---

56. The *Republic* is generally quite conscious of the need for the desires to be restrained so that reason can rule. See *Rep.* 4.431c: "But the simple and moderate desires, pleasures and pains, those led by calculation accompanied by intelligence and right opinion, you will come upon in few; and those the ones born with the best natures and best educated." Note the emphasis here on nature and nurture.

doing so will help him and Protagoras learn about courage as it relates to the other parts of virtue (353b1–3). If being virtuous has now turned out to require mastery of the *technē* of measuring pleasures and pains, will courage not require the same? Protagoras, as we know, had sought to place courage within the realm of nature and nurture and outside the realm of *technē*. Will he now have to accept that courage, like the rest of *aretē* from which he struggled to divorce it, is a matter not of nature and nurture but, alas, of *technē*?

Socrates in this section subjects Protagoras to a second examination of his views on courage and wisdom. Whereas the first argument sought to establish that the courageous, though confident, must also have wisdom, the new argument severs the connection between courage and confidence; it contends that whether confident or afraid the courageous know what is and is not fearful.[57]

The reason the first argument linked courage with confidence is that Protagoras had just insisted that courage was wholly unlike any of the other virtues. In that context it made good sense for Socrates to seize on something that the popular imagination associates uniquely with courage, namely, confidence. Indeed, in the first argument, the knowledge that was said to distinguish the courageous from the merely confident was knowledge of such things as how to dive, ride, and fight—that is, mastery of danger-related skills. And in the first argument, the courageous man, like all confident men, faces danger intrepidly. The courageous man is thoroughly unlike the coward who shrinks in fear at the first sign of danger. Dispositionally, the brave man and the coward are opposites: the former "goes toward" (*itas epi*) the very things toward which the many (the cowardly) fear to go (*kai itas ge . . . eph' ha hoi polloi phobountai ienai* [349e3]). It is much easier to differentiate the brave man from the coward than from the man who is confident. The brave man and the confident man behave similarly and can only be distinguished in terms of their respective training in and mastery of danger-related skills.

In the second courage argument, by contrast, the knowledge that distinguishes the courageous man is knowledge of good and bad, noble and shameful, pleasant and painful, fearful and not fearful—these pairs of terms all being interchangeable with one another. The courageous and cowardly both go toward (*itas epi* [359c3]), and are willing to go toward (*ethelousin ienai* [359e4, 360a1, a4]), the same things (359d7–e1). The dispositional difference

---

57. A similar shift in the type of knowledge associated with courage occurs in the *Laches*. See Schmid 1985.

between the courageous and the cowardly in the first argument is entirely absent from the second, and the only difference that remains is epistemic: the brave man is better able to assess the degree of badness or fearfulness or unpleasantness in his alternatives than is the coward. Interestingly, in this second argument, the brave man resembles the confident man not at all. He is confident when appropriate and fearful when appropriate; he is not necessarily likely to be confident more frequently than he is fearful. What is distinctive of the brave man, whether he is confident or fearful, is that he *knows*.

The transition from the first characterization of courage to the second is facilitated by the hedonism that intervenes, along with the consequent denial of *akrasia*. When the pleasant is the only criterion for goodness, when no one can be overcome, when everyone does what seems to him best/most pleasant, then courage is eviscerated, emasculated. When all people are the same, when all prize pleasure, when all seek to maximize pleasure and minimize pain, and when no irrational influences can interfere with the pursuit of maximal pleasure and minimal pain, then all men, both the brave and the cowardly, go toward the things that inspire confidence (*ta tharralea*) and avoid the things that inspire fear (*ta deina*). No longer is it the case that the brave man goes toward *ta deina* when he believes doing so to be noble and good; no longer is it the case that the coward avoids *ta deina* despite believing that going toward them would be noble and good. The only thing that can distinguish a brave man from a coward now is how successfully he determines what is most fearful and what is least so, what is most pleasant and what is least so. The courageous man is none other than the man who has mastered the hedonic calculus. Gone are the intrepid souls who dare to go where the many fear to tread (349e3).

It is inconceivable that Socrates should subscribe to all that he has argued for. For Socrates, courage is doing what justice requires regardless of cost, in spite of pain, in spite, even, of death. Why is the temperate man brave? Because, as Socrates says at *Gorg.* 507a–c, "it is not the part of a temperate man either to pursue or to flee things that are not fitting, but to flee and pursue what he ought—affairs, human beings, pleasures and pains—and to abide and be steadfast where he ought." Courage, then, is persisting in the face of whatever fearful things confront one, refusing to fear them, and standing firm in one's convictions about the just. "A man who is not totally bereft of reason," Socrates says at *Gorg.* 522e, "is afraid not of dying but of committing injustice." Courage is the refusal to fear what is unworthy of fear; it is standing firm for justice come what may. At *Ap.* 29b Socrates declares: "Then compared to the bad things I know are bad, I will never fear or flee the things about which I do not know whether they even happen to be good." And at *Rep.* 4.442c: "we call an individual courageous . . . when his spirited part preserves, through pains and pleasures, what has been proclaimed by reason(s) to be fearful and not."

Protagoras, who had wanted to consign courage to the realm of nature and nurture, is utterly at a loss. He resists the idea that "the cowardly and the courageous go toward the same things" (359d8–e1), protesting: "But, Socrates, what the cowardly go toward is completely opposite to what the courageous go toward. For example, the courageous are willing to go to war, but the cowardly are not" (359e1–4). Socrates quickly counters that, if going to war is more honorable, hence better, hence more pleasant than not going, then surely the cowardly would wish to go to war; if they do not it can only be because they fail to recognize that war is more honorable, hence better, hence more pleasant.[58] The willingness of the brave to go to war is attributed solely to their awareness that going to war is more pleasant than avoiding it.[59] Protagoras admits that the things that have been agreed on compel the conclusions Socrates reaches (360e4–5). But his assent to Socrates' conclusions becomes increasingly more reluctant (360d3–4) until he finally falls silent (360d6).[60]

58. That courage and pleasure cannot be linked in this way has not gone unnoticed. See Sesonske 1963, 73–79; Wolz 1967, 216–17; Tennku 1956. Sesonske recognizes that no one thinks that since courage is noble it is also pleasant. Plato, Sesonske reasons, must be showing here that pleasure is *not* the good, for if it were, then, per impossibile, either courage would not be noble or a courageous act would be the knowing performance of that which is most pleasant. Since neither of these consequents is true, the antecedent must be false. Wolz thinks it is absurd to link courage and pleasure because there would then be no way to distinguish the courageous man from the coward: neither one would be willing to face the fearful in a dangerous situation. Tennku notes that we do not admire a courageous man for seeking pleasure and avoiding pain, but rather for choosing the most honorable course of action in spite of anticipated pains and risks. Irwin (1977, 112) acknowledges that it is simply not true that men are brave only because bravery yields pleasure. Since, however, he fails to see that Socrates' argument is a reductio ad absurdum of Protagoras's pretensions to teach *aretē*, he thinks the argument fails.

59. This argument is strikingly similar to Socrates' second argument against the identification of pleasure and good in the *Gorgias* (497e–499b). There the brave man is pleased when the enemy retreats; the coward is, if anything, even more pleased. With respect to pleasure, then, the coward and the brave man are fairly indistinguishable; it is only with respect to goodness that they can be differentiated from one another. Since in the *Protagoras* good has already been reduced to pleasure, nothing is left but skill at calculation.

60. Rather than graciously accept defeat, Protagoras accuses Socrates at 360e3 of being a lover of victory. It is, of course, Protagoras who is a lover of victory. See 335a.

Socrates, of course, had maintained all along that *aretē* could not be taught. Protagoras had maintained that it could. Why, then, is Protagoras unhappy with the outcome? Has it not been shown that *aretē,* indeed that even courage, is teachable? Has it not in fact been shown that the sophists are its teachers? The reason Protagoras is unhappy is that the courage sophists have been shown to be able to teach is no courage at all. It has been mangled and distorted beyond recognition. By making courage a matter of knowledge, Socrates has all but effaced the difference between courage and cowardice: the courageous man is simply a coward who is adept at measuring pleasure and pain. Socrates has made a laughingstock of Protagoras and of his profession, and Protagoras, for one, knows it.

The Paradox

In the *Protagoras* Socrates deliberately contorts and impoverishes the human personality, turning people into purely rational pursuers of pleasure. His denial of *akrasia* produces a version of the Socratic paradox that is anomalous and "un-Socratic": when Socrates says in the *Protagoras* that "no one does bad things willingly," he means that no one who is able to choose what is in his judgment a better alternative will ever choose a worse one. The paradox in this perverse form plays a critical part in Socrates' project to discredit in Protagoras's own eyes his claim to teach *aretē.* The sophist who teaches clever speaking in the guise of manly and civic excellence, who, with the promise of helping young men to rise to political preeminence, lures them away from those who nurture their souls, and who holds in esteem not the *aretai* of justice, temperance, and holiness that he professes to teach—if only "a bit better than others"— but the wisdom and courage that he knows full well that he cannot teach, must be exposed for the sham that he is. By setting forth the improbable conditions for successful sophistic education, Socrates exposes the uselessness—even by the sophist's own lights—of such education for real people who are to be genuinely made virtuous. Real people are not pleasure-calculating automatons but are vulnerable to the tug of passion, pleasure, pain, love, and fear— that is, they are subject to *akrasia.* And some real people care about things other than maximizing pleasure: brave people, for example, really do "go toward" things different from those toward which cowards go. Moreover, even those real people who care exclusively about maximizing pleasure are able to recognize, if not always to pursue, other goods besides pleasure. So long as people are real people, sophists cannot teach *aretē*. In order for real people to acquire *aretē* neither a hedonic calculus nor skill at speaking is required. What real people need in order to be truly good is nurture of the soul and critical reflection. Of course, if doing well (*eu prattein*) depended on getting the biggest pleasures and smallest pains (356d), and if getting the biggest pleasures and smallest pains required nothing but mastering the hedonic calculus, then it would make good sense for sophists to be sought after and handsomely paid. But if, as Socrates suggests to Hippocrates, what doing well (*eu prattein*) depends on is whether the soul becomes good or bad, then not only should sophists not be sought after and paid well but they should be avoided at all costs (313a).

It is, then, in souls that are properly nurtured that knowledge of good and bad rules the soul and is not dragged around like a slave by passion, pleasure, pain, fear, and love. Such knowledge, however, is not the hedonic calculus. For the hedonic calculus, as an instrument for pleasure maximization, is the servant of desires and appetites and not their master. The hedonic calculus thus does nothing to improve people; it fails to "take the desires in a different direction" (*Gorg.* 517b5–6).

3

THE *GORGIAS*:
HOW OUGHT A HUMAN
BEING TO LIVE?

The *Gorgias* contains at 509e5–7 the classic formulation of the Socratic paradox: "no one does wrong willingly, but it is unwillingly that all who do wrong
do wrong" (*mēdena boulomenon adikein, all' akontas tous adikountas pantas adikein*).
Although Socrates addresses the paradox to Callicles, he points out that Polus
had already agreed to it (509e4–5).[1] The paradox is not, then, intended for Callicles alone. Facing two interlocutors cut from the same cloth, Socrates aims
his paradox at both.

Of the two, however, there can be little doubt that Callicles poses the
greater danger. For it is he who raises to the level of theory the lack of restraint
and the appetitive excesses that he and Polus share. He elevates the basest of
desires and the most egregious deficiencies of character to an ideal—indeed,
to nature's ideal. Although Callicles is not a sophist, he subscribes to and is a
proponent of every one of the sophistic views that give rise to Socratic para-

1. Scholars disagree on the identity of the passage containing the referred-to agreement.
Among those who think it is 466–468 are Gulley (1968, 120); Kahn (1983, 114); Kraut (1984, 314,
n3); Nakhnikian (1973, 15). Irwin (1979, 229) seems to think the passage being referred to is 474–
480. That was at one time my view (1992b, 312–13). I now think that when Socrates speaks of what
he and Polus earlier agreed to, he is referring not to any one specific agreement with Polus but,
rather more vaguely, to the whole of their discussion.

doxes.[2] He believes that the wise are unjust and intemperate, and the fools temperate. He thinks the right way to be, the best way to be, is intemperate, that intemperance is the way to happiness. He thinks that only the weak praise justice and denounce injustice, but that even they are just not because they hold justice in esteem; it is only their ineptitude that prevents them from practicing injustice successfully. In other words, from Callicles' perspective, no one does right willingly. Callicles regards courage and intelligence as the virtues of superior men, seeing in justice, temperance, and piety the impotence of the inferior masses.

Because of the theoretical scaffolding on which Callicles drapes his own intemperance, he is a greater threat to the hearts and minds of others than is Polus. But in both of these characters one senses how tenuous is the hold of *nomos,* of traditional conventions and pieties, on the ambitious young men of fifth-century Athens. As Plato sees it, the blame for the widespread indifference of the young to the rudiments of decency may be laid, at least to some extent, at the door of professional teachers of rhetoric. It is no accident, therefore, that before turning to Polus and Callicles, Socrates confronts their teacher Gorgias.

Gorgias

Gorgias is not at all like his successors in the argument. Specifically, and significantly, he disapproves of injustice. The Gorgias of our dialogue betrays no personal ambition. As far as the reader can tell, he is content to be a wealthy and famous teacher of rhetoric. It would appear that he aspires neither to political office, nor to committing atrocities against others, nor to the unlimited indulgence of appetite. And he is not an unjust man.[3]

Nevertheless, what Gorgias sells is raw power—power in the form of freedom and political prominence, or, perhaps more accurately, political domi-

---

2. As Plato depicts Callicles, he is, if not a professional teacher of rhetoric, nevertheless, qua politician, a practicing rhetorician. In urging Socrates to become a political man, he in effect urges him to abandon philosophy for rhetoric. Also note that Gorgias is a guest in Callicles' home (447b).

3. Gorgias willingly helps his physician brother as well as other physicians to persuade their patients to undergo the treatment prescribed (456b). It is difficult to imagine either Polus or Callicles doing the same. See Weiss 2003, 198–201.

nance (452d).[4] Although he eventually identifies "the just and unjust" as the subject matter of rhetoric (454b)—rhetoricians do, after all, do their work largely in the law courts and other places where matters of justice and injustice occupy center stage—he does so only when pushed. On his own, Gorgias specifies *logoi* (words or speeches [449e1])—that is, persuasion by way of *logoi* (452e1)—as the subject matter of rhetoric.[5] And even when he singles out "the just and unjust" as what his persuasive *logoi* are about, he continues to maintain rhetoric's versatility: the rhetorician is more persuasive than the expert on *every* subject—at least when addressing those who do not know (455d–456a). As Gorgias sees it—and despite the admission to the contrary that Socrates manages to extract from him later on (at 460a)—the rhetorician's professional relationship to justice and injustice is indeed precisely the same as his professional relationship to all other subjects: with respect to all subjects he does no more than teach his pupils to speak more persuasively than anyone else. Gorgias's art, as he himself portrays it (456d1), is an agonistic one like boxing and wrestling.[6] And although he maintains that the instructor of rhetoric, like instructors of boxing and wrestling, imparts his skill to his students to be used justly by them (456e), he makes it clear, through this comparison, that the instructor of rhetoric is no more (and no less) attentive to justice than the others.

Why does Socrates not relent until Gorgias has identified the just and unjust as the special subject matter of rhetoric?[7] Why does he in effect force

4. Cooper (1999, 41) contends that when Gorgias credits the rhetorician with producing something that is the cause of "freedom for men themselves" (452d6–7), he means by freedom "their capacity to rule themselves as a free people, in accordance with their considered judgment of what is just and best, without falling into inarticulate quarreling and the exercise of brute force against one another." When Socrates' interlocutors speak of freedom, however, they always mean the power to dominate others and to avoid being dominated oneself. See *Meno* 86d; *Rep.* 1.344c; *Lysis* 210b. At *Meno* 73c9, Gorgias is said to define virtue as "the ability to rule men." Were rhetoric's aim the enhancement of free political self-governance, would Gorgias boast that with it the rhetorician will have the doctor, the trainer, and the businessman as his slaves (452e)? Note, too, that the crafts to which Gorgias compares rhetoric are boxing, wrestling, and fighting in heavy armor.

5. When Socrates defines rhetoric at 465a, he says not that it is *peri logous* but, on the contrary, that it *ouk echei logon* (has no logos [465a3]), and that it is an *alogon pragma* (a logos-less thing [465a6]).

6. The dialogue's opening word is "war" (*polemou* [447a1])—a hint perhaps at the competitive nature of rhetoric or perhaps at the combative nature of Socratic discussion.

7. Is it coincidental that Socrates uses the term *dikaiōs* (justly) four times just before Gorgias identifies his subject matter as the just and unjust? See 453c5: "Now consider if I seem to question

Gorgias to concede, contrary to what he really believes, that the rhetorician is not "in the same situation in regard to the just and unjust, the shameful and noble, and the good and bad, as he is in regard to the healthy and the other things belonging to the other arts" (459d)? From Socrates' perspective, it is, to be sure, no trivial matter for a man to speak before the public about what is just and unjust, noble and shameful, or good and bad while "not knowing the things themselves but, having devised persuasion about them . . . to seem to know more than the one who knows, among those who do not know" (459d). If rhetoricians are trained to speak primarily about matters of justice without knowing what they are talking about, and if they simulate expertise on justice before "mobs" who themselves know nothing,[8] then rhetoric is hardly the blameless occupation that Gorgias makes it out to be. Inasmuch as the soul is more important than the body, false speech about justice is more detrimental than false speech about anything else. By making Gorgias pinpoint justice and injustice as the subject matter of rhetoric, and by putting Gorgias in a position where he must then ask himself whether the same rules apply to persuading people about matters of the greatest import as to persuading them about other matters, Socrates compels Gorgias to confront and acknowledge the ugly underside of his rhetorical practice.

But why does Gorgias capitulate to Socrates, saying, contrary to what he really believes, that his relationship with justice and injustice is special, that it is different from his relationship with all the other subjects about which his students are able, solely by virtue of their verbal skill, to speak well? As Polus will soon point out, Gorgias is ashamed to admit that although he teaches his students to hold forth about justice, he neither knows nor teaches it: who, after all, admits to not having knowledge of the just things and to not teaching them (461b–c)?[9] Can Gorgias afford to acknowledge openly that he is as ignorant about justice as he is about the other things he speaks cleverly about,

---

you justly?"; 453c7: "wouldn't I justly ask you?"; 454a7: "we might after this justly ask"; 454a9–b1: "Or doesn't it seem to you just (*dikaion*) to ask further?"

8. Although Gorgias had said at first that the teacher "persuades most of all" (453d11), it is not the teacher but the rhetorician whom he credits with being the most persuasive "in a mob" (459a3).

9. The obvious answer is: Socrates. It is Socrates who famously and repeatedly denies having knowledge of virtue and teaching it. See *Ap.* 21b, where Socrates says that he knows he is not wise, and 33b, where he declares that, because he does not teach, he is not responsible for how those who hear him turn out.

and that he therefore does nothing to improve the character of those who come to him, providing them only with the skill to *seem* just when they are not and to speak about justice when they, too, know nothing about it? Socrates in effect drives Gorgias to accept a role he eschews (especially if one trusts the *Meno* on this),[10] the role of sophist or teacher of virtue.

Unlike Protagoras, then, who professes to make his students better but actually teaches them to speak well, Gorgias professes to teach his students to speak well and does not, at least initially, claim to make them better.[11] The lie that comes easily to Protagoras, namely, that he teaches justice and temperance, comes much harder to Gorgias—but it comes: Gorgias cannot long publicly sustain his claim that he, like all other teachers of agonistic skills, bears no responsibility for its unjust use by his pupils. Once he admits that his *technē* deals specifically with justice and injustice, he feels constrained to say that he knows justice and teaches it.

As Socrates sees them, both Protagoras and Gorgias are remiss in the same way. They instruct young people but without nurturing them.[12] They impart skills but neglect souls. Moreover, they lure young people away from those who would, however imperfectly, care for their souls. At *Ap.* 19e–20a Socrates names Gorgias, Hippias, and Prodicus as men who are "able to go into any one of the cities and persuade the young men, who can associate for nothing with whomever they wish among their own fellow citizens, to give up the as-

10. There is reason to think that the *Meno* may have this right. For Callicles, too, prides himself on being a rhetorician rather than a sophist and indeed mocks sophists. Socrates, however, seems determined to disallow the distinction. He argues that rhetoricians and sophists are pretty much the same (465c) and, if anything, the sophist is superior to the rhetorician as the physical trainer is superior to the doctor and the legislator to the judge (520a–b). In each of these pairs, the former does his work before the damage is done; the latter does his after. (Socrates calls Gorgias a sophist at *Ap.* 19e–20a.)

11. As we saw in chapter 2, the virtues Protagoras says he teaches are the cooperative ones: justice, temperance, and justice, though what he actually teaches are competitive skills required for getting ahead. Gorgias openly acknowledges that it is clever speaking that he teaches, and so makes no claim to teach virtue. Virtue, or justice, is something Gorgias expects people to bring to whatever skill they are taught.

12. By saying at 455a that the rhetorician "would not be able . . . to teach so large a mob such great matters (*houtō megala pragmata*) in a short time," Socrates both provides Gorgias with an excuse for not teaching but merely persuading in the law courts about the just and unjust, and suggests at the same time that teaching justice is not something that can be done in a few short lessons. Yet Protagoras boastfully assures Hippocrates that "the very day you start [studying with me], you will go home a better man" (*Prot.* 318a).

sociation with those men to associate with them and pay them money and be grateful besides." And Protagoras is characterized in precisely this way at *Prot.* 316c–d. That sophists and rhetoricians promote their *technai* as substitutes for the moral training young people get from relatives and friends makes them more blameworthy for their pupils' injustice than are teachers of other agonistic skills such as wrestling and boxing. And since the subject matter about which Protagoras and Gorgias enable their students to speak eloquently and persuasively is justice, they cannot as easily as wrestling and boxing instructors escape culpability when their students put their *technē* to unjust use.

Much has been made of the presumed inadequacy of Socrates' brief argument for the conclusion that a man who has learned justice is a just man, that is, a man who does not *wish* to commit injustice (460c3). But if a man who has learned medicine is a doctor, a man who has learned carpentry a carpenter, and a man who has learned music a musician, why is not a man who has learned justice a just man (460b)? And is not a just man indeed a man who does not wish to do wrong, a man whose desires have been properly trained? The skilled and good rhetorician, Socrates says at 504d–e, will always direct his mind toward "how he may get justice to come into being in the citizens' souls and injustice to be removed, temperance to arise within and intemperance to be removed, the rest of virtue to arise within and badness to depart." The good politician, he says later at 517b, will seek to make the citizens in his care better citizens, that is, to "take their *desires* in a different direction." One need not press the analogy with other learners too hard. A man who has learned medicine may use his skill for good or ill, but what he has learned is medicine, not justice. At 519c–d Socrates maintains that a teacher of virtue could not be mistreated by his pupils, for how could "human beings who have become good and just, who have been delivered from injustice by the teacher, and possess justice, do injustice with this thing [injustice] that they do not have?" Indeed, the person who has been made better, Socrates says, "*desires* to do good in return" (520e). Had Gorgias's students learned justice from him, they would indeed not be unjust, and they would, consequently, have no wish to use their skill in speaking *about* justice to further unjust ends. [13]

---

13. Readers have tended to read this argument of the *Gorgias* as if it fails to recognize the point made in the *Hippias Minor* that a *technē* enables one to speak both truly and falsely and to do good or bad at will. But perhaps it is the *Hippias Minor* that needs to be read in light of the *Gorgias*. See *Rep.* 1.334d3: "Yet the good men are just and are not the sort to do injustice?"; and 1.335d11–12: "It

Gorgias is a decent man, whose preference is that his students wield power in the city but not abuse that power. Insofar, however, as he does nothing to shape his students' character or even to alert them to the moral pitfalls that come with power, he is not guiltless when he produces a Polus or a Callicles. By teaching his students to craft their speeches well, he helps them to benefit themselves—not to benefit the crowds whom they address, and not to further the interests of justice and truth. So, the rhetorician is neither like the doctor, the gymnastics trainer, and the businessman who help others achieve health, fitness, and wealth, nor like the many other craftsmen who use their craft to benefit others.[14] Indeed, Gorgias boasts that the power of rhetoric is so great that the rhetorician will have even the doctor and the gymnastics trainer as his slave (452e); the businessman will be making money for the rhetorician and not for himself (452e); and experts in all fields will be at the rhetorician's mercy when they compete before the public (457a–b).[15] Promises such as these are guaranteed to attract those who covet the kind of power that will enable them to advance themselves even as they exploit others.

Polus

From the very outset the Polus we encounter in the *Gorgias* is immodest and undisciplined. He usurps Gorgias's place when Chaerephon wishes to question Gorgias about his *technē* (448a). He rushes to defend rhetoric as if it were under attack rather than say, as he was asked, what it is (448e).[16] And Socrates has to instruct him to conduct himself with a measure of restraint (461d). But

---

is not the work (*ergon*) of the just man to harm either a friend or anyone else . . . but of his opposite, the unjust man." Indeed, "it is never just to harm anyone" (1.335e5). Cf. *Crito* 49b–e.

14. Not all crafts are alike. Gorgias likens rhetoric to boxing and wrestling, that is, to agonistic arts whose practitioners benefit themselves. Socrates, however, challenges him to compare rhetoric to crafts that benefit others (medicine, gymnastics, and, in this context, even money-making). In all of Socrates' cases the "human beings" (*tois anthrōpois* [452a5, 452b1, 452c5, 452d3–4]) who benefit are distinct from the craftsmen. In the case of rhetoric, however, the beneficiaries (*tois anthrōpois* [452d6–7]) are the rhetoricians themselves.

15. See *Philebus* 58a–b, where Protarchus remarks that Gorgias frequently claimed that "the art of persuasion (*peithein*) is superior to all others because it makes them all its slaves"—albeit with their consent and not by force.

16. Gorgias does the same. When asked at 451d "Of the things that are, what is this thing that these speeches used by rhetoric are about?" he responds: "The greatest of human affairs, Socrates, and the best." Unlike Polus, however, Gorgias is not reprimanded.

Polus is more than merely impolite and impulsive, more than merely psychologically, emotionally, and temperamentally immature. He is the first of two bad apples that fall from the Gorgias tree. (Callicles is the second.) For not only is Polus enamored of the power that Gorgias hails as the great benefit of rhetoric but, because of his impulsiveness and immaturity, what he especially likes about power is that it makes it possible to do wrong and get away with it. If, as Socrates and Gorgias agree at 460c3, a just man is one who wants never to commit injustice, then Polus is certainly no just man. And if what a teacher of justice teaches his pupils is not to want to do injustice, then Gorgias is certainly no teacher of justice. In Polus, Gorgias gets to see up close the moral failure of his nonmoral instruction.[17]

Polus's ideal human being is the tyrant, whom he furthermore believes to be the envy of all men, including Socrates. What all men envy in the tyrant, Polus thinks, is his ability to kill, confiscate, and banish. And Polus certainly does not mean only justly. As is clear from his description of the immoral excesses of his idol Archelaus, Polus regards this most unjust of human beings as—deservedly—the object of universal adulation.

Socrates surely has his work cut out for him as he confronts Polus. He must devise arguments suited to someone who foolishly and childishly lusts after injustice for its own sake, who craves power for the sheer thrill of visiting harm on others at whim. Polus is not one to name such goods as health or even gold and silver and high office (as, say, Meno does [*Meno* 78c6–7]) as the ends tyrants achieve and on account of which they are enviable. When Polus looks at a tyrant, he sees what he wants to be: a man who can do whatever he wants to whomever he wants and not have to pay the consequences. Polus's expressions *hon an boulōntai* (whomever they want [466c1]) and *hon an dokēi autois* (whomever they please [466c2]) reveal the utter capriciousness of Polus's desires.

Socrates marshals four arguments as he confronts Polus. Of these, the second and third are notoriously weak.[18] Only the fourth has any real substance,

17. See Nichols 1998, 138.

18. See Kahn 1983, 113, n62, who recognizes that Socrates generally is not reluctant to use false or inadequate premises in support of a conclusion he regards as true. Gentzler (1995, 27), by contrast, argues that an interlocutor can count as having been "genuinely refuted" only if defeated by a sound argument. In my view, Socrates frequently argues for conclusions he himself regards as false. Nor is it generally his intent to offer sound arguments to refute his interlocutors. Indeed, when it comes to certain interlocutors, Socrates is not averse to using any argument

yet even it trades on the doubtful premises to which Polus had earlier prematurely committed himself. We shall examine each of the four arguments in turn, with an eye toward discerning how they collectively both reflect the particular deficiencies of the character Polus and prepare the ground for the "no one does wrong willingly" paradox as formulated at 509e in the subsequent discussion with Callicles.

THE FIRST ARGUMENT: TYRANTS AND RHETORICIANS DO NOT HAVE GREAT POWER (466a9–468e10). The conclusion of this first argument is: "It is possible for a human being who does in the city what he pleases not to have great power nor to do what he wants" (468e3–5). To establish this conclusion Socrates argues first that killing, confiscating, and banishing are not things that are wanted.[19] He argues next that for the sake of their benefits, one might nevertheless want *to* kill, confiscate, and banish. And he argues finally that if these activities turn out not to be beneficial, even though the one who did them thought they were, then the one who did them has not done "what he wants" and has no great power.[20]

In order to make the first point, Socrates introduces the categories of the bad (*kaka*) and the intermediate (*metaxu*). Just as medicine or surgery or dangerous and uncomfortable sea voyages are bad things that, qua bad things, are not wanted—only the good things for the sake of which one does the bad things are wanted—so, too, Socrates argues, killing, confiscating, and banishing are bad things that are not wanted; only the good things for the sake of which these bad things are done are wanted.[21]

---

that will work to get them to contradict themselves, to make them appear ridiculous in their own eyes. All Socrates requires in order to bring an interlocutor to self-contradiction is the interlocutor's stated commitment to the view being challenged; the interlocutor need not sincerely believe it. Socrates invokes the "say what you believe" rule only when the interlocutor seeks suddenly to dissociate himself from the belief being tested. See note 42.

19. It can be no accident that Socrates names specifically killing, confiscating, and banishing as what rhetoricians and tyrants do. The three punishments from among which he is forced to choose at his trial are death, fine, and exile.

20. This final point is reminiscent of a similar one in *Rep.* 1: if rulers err regarding their own advantage, and if it is just to obey the rulers, then, at least when rulers err, justice is not "the advantage of the stronger."

21. The things in *Rep.* 2's third class of "goods," namely, gymnastic exercise, medical treatment, and the various money-making practices, are characterized by Glaucon as "drudgery" (*epipona* [357c7]) and thus as things "we would not choose to have for themselves" (*heautōn heneka ouk an dexaimetha echein* [357c8]), but only for the sake of whatever else results from them. These are the

Many commentators simply assume that killing, confiscating, and banishing are neutral intermediates rather than bad things and that it is for that reason that they are not wanted.[22] Yet Socrates expends considerable effort in showing—indeed this is what he shows first—that *bad* things (drinking a drug, suffering pain, money-making activities such as sailing when it involves danger and troubles) are not wanted; only the ends for the sake of which these things are done are wanted: health in the case of activities involving pain; wealth in the case of dangerous activities (466c7–d1; 466d1–6). Although Socrates does not explicitly call these bad things "bad," it is nevertheless clear that he does so regard them. For at 467e1–3 he introduces intermediates as a new and distinct category of things that are not wanted. If the new category contains things neither good nor bad, then the old can only contain bad things. Indeed, the introduction of the class of things neither good nor bad serves to strengthen Socrates' case concerning the unwantability of bad things: if we walk and stand (activities that are neither good nor bad) not because we want the walking and standing, doing them only for the sake of some good or because we think it better for us, then, a fortiori, we do not drink a drug and undertake dangerous sea voyages (activities that are bad) because we want *these* activities. To which of these two classes, then—that of bad things or that of things neither good nor bad—do killing, confiscating, and banishing belong? Note that Socrates does not list these three activities with the purely neutral ones. Instead, he groups them together, apart from the intermediates. And when, after having considered the intermediates, he goes on to say that we want killing, confiscating, and banishing not just like that (*haplōs houtōs*), though we do wish *to do* them (*prattein auta* [468c8]) if they are beneficial,[23] he explains: "for we want neither the things that are neither good nor bad *nor the*

---

same "good things" that in our argument are "bad things" (*kaka*). Heinaman (2002, 312–14) rightly sees that the goods in Glaucon's third class are "intrinsic evils."

22. See, e.g., O'Brien 1967, 88.

23. Those who drink a drug, Socrates says, do not want "this thing that they are doing" (*touto . . . hoper poiousin* [467c8–9]); those who sail do not want this "thing that they do on each occasion" (*touto . . . ho poiousin hekastote* [467d2–3]); and generally whenever someone does one thing for the sake of another, he does not want "this thing that he does" (*touto . . . ho prattei* [467d7]), but the other thing for the sake of which he does it. (This idea is repeated at 468b8–c1.) But, Socrates continues, although we do not want killing, banishing, or confiscating just like that, nevertheless, when they are beneficial to us we do wish *to do* them (*prattein auta* [468c4]). Irwin (1979, 141), Nakhnikian (1973, 16), and Vlastos (1985b, 19, n80) all insist, against Socrates, that when one does or undergoes a bad thing for the sake of a good, one does indeed want

bad things" (468c6–7). Surely, then, killing, confiscating, and banishing qualify as bad things.

Further evidence for the view that for Socrates killing, confiscating, and
banishing are no mere intermediates comes just a bit later at 468e6–469b2.
Were they mere intermediates Socrates would have no reason to say that the
man who kills even justly is, like the man who kills unjustly, unenviable (469b).
Would he assert that a man who, say, walks justly or stands justly is unenviable? The only reason that the man who kills justly is unenviable is that he en-
gages in an act that is in itself abhorrent, an act of killing. The man who kills
justly, like the man who undergoes painful and debilitating surgery in order to
improve his health, is, though hardly wretched, "not enviable either" (469a).

Since Polus, as we observed, does not think in terms of advantage but
wants to kill, confiscate, and banish just like that, and since he thinks those
men most powerful who do kill, confiscate, and banish just like that, it is important that Socrates try to show him that even those who kill, confiscate, and
banish do so thinking that these acts are to their advantage. Unlike Glaucon at
Rep. 2.360a–b, who contends that anyone lucky enough to possess Gyges' ring
with its invisible-making powers would, even if he were "just," proceed without a moment's hesitation to commit adultery and homicide and all manner
of injustice because he thinks injustice is profitable (*lusitelein* [*Rep.* 2.360c8]),
Polus thinks that what we would all like is to be able, just for their own sake,
to kill, confiscate the belongings of, and banish whomever we please.[24]

That Socrates hopes to get Polus to think in terms of good, benefit, and advantage, ideas that are foreign to his way of thinking, is clear from the argument's very inception. In characterizing what tyrants do (466b11–c2), Polus
uses interchangeably the expression *hon an boulōntai* (whomever they want
[466c1]) and *hon an dokēi autois* (whomever they please [466c2]). Socrates, in
arguing for a distinction between these expressions, actually changes the latter one. He substitutes for *hon an dokēi autois* the closely related yet significantly different *hoti an autois doxēi beltiston einai* (what seems best to them
[466e2]). He thus unobtrusively introduces into Polus's expression the new

---

the bad thing. My intuitions, however, coincide with Socrates' on this matter. The person who undergoes surgery for the sake of health does not want the surgery.

24. To prove just how happy the tyrant is Polus points not to the good things that Archelaus
acquires but to the horrific acts of injustice that he commits. See 471a–d. Rudebusch (1989, 36)
observes that tyrants sometimes "desire to murder not as part of a plan. They may develop an
appetite for murder for its own sake." This, I would argue, is precisely Polus's condition.

dimension of thinking something *best*. Even tyrants, Socrates suggests, do what they think best, that is, they think in terms of advantage, of self-interest. They do not, as Polus seems to think, simply do as they please, thoughtlessly pursuing whatever strikes their fancy.

Socrates repeats "best" at 466e10, and although he drops it later at 467a3 and 5, he by then may presume it to be understood: not only has Polus already heard it twice but he has apparently accepted it as a friendly amendment, since he says at 467b3–4 that he and Socrates were just now agreeing that rhetoricians and tyrants do what seems to them to be best. Nevertheless, since the full significance of the expansion of his expression is surely lost on Polus (he reverts at 467b8, apparently unawares, to his original formulation), Socrates now makes it plain: bad and intermediate things are things that those who do them want to do only because they think it *better* (*beltion* [468b2]; *ameinon* [468b6]).

Contrary to what is widely believed, the first argument against Polus does not make the claim that *all* things are done for the sake of good things or for the sake of "the good," but only the claim that bad and intermediate things are done for the sake of good things.[25] When Socrates says that "all these things" (*hapanta tauta* [468b8]) and that "those things" (*ekeina* [468b9]) are done for the sake of the good or for the sake of something that we do want, he is clearly referring not to all things but specifically to the bad and intermediate things, respectively, that he has just discussed.[26] It is not legitimate, therefore, to sup-

---

25. Early on in the argument, at 467b6–e1, Socrates asks: "So is it not also this way concerning *all things*: that whenever someone does something for the sake of something, he wants not the thing that he does but the thing for the sake of which he does it?" Socrates is surely not saying here that all things are chosen for the sake of other things. His claim is rather that since in the case of all things, when *x*'s are chosen for the sake of *y*'s it is not the *x*'s that are wanted but the *y*'s, it is not only in the case of bad things but in the case of intermediates as well that it is not they that are wanted but the goods for the sake of which they are chosen. Bad things and intermediate things, taken together, exhaust the class of *x*'s chosen for the sake of *y*'s. Pleasant things will later, in the discussion with Callicles, join bad and intermediate things in the class of things that are *to be* chosen for the sake of good things. Socrates recognizes that pleasant things—unlike bads and intermediates—need not be chosen for the sake of other things, so that even when they are, they are not chosen *simply* for the sake of other things.

26. In this dialogue, unlike in the *Meno,* as we shall see, "bad" means not harmful but rather repugnant or repulsive. The intermediates, then, things that are neither good nor bad, are things that are neither repugnant nor attractive. "Bad" as used here in the *Gorgias* must mean repugnant rather than harmful because Socrates' point is that these bad things might well be beneficial and be chosen for the sake of the benefit they bring despite their badness. The intermediates, too, since they

pose on the basis of this argument that Socrates thinks people always act for the sake of achieving what they take to be their own interest. Socrates is perfectly well aware that people can and do want and choose in and for themselves things they find attractive, whether they judge them beneficial or not. The problem he identifies as Polus's is not simply that Polus wants and chooses things that he finds attractive but does not judge beneficial, but that he finds attractive even things that are thoroughly repulsive, things that it is therefore not possible to want. The same Polus who wants what is unwantable will soon envy those who are unenviable (469a). And just as he will have to be told not to envy the unenviable, so he has first to be told not to want the unwantable. By slipping killing, confiscating, and banishing into the class of things that Polus agrees are bad, the class containing such things as drinking a drug and undertaking dangerous sea voyages, Socrates tries to make Polus grow up and wise up: who could want to kill, confiscate, or banish for its own sake? To anyone but a fool or a child, only the perceived benefits of such activities could make engaging in them desirable.[27]

Polus is now ready for the next point. When someone does such bad things as killing, confiscating, or banishing, these bad things are not wanted "just like that" (*haplōs houtōs* [468c3]), but "when these things are beneficial for us we want *to do* them (*prattein auta* [468c4]), and we do not want [to do them] when harmful" (468c2–5). This is because "we want the good things . . . but we do not want the things that are neither good nor bad nor the bad things" (468c5–7). In other words, since we do not want the things that are neither good nor bad *nor the bad things,* we do not want the killing, confiscating, and banishing (which are bad things) "just like that." But since we do want the good things, we do want *to do* these bad things *if they are beneficial,* that is, if they bring us good things.

But, Socrates asks—and this is his third point—what if the things for the sake of which a man kills, confiscates, and banishes, things he *thinks* are good,

---

neither attract nor repel, are not themselves things that are wanted: one chooses them, therefore, for their perceived benefits. "Bad" as used in the *Protagoras* is closer to the *Gorgias*'s usage than it is to the *Meno*'s. In the *Protagoras,* bad means painful. We shall see in chapter 6 that in *Rep.* 4 "good" is the opposite of "bad" as used in the *Gorgias:* it means attractive—not beneficial.

27. Had Polus resisted Socrates' attempt to characterize killing, confiscating, and banishing as bad things, protesting that these things are good things, things indeed desirable in themselves, Socrates' argument could not have succeeded. Socrates often counts on his interlocutors' not having the presence or clarity of mind to reject his suggestions.

turn out to be not good but worse (*tunchanei de on kakion* [468d3-4])? Can he then be said to "do what he wants" ([*poiei*] *ha bouletai* [468d5])? And can he be said, on the assumption that having great power is something good, to have great power in the city? (468d7–e2). Since he cannot be said either to do what he wants or to have great power in the city, it follows that "it is possible for a human being who does in the city what he pleases not to have great power nor to do what he wants" (468e3–5).

Two distinct ideas are thus presented in Socrates' first argument against Polus, two lessons for Polus to ponder: first, that bad things—killing, confiscating, and banishing among them—are not wanted "just like that" and, second, that when someone wants *to do* bad things for the sake of benefit, he fails to "do what he wants" if the things he thought good are not really good. For when someone wants good things and not bad, does he not want *truly* good things? The tyrant fails to do what he wants and fails to have great power because, though he does bad things for the sake of true benefit, he lacks the intelligence to discern which things are truly good (466e10), and thus fails to attain his true benefit.[28]

Socrates identifies in this argument two different kinds of things that people want. On the one hand, people want *to do* even bad and intermediate things for the sake of good ones. On the other, they want good things—that is, things that are neither bad nor intermediate. Among these are (1) things that are simply attractive or appealing, (2) things people regard as being good and of benefit to themselves, and (3) things that are truly good. Although no examples of (1) are given—we are given only examples of unattractive and unappealing bad things: drinking a drug, suffering pain, sailing when it is dangerous and troublesome[29]—examples can be easily supplied: eating a delicious meal, feeling pleasure, sailing for recreation. Examples of (2) are wis-

---

28. Polus has in effect admitted that rhetoricians have no knowledge. On the one hand, he does not dispute Gorgias's description of the business of rhetoricians as one of persuading, without knowledge, others who also lack knowledge—a business in which, one might say, the blind lead the blind. And, on the other, in the one matter in which Gorgias reluctantly concedes that he has knowledge and will teach those who do not, namely, justice, Polus berates him for saying out of shame what is not so. We may assume, then, that Polus subscribes to the conception of the rhetorician as a know-nothing whose power lies in his ability to persuade with respect to all things despite his ignorance. Socrates is convinced that tyrants are ignorant, but for an entirely different reason. As he sees it, men who are truly wise do not choose to lead lives of injustice and unrestraint.

29. Sailing is otherwise an intermediate (468a2) or even, perhaps, a good thing.

dom, health, and wealth (467e4–5).[30] The actual content of the goods in (3) is left unspecified; these goods are wanted—but in the abstract.[31]

To say that people want things that are good and are not bad or intermediate is to say that it is possible for them to want anything they *perceive* as good and not as bad or intermediate. And, if this is so, it cannot be correct to say that people do not want anything that is not truly good.[32] Nor can it be right to say that if a particular thing *is* truly good then people *must* want it. In fact, nothing that Socrates says suggests either the unwantability of the things merely thought good or the necessity of wanting those concrete things that in fact satisfy the description "truly good." Although the tyrant cannot want, because it is not something that anyone can want (or at least so Socrates argues), the killing itself—a bad, that is, repulsive, thing—the tyrant may indeed want *to* kill, confiscate, and banish for the sake of wealth and power. As Soc-

30. It is not Socrates but his interlocutor for whom the good things are "wisdom, health, and all other such things" (467e4–5). So, too, at *Meno* 78c5–6 and *Euthyd.* 279a7. Note that *boulesthai* is used for wanting even things like wealth; how can it be right to say, then, that *boulesthai* is reserved in this dialogue (or generally in Plato) for the kind of wanting whose object is the true good? Among those who attribute to *boulesthai* a restricted sense in the *Gorgias* are Dodds (1959, 236); Gosling (1973, 77); Penner (1991, 150); Santas (1979, 315–16, n16); Cornford (1927, 306); Gulley (1965, 83); Kahn (1983, 114). Irwin (1979, 141–42), McTighe (1984, 216), and Nakhnikian (1973, 14), however, argue against such a restrictive sense of *boulesthai* in the *Gorgias.*

31. Penner and Rowe (1994) think that desire, throughout this argument, is for what is really good for us, by which they mean the actual things that fit the description "truly good." But if among the goods we are said to want are not only wisdom and health but also wealth and any of the other standard "goods" one might name (467e4–6), then surely we can be said to want even what is not actually good for us. Hall (1971, 205–6), by contrast, thinks "good things" and even "the good" throughout this passage refer to "the good things which are the objects of our desires." On Hall's view it would have to be the case that tyrants and rhetoricians lack power because they fail to obtain the goods that are the objects of their desires. But why would Socrates assume that they would fail in this way? Is it not more likely that he would think that because they lack intelligence they would fail to obtain the things that are really good?

32. Aristotle expresses the difficulty of Socrates' position as follows: "Those, however, who say that what is wanted is the truly good, are faced with the conclusion that what a man who chooses his end wrongly wants is not truly wanted at all" (*EN* III.iv. 1113a17–18). Aristotle finds the alternative to this position troubling as well: if it is right to say that what appears good to each person is what that person wants, then is there no such thing as being wanted by nature (*mē einai phusei boulēton* [1113a21])? Socrates' solution to this puzzle is that when we choose things that seem good but are not, we do want those things yet do not "do what we want": in choosing what seems good but is not, we satisfy our desire for that thing but not our other and deeper desire for the happiness and fulfillment that come only from having what is truly good by nature. Cf. *Rep.* 9.577e: the soul that is under tyrannical rule "least does what it wants" (*hēkista poiēsei ha an boulēthēi*). For further discussion, see chapter 1, note 42.

rates will later say, the tyrant will kill *if he wants* (511a–b). In both these instances Socrates uses "want" perfectly ordinarily. Where he deviates subtly but importantly from ordinary usage is when he uses the expression "does what he wants." Socrates will not permit the tyrant to be described as "doing what he wants" if what he achieves through what he does is not his own *true* good. In other words, when a person who chooses attractive and pleasant things that he wants, or undertakes a specific course of action for the sake of perceived benefits that he wants, but does not by his choices achieve his true advantage, he fails, according to Socrates, to "do what he wants." For in addition to all the other things a person wants, there is something else, something of overarching importance, that he also wants—namely, to secure for himself the things that are truly good.[33]

Socrates' first argument against Polus is, to be sure, less than satisfying. It does not reveal the nature of the really good things whose attainment by tyrants and rhetoricians would confer on them real power. It does not so much as hint that the truly good things that Socrates has in mind are the goods of the soul: temperance and justice and courage. Indeed, although Socrates had spoken with Gorgias about a good condition of the body and a good condition of the soul (464a1–465e1), Socrates makes no mention of the soul when speaking with Polus until he gets to his fourth argument (at 477a6).[34] But nor

33. Socrates uses other terms idiosyncratically as well. "Power" (*dunamis*) is one such term. Since the argument with Polus assumes that power is a good thing, Socrates contends that people cannot have power unless they attain what is truly good for them. This special use is abandoned later, however (510d–e, 513b, and 525d–526b), as Socrates observes that kings and tyrants are most powerful and that those who are most powerful are most wicked. (One consequence of Socrates' equivocation on "powerful" is that those who are most powerful in the ordinary sense are least powerful in the idiosyncratic Socratic sense. Those who repeatedly and with impunity commit the gravest injustices do the most serious damage to their souls and hence least do what they want.) A second such term is *technē*. *Technē* is at first assigned so restrictive a sense that it excludes not only rhetoric but even (at 501–502) the paradigmatic *technē* of flute-playing (see *Prot.* 318c; *Meno* 90d7–e1). By the end of the *Gorgias*, however, rhetoric is called a *technē* (511b–c), as is cookery, even though as late as 500b cookery is regarded as the counterfeit counterpart of the genuine *technē* medicine. At 509d–510a, both avoiding suffering injustice and avoiding committing it are regarded as *technai*.

34. Since Gorgias actually asks Socrates to disregard Polus and to explain just to him what he means by saying that "rhetoric is a phantom of a part of politics" (463e), Socrates ends up addressing Gorgias alone when he introduces the distinction between the true and false arts that apply to body *and soul*. In the *Crito*, too, Socrates avoids use of the word "soul," resorting to the circumlocution "that which the unjust maims and the just profits" (47e).

does Polus ask Socrates what he means.[35] Instead, he impugns Socrates' integrity: "As if indeed you, Socrates, would not welcome the possibility of doing what you pleased in the city" (468e). Until Polus has been made far less certain of the self-evidence of his own views, he is not ready for an account of the good from the Socratic perspective.

THE SECOND ARGUMENT: IT IS WORSE TO DO INJUSTICE THAN TO SUFFER IT (468e10–476a3). Despite Socrates' efforts in the first argument to persuade Polus that tyrants and rhetoricians are unenviable because they do not do what they want, Polus remains unconvinced. He continues to believe that he and everyone else, including Socrates, envy those who kill, confiscate, and banish at whim, and, furthermore, that it makes no difference whether they do so justly or unjustly. That he believes it makes no difference whether those who kill, confiscate, and banish do so justly or unjustly elicits from Socrates a "Bite your tongue, Polus" (*Euphēmei* [469a2]). As Socrates sees it, such an idea is nothing short of blasphemy.[36] Yet Polus truly has no idea why Socrates would regard those who kill unjustly as wretched and pitiable. For Polus actually envies (and admires) those who kill unjustly far more than he does those who kill justly. Indeed, Polus seems shocked to hear that Socrates would choose suffering injustice over committing it if he had to, since that preference entails not welcoming (*dexaio*) the prospect of "tyranting" (469c3).[37] Wrongdoing is for Polus both the essence of tyranting and what makes it so desirable. In response to Socrates' having said that "when someone does those things [killing, confiscating, and banishing] justly, it is better, but when unjustly, worse," Polus sneers: "It is really hard to refute you, Soc-

---

35. By contrast, Gorgias wants to know what Socrates means by characterizing rhetoric as "an image of a part of politics" (463e). And Meno asks Socrates to clarify for him the notion that "all learning is recollection" (*Meno* 81e).

36. For other "blasphemous" utterances that elicit the *euphēmei* response, see *Prot.* 330d7; *Meno* 91c1; *Euthyd.* 301a7; *Rep.* 1.329c2, 6.509a9; *Laws* 3.696c1, 10.907a1.

37. See also 468e, where Polus uses *dexaio* to express his confidence that everyone, including Socrates, would welcome doing as he pleased in the city and would envy those who killed, confiscated from, and banished whomever they pleased. Cf. 474b7, where Polus says to Socrates: "So you would welcome (*dexai'*) suffering injustice rather than doing it?"; 471d1: "and perhaps there is some one of the Athenians, starting with you, who would welcome becoming anybody else whatsoever of the Macedonians rather than Archelaus." At 475d4 and 475e5, Socrates turns *dexaio*, *dexaimēn*, and *dexait'* back on Polus.

rates. But would not even a child refute you, and show that what you are say-ing is not true?" (470c). And at 471a Polus erupts: "But how on earth could he [Archelaus] not be unjust?" proceeding in exhilaration to enumerate the ma-licious and dastardly deeds of the vicious tyrant. Nothing but Polus's fascina-tion with freewheeling injustice can account for his impassioned admiration for the ruthless tyrant Archelaus.

Whereas Socrates' first argument asked whether tyrants and rhetoricians who kill, confiscate, and banish as they please have power, it is not until the second argument that the element of injustice is introduced. For Socrates, what determines if killing, confiscating, and banishing are the better course of action is whether one does these things justly (470c; 472e). Polus's criterion, however, is whether one escapes punishment (470a–b; 472d–e).[38] Polus thinks Socrates' criterion cannot be right because surely the villainous Archelaus, the tyrant who commits injustice upon injustice with impunity, and others like him are happy.[39] But Socrates thinks Polus's criterion cannot be right; as he sees it, only "the fine and good man and woman are happy; the unjust and base, wretched" (470e9–11). And each insists that it is his view that is shared by everyone (471c–e; 474b; cf. 475e3–6).[40]

Although Polus maintains that he and everyone else secretly or not so se-cretly crave the lawless excesses of the tyrant, he nevertheless concedes that committing injustice is more shameful than suffering it. Just as Gorgias's ad-

---

38. In order to get Polus to admit that it is not always good to kill, confiscate, and banish as one pleases, Socrates illicitly trades on an ambiguity in the phrase "as one pleases." Whereas Polus takes the phrase to imply that one acts with impunity, Socrates treats the phrase as if all it implies is that one acts freely. He asks (469d–e): do I not lack power despite doing "as I please" if I have to pay the penalty for entering a crowded marketplace with a dagger under my arm and killing anyone who strikes my fancy (*kata tēn autou doxan* [469c7])? For Polus, a person who has to pay a penalty does not do "as he pleases."

39. Although Polus says only that "*many* human beings who do injustice are happy" (470d), what motivates the qualifying "many" is surely that not all who do injustice get away with it.

40. Polus thinks that Socrates is lying when he claims to disagree with him (471e1). But Socra-tes recognizes both that all would *say* they agree with Polus (472a–b; see also 575e8–9 and 482b–c) and that they would really mean it (see 472d, 473a, 475e8–9, 482b–c). Since Socrates believes, however, that most people would admit to holding at least some views that entail his, he feels justi-fied in saying that everyone agrees with him (see 516d). McKim (1988, 48) suggests that Socrates shames his interlocutors into saying not what convention requires, but rather what they really do believe. It seems clear, however, that Polus and Callicles do not really believe—nor does Socrates think they do—the views to which they finally agree.

mission that he knows justice and teaches it to his students caused his downfall, so Polus's concession that the commission of injustice is shameful proves his undoing.[41] The argument that Socrates devises to refute Polus exploits his concession and uses it against him but makes no effort to understand what Polus means by it. Instead of exploring Polus's views on committing injustice and on suffering it, instead of seeking to determine what Polus means by shameful as distinct from bad, and instead of explaining why Polus's views are wrong, Socrates opts for a cheap verbal victory. He educates Polus not at all; all he does is trip him up.[42]

Let us look at the argument. It begins with Polus's view that *kalon* is not the same as *agathon,* nor shameful the same as bad (474c9).[43] Even though the question at hand is whether Polus is right to believe that doing injustice is more shameful but suffering it worse, Socrates immediately steers the discussion away from shameful (*aischron*) and bad (*kakon*) and toward their opposites *kalon* and *agathon.*[44] Why? Because whereas Polus is quite clear about what he means by shameful and bad, and about why he considers committing injustice more shameful and suffering it worse, he is, as Socrates no doubt hopes, less clear about what he means by *kalon* and *agathon* and, in particular, about what the difference is between them. Indeed, Socrates has reason to think that Polus may not draw a sharp distinction between *kalon* and *agathon,* since earlier he not only placed Gorgias's art among the best (*aristōn*) arts (448c8), but also

41. Cf. *Rep.* 1.348e, where Socrates says to Thrasymachus: "For if you had set injustice down as profitable but had nevertheless agreed that it was badness (*kakian*) or shameful, as do some others, we would have something to say, speaking according to customary usage."

42. This argument ought to give pause to those who believe that Socrates takes seriously the "say what you believe" constraint (a term coined by Vlastos [1983, 35–37]). See, e.g., Benson 2000, chap. 4. In this argument, Socrates is determined from the outset to get Polus to say the very opposite of what he believes. See Kahn (1992, 256), who recognizes how readily Socrates dispenses with the "say what you believe" constraint. See also note 18.

43. Crito, too, distinguishes shameful from bad. At *Crito* 45e, he regards as bad the misfortune of losing such a friend as Socrates but as shameful the failure of Socrates' friends to save him while still possible. The judgment that something is shameful is a judgment about how it looks. As I understand it, something can be *aischron* by being ugly to look at, regardless of whether anyone actually looks or is expected to look.

44. Socrates uses a similar tactic in his argument concerning temperance and wisdom at *Prot.* 332. Since it is hard to see how temperance and wisdom are the same, Socrates draws Protagoras's attention to the opposite of temperance and the opposite of wisdom, which, he argues, are the same: both are *aphrosunē,* folly.

called it, in the very next line (448c9), *tēs kallistēs* of the arts. It might even be fair to say that the distinction between *kalon* and *agathon* is generally less clear than that between *aischron* and *kakon*.

One way to discern Socrates' agonistic strategy in this second argument is to begin by asking, as Socrates deliberately does not, what it is that Polus means when he says initially that doing injustice is more shameful but less bad than suffering it. We need to ask, in other words, what Polus's criteria are for badness. There can be no doubt that what he means by "bad" is: painful or harmful or both. That is why he regards suffering injustice as obviously worse than committing it: suffering injustice is more physically painful or more materially harmful to the sufferer than committing injustice is to the committer. (See, for example, Polus's description at 473c of what happens to someone who is caught attempting to displace a reigning tyrant.) If indeed, as he says, he views bad and shameful as distinct, then his criteria for bad, namely, painful or harmful or both, cannot be his criteria for shameful, nor can the opposites of his criteria for bad, namely, pleasant or beneficial or both, be his criteria for *kalon*. Nevertheless, Socrates induces Polus to agree to a definition of *kalon*, the opposite not of bad but of shameful, in terms of pleasure or benefit or both.

Polus, had he had his wits about him, would have resisted Socrates' definition of *kalon* in terms that, given his understanding of *kakon* and his insistence that *kakon* and *aischron*, *agathon* and *kalon* are not the same but different, surely better suit *agathon*.[45] (Indeed, in Socrates' next argument against Polus [see 477a1–2] fine things are determined to be good things because they are pleasant or beneficial! Pleasant and beneficial are there simply assumed to be the criteria for *agathon*.) Socrates, however, exploits Polus's dimwittedness, never raising for him the possibility that it might be *agathon* to which the criteria of pleasure and benefit would be better suited. Note that once Socrates gets Polus to agree that *kalon* and *agathon* are not the same, he never again mentions *agathon* at all.

Observe, too, that in defining *kalon* in terms of pleasure or benefit or both, Socrates has recourse to a kind of pleasure and benefit that could never be the counterpart of the kind of pain and harm that Polus associates with bad. For Polus, the reason suffering injustice is worse—more bad—than

---

45. Callicles will define, not *kalon,* but *agathon,* first in terms of pleasure and then in terms of benefit (495a; 499d).

committing it is because it involves physical pain and material harm. Yet the pleasure and benefit that Socrates assigns to things that are *kalon* are neither physical nor material.[46] They are instead the rarefied pleasures of art and music and laws and practices and subjects of learning. Polus, to be sure, could never have associated *kalon* with the feel-good pleasures of eating, drinking, or sex, the arguably more direct counterparts of the feel-bad pains of being tortured on the rack, castrated, having one's eyes burned out, being mutilated, and being impaled or tarred or burned (473c). Nor could he have associated *kalon* with such material benefits as power, health, and wealth, the arguably more direct counterparts of such material harms as impotence, sickness, and poverty. For just as Polus associates physical pain and material harm with bad rather than with shameful, so would he surely associate physical pleasure and material gain with *agathon* rather than with *kalon*. The ethereal pleasures and benefits in terms of which Socrates defines *kalon* prevent Polus from seeing that it is *agathon,* and not *kalon,* that is best defined in terms of pleasure and benefit.

Another way of thinking about the difference between Polus's sense of pain

---

46. Vlastos (1967) and Santas (1979, 233 ff.) think the fallacy in the argument lies in the shifting "for whom": whereas in the case of beauty it is the observer, not the thing observed, that experiences the pleasure, it is the sufferer who experiences the pain in the case of suffering injustice. But, they ask, is it clear that the observer of suffering experiences more pain at the suffering of the sufferer than at the cruelty of the committer? Moreover, as Guthrie (1975, IV, 312) notes, it is not all that simple in the act of observing to separate out the suffering from the infliction of suffering. Several considerations tell against the Vlastos-Santas view. First, as McKim (1988, 45) points out, some of Socrates' examples of *kalon* do not involve an observer. Second, it is possible that those who identify the fallacy in this way are responding unawares to the incommensurateness of the pleasures and pains being opposed: none of Socrates' examples of pleasant things involves the sort of physical and material pleasure that is the natural counterpart of the physical and material pain of suffering injustice. And, third, it is likely that Socrates intends the pleasure or pain in each case to be assessed in relation to the *primary* experiencer: in the case of suffering injustice the primary experiencer is the sufferer and in committing it the primary experiencer is the committer—in neither of these cases is the primary experiencer the observer; in the case, however, of a beautiful color or sound, the primary experiencer is the observer or hearer, in the case of laws it is the one governed by them, and in the case of subjects of learning it is the student. Mackenzie (1981, 243) argues, against Vlastos and Santas, that it is permissible to leave unspecified who the sufferer of the pain and harm is because *everyone* calls doing injustice shameful insofar as it is painful or harmful to each in his own way. It must be said, however, that even though everyone—including the committer, the sufferer, and the observer—calls committing injustice *aischron,* what they all mean is that it is *aischron* for the committer (since what he has done is ugly), on account of the pain and harm he has caused the sufferer.

and harm and the sense of pleasure and benefit that Socrates foists on him is that Polus's sense is natural and Socrates' conventional. Indeed, it is in precisely these terms that Callicles later (at 483a) diagnoses the Socratic "mischief" (*kakourgeis*) that he detects in the arguments: "if someone speaks of things according to convention, you slip in questions according to nature, and if he speaks of the things of nature, you ask about the things of convention." The pain and harm that Polus has in mind when he pronounces suffering injustice worse than committing it are natural; their badness is not measured against any cultural standard. Yet Socrates "slips in" their conventional counterparts—pleasures and benefits that are, as he expands his list of *kala,* increasingly matters of taste, judgment, and sensibility. Moreover, just when Polus begins to think in terms of conventional pleasure and benefit, Socrates reverts to the natural sense of pain in asserting that surely committing injustice is not more painful than suffering it.[47]

If we now focus our attention squarely on the matter of benefit we can see even more clearly how Socrates misleads Polus by the definition of *kalon* that he suggests: could Socrates or anyone else seriously entertain the idea that for those who, like Polus, distinguish between *kalon* and *agathon,* benefit belongs with *kalon?*[48] Does not beneficial (*ōphelimon*) naturally align itself with good (*agathon*)? Of course it does.[49] And because it does, Polus himself immediately and automatically makes the substitution of *agathon* for *ōphelimon* at 475a2–4, thereby giving Socrates just what he needs.[50] With this substitution in place Socrates is able to conclude that if committing injustice is more shameful (the

---

47. Callicles says: "when Polus spoke of the more shameful according to convention, you pursued convention according to nature" (483a6–7). Some editors (Riemann) emend the *nomon* in the manuscripts to *logon,* and read "you pursued the argument according to nature," apparently not seeing what it could mean for Socrates to be "pursuing convention according to nature." But "pursuing convention according to nature" is precisely what Socrates does. Socrates' "mischief" far exceeds simply (deliberately) mixing up a conventional term (*aischron*) with a natural one (*kakon*).

48. So Adkins (1960, 250), who points out that *agathon* can be connected with advantage and benefit in a way that *kalon* cannot. Whereas *kalon,* he says, smacks of the conventional, *agathon* does not, nor does benefit. "No thing can be beneficial 'by convention': it either is beneficial or it is not."

49. See 499d, where Socrates says: "So are the beneficial [pleasures] therefore [that is, now that it has come to light that there are both good and bad pleasures] good and the harmful ones bad?"

50. If Polus hadn't himself made the substitution, it would surely have been easy enough for Socrates to get him to. All Socrates would have had to say is: "And is something that is *ōphelimon*

opposite of more *kalon*) than suffering it, yet committing injustice does not exceed suffering it in painfulness (the opposite of pleasure), then committing injustice can only exceed it in badness, *tōi kakōi* (the opposite of benefit, now equated with good) (475c7). *Kalon* as beneficial is no longer distinct from *agathon,* and thus *aischron* as harmful is no longer distinct from *kakon.* This reversal of Polus's initial separation of *kalon* from *agathon* and of *aischron* from *kakon* comes to pass only because Polus is duped into associating benefit with *kalon* instead of with *agathon.* Had Socrates from the start attempted to define *kalon* strictly in terms of benefit rather than in terms of pleasure or benefit or both, Polus might have had some chance, however slim, of noticing that he was actually defining *agathon.*[51] By coupling benefit with pleasure, however, and in particular with genteel pleasure, Socrates effectively obscures the natural link between benefit and *agathon.*[52]

In his attempt to ensnare Polus, then, Socrates has set for him at least seven traps. First, he does not ask Polus what he means by *kakon* and *aischron,* thereby preventing Polus from making clear to himself the criteria he assigns to each. Second, he shifts the discussion away from *kakon* and *aischron,* where Polus may well have been able to articulate the difference between the terms, to *kalon,* the opposite of *aischron,* where Polus is less clear and is hence more

---

not *agathon?,*" to which Polus no doubt would have responded: "Certainly." It is striking, however, that Polus does make the substitution on his own: so obvious is it that *ōphelimon* is interchangeable with *agathon.*

51. The association of benefit with *kalon* is so jarring that Socrates does not at first use the term *ōphelimon.* He says instead that the reason a body is called *kalon* is because of a use (*chreia*) it has for which it is useful or to which it is suited (*chrēsimon*). To say that a body is *kalon* because it has a use for which it is useful or apt is not quite the same thing as to say that it is *kalon* just because it is useful: a knife, for example, may be something *kalon* because it is particularly useful for or well suited to the use it serves; it would not, however, be *kalon* just because it is useful. There is beauty or nobility in the fittingness of things to their purpose—not in their having a purpose simpliciter.

52. Most commentators direct their criticism of Socrates' argument to the pleasure element in his definition of *kalon.* But they fail to notice, just as Socrates intends Polus to fail to notice, that Socrates' having defined *kalon* in terms of pleasure matters hardly at all to the argument, since it is not by virtue of its being more painful that committing injustice is said to be more *aischron* than suffering it. Socrates talks about pleasure for two reasons: first, to keep Polus from noticing that he is defining *kalon* in terms of benefit, something that, as Polus instinctively senses, is more naturally suited to *agathon;* and second, to provide himself with an alternative he can dismiss (viz., more painful), so that all that is left to account for why committing injustice is more shameful than suffering it is that it is "more *kakon,*" the opposite of "more *ōphelimōn/agathon.*"

easily taken in. Third, Socrates defines *kalon* in terms of pleasure or benefit or both, terms that for Polus (or anyone else who distinguishes between *agathon* and *kalon*) would more naturally define *agathon*. Fourth, Socrates makes no mention of *agathon*, thereby making it more difficult for Polus to resist Socrates' definition of *kalon* in terms of pleasure and benefit. Fifth, Socrates identifies *kalon* with a rarefied kind of pleasure and benefit foreign to the pleasure and benefit that are the opposites of the pain and harm that Polus no doubt has in mind when he asserts that suffering injustice is worse than committing it. Sixth, Socrates switches the sense in which pleasure—and by implication its opposite, pain—is to be understood. He uses it in its more ethereal sense when he seeks to define *kalon* but reverts to its cruder physical sense when he wishes to eliminate "because it is more painful" as the reason that committing injustice is more shameful than suffering it, and to leave as the only viable explanation "because it is worse." And seventh, Socrates associates benefit with *kalon* rather than with the *agathon* with which it naturally belongs, knowing that he can count on Polus to make the critical substitution of *agathon* for *ōphelimon*.

Socrates himself—but for his own reasons, reasons as yet not shared with Polus—frequently pairs *kalon* with *agathon*. For example, Socrates thinks "the fine and good man and woman are happy" (470e9–10); he advocates the pursuit of "what is good and fine" (480c); and he says of the man who imitates the tyrant that when he kills whomever he wants he will be a base man killing "a fine and good one" (511b). (See also 490e6, 514a1, 515e13, 518b1, 518c4, 526a7, and 527d2.) Moreover, Socrates has made it clear from early on that he thinks shameful things (*aischra*) are bad things (*kaka*). For when Polus asked him if rhetoric is *kalon* or *aischron* (463d3), he responded: "I say *aischron*—for I call things that are *kaka*, *aischra*" (463d4). Indeed, the very way in which Socrates poses his question to Polus: "So then it is also worse if indeed it is more shameful?" (474c8–9), shows that for him these two terms belong together. And Socrates will continue to join *kakon* and *aischron* until the dialogue's end: at 521b–c he will say of the bad man who will likely do him harm that if such a man confiscates Socrates' possessions "he will use them unjustly, and if unjustly, then shamefully, and if shamefully, badly" (521b–c).

If, then, among the things Socrates finds objectionable in Polus's position is his sharp division of *kalon* from *agathon* and *aischron* from *kakon*, he is nevertheless content at this stage of the discussion simply to trick Polus into conflating these terms. Illumination will come, but only in connection with the fourth argument, where Socrates will show that considerations of *kalon* and *aischron* are assimilable to considerations of good and bad, benefit and harm, in determining the relative worth of committing and suffering injustice and of escaping and undergoing rightful punishment.

THE THIRD ARGUMENT: HE WHO IS PUNISHED JUSTLY SUFFERS GOOD THINGS AND IS BENEFITED (476b1–477a4). By the time Socrates completes the second argument, he has Polus agreeing that, "at least according to this argument" (475e2–3), no human being, including Socrates and Polus, would welcome doing injustice rather than suffering it.[53] All that remains then for Socrates to do is to show Polus that it is better to be punished justly than to escape just punishment. (Recall that for Polus, what determines whether it is better to kill, confiscate, and banish is whether one escapes punishment.)

Before actually addressing the question of whether it is better to be punished justly than to escape just punishment, Socrates presents a short argument to establish that he who is punished justly suffers good things and is therefore benefited. Although this brief argument is generally seen as part of the larger argument whose aim is to show that being punished is far better than not being punished, the larger argument actually stands on its own.[54]

Here, then, is the third argument:

1. All just things (*dikaia*) are fine things (*kala*). (476b1–2)
2. It is always the case that the thing that suffers suffers what it suffers in the same manner as the doer does it. (476b5–6)
3. He who punishes correctly, punishes justly.[55] (476d8–e1)

---

53. The effect on Polus of Socrates' refutation is indeed precisely that described by Aristotle as the effect of sophistic refutation: "the mind is fettered, being unwilling to stand still because it cannot approve the conclusion reached, but unable to go forward because it cannot untie the knot of the argument" (*EN* VII.ii. 1146a25–27).

54. Although the larger argument that I am calling the fourth takes as its point of departure the conclusion of the brief argument ("the third") that precedes it, it is nevertheless fully independent of the earlier argument. Indeed, its conclusion, namely, that one who suffers just punishment is benefited, depends on the entirely new premiss that there is a good and a bad condition of both body and soul.

55. Those who think that justice is helping themselves and their family and friends not to suffer at the hand of others (*Crito* 45c) are not likely to believe that the correctness of a punishment has much to do with its being just. Those who impose punishment—whether correctly or

4. He who punishes justly does just things. (476e1–2)
5. He who is punished justly suffers just things. (2, 4; 476e2–3)
6. He who punishes justly does fine things. (4, 1; 476e3–4)
7. He who is punished justly suffers fine things. (5, 1; 476e5)[56]
8. Fine things are pleasant or beneficial. (477a1–2)
9. Things that are pleasant or beneficial are good things. (implicit in 77a1–2)
10. Fine things are good things. (477a1)
11. He who is punished justly suffers good things. (7, 10; 477a2–3)
12. To suffer good things is to be benefited. (implicit)
∴ 13. He who is punished justly is benefited. (11, 12; 477a3)

Note that this argument rides roughshod over the distinction between *kalon* and *agathon* with which the previous argument began. In propositions 7 through 9, and without any fanfare, Socrates associates with *agathon* the very features that he had, in the previous argument, associated with *kalon*—namely, pleasant and beneficial. Indeed, he uses these features of *kalon* to link it to *agathon:* "So, if fine, then good? For they are pleasant or beneficial" (477a1–2). Of course, without the distinction between *kalon* and *agathon,* the game is up for Polus the moment he agrees that all just things are *kala.* Yet how could he fail to agree to that? After all, he is the same Polus who believes that committing *in*justice is shameful.

Polus's defeat in the third argument is ensured, then, not by any substantive philosophical point that Socrates makes but rather by Polus's concession that all just things are fine things. It is perhaps worth noting that, because the argument is purely formal, saying nothing of substance, Socrates could equally well have used it against a position of his own. At 469b Socrates famously maintains that those who are killed unjustly are less wretched and pitiable than those who kill unjustly. But he also asserts in that passage that

---

not—are seen to be inflicting harm and hence are regarded as an enemy, so that one who suffers punishment, whether it is correct or not, is suffering injustice at his enemy's hand. See *Crito* 50c1–2, where Socrates has to introduce Crito to the idea that the correctness of a punishment, that is, whether it is merited or not, determines its justness.

56. Mackenzie (1981, 244) thinks this argument is fallacious because although the judge experiences pleasure when he punishes justly, it is not the case that the man punished does. Yet it is not because the judge experiences pleasure that punishing justly counts as *kalon*. Punishing justly is *kalon* because all just things are *kala.* And if all just things are *kala,* then being punished justly is similarly *kalon,* and if *kalon,* then either pleasant or beneficial or both.

those who are killed unjustly are less wretched and pitiable than those who are killed justly. Using the same line of reasoning he uses against Polus, Socrates could have argued—against himself—that he who is killed unjustly is *more* wretched and pitiable that he who is killed justly. The argument might have gone something like this:

1. He who kills incorrectly does unjust things (*adika*).
2. Unjust things are shameful things (*aischra*).
3. The sufferer suffers as the doer does.
4. He who is killed unjustly suffers unjust things. (1, 3)
5. He who is killed unjustly suffers shameful things. (4, 2)
6. Shameful things are painful or harmful.
7. Things that are painful or harmful are bad things.
8. He who is killed unjustly suffers bad things. (5, 6, 7)
9. He who kills correctly kills justly.
10. He who kills justly does just things (*dikaia*).
11. Just things are fine things (*kala*).
12. The sufferer suffers as the doer does.
13. He who is killed justly suffers just things. (10, 12)
14. He who is killed justly suffers fine things. (13, 11)
15. Fine things are pleasant or beneficial.
16. Things that are pleasant or beneficial are good things.
17. He who is killed justly suffers good things. (14, 15, 16)
18. He who suffers bad things is more wretched and pitiable than he who suffers good things.
∴ 19. He who is killed unjustly is more wretched and pitiable than he who is killed justly. (8, 17, 18)

When arguments are merely formal—one might even say sophistic—the same premisses might yield a true conclusion *and* a false one. Only once Socrates *explains* that what makes just punishment *kalon* and *agathon* is that it re moves the evil from one's soul does his assertion that even just punishment is *kalon* and *agathon* start to mean something. And it is not until it becomes clear that it is more *kalon* and more *agathon* not to have sinned at all and not, there-fore, to have a soul in need of repair that Socrates' seemingly bizarre view that he who is killed justly is more wretched and pitiable than he who is killed unjustly begins to make sense. Socrates will eventually share with Polus the substance of his thinking, but evidently not before Polus has been defeated in a game of words.

Returning now to the third argument, we note that it makes no mention of the painfulness of punishment. Indeed, the expected move—namely, "All *dikaia* are *kala;* all *kala* are pleasant or beneficial or both; just punishment is not pleasant; therefore, just punishment is beneficial and hence good"—is conspicuously absent. Yet surely it is the painfulness of punishment—and even of just punishment—that for Polus renders it bad. By avoiding all consideration of the one feature of punishment that for Polus makes it decidedly bad, does not Socrates once again fail to engage or challenge Polus's view in any serious way?

Socrates' first argument, although it was surely incomplete and overly cryptic, did not treat Polus with the flagrant disrespect so evident in the second and third. Why are the second and third arguments such shoddy ones? Why is Socrates content to gain through them a merely superficial, hollow, strictly verbal victory? Why does he not mount a substantive offensive against Polus's views? Why does he say nothing to explain why committing injustice is worse than suffering it? Why does he make no reference to the soul?

Recall that Socrates' second and third arguments are occasioned by Polus's having championed not merely killing, confiscating, and banishing for their own sake, as he did in the first argument, but their *unjust* commission—a shameful and thoughtless position. Moreover, Polus dismisses the first argument's conclusion as preposterous and Socrates' apparent endorsement of it as disingenuous. Indeed, Polus proceeds to scoff at all the positions Socrates adopts as if they are so patently ridiculous and indefensible that "would not even a child refute you?" (470c4–5). But just how does Polus propose to refute Socrates, to do what even a child could do? Polus's idea of refutation, as Socrates observes, comprises (1) producing many witnesses in support of his own point of view and in opposition to his opponent's (471e); (2) "spooking" his opponent (*mormoluttei* [473d]); and (3) laughing (473e). Indeed, with respect to the last of these Socrates is moved to ask: "Is this yet another form of refutation?" (473e2–3). To Polus's flagrantly rhetorical tactics Socrates opposes one of his own, calling it, too, "another way of refutation" (472c3–4)—as if to say that his style of refutation will be no more serious, no more substantive, than Polus's. It will consist, as Socrates explicitly states, in just trying to make Polus *say* the same things as he (*peirasomai de ge kai se poiēsai . . . tauta emoi legein* [473a]), to get Polus to, as it were, "witness" against himself (472b–

c). In other words, a victory in words is all Socrates is after. Why is his professed goal so modest? Because a man like Polus cannot be improved until he is humbled. The second argument, therefore, explains not at all why it is that doing injustice is a bad thing, a thing worse than suffering it. Nor does the third argument indicate in any way how the man who is punished justly is benefited. Although Socrates explains in his fourth argument (beginning at 477a5) and later on as well why doing wrong is bad for the one who does it, and why one who is punished benefits by being punished, he does not do so until Polus has been tamed, until Polus observes himself sheepishly endorsing views that are diametrically opposed to those he had previously affirmed with such belligerent assurance. Not until then does Socrates dignify Polus's views with an account of why they are wrong. Polus has laughed at Socrates, but Socrates, if he is to benefit Polus at all, must have the last—and heartier—laugh.

THE FOURTH ARGUMENT: IT IS BETTER TO SUFFER JUST PUNISH-MENT THAN TO ESCAPE IT (477a5–479e9). Once Socrates has secured Polus's assent to propositions that Polus had initially found ludicrous (and probably still does), once Socrates has gotten Polus to relinquish, if only in word, his ugly opinions about the glories of committing injustice with impunity, he is prepared, at long last, to reveal what it is that constitutes true benefit—to reveal, that is, what *he* regards as true benefit. At 477a5, Socrates rather strikingly asks: "Then what do *I* suppose (*egō hupolambanō*) the benefit [of just punishment] to be?" Whereas up to now Socrates had derived the implications of premisses to which he secured Polus's assent, Socrates now presents his own position. And now, too, for the very first time, he speaks to Polus of the soul: "Does he become better in respect to his soul if he is justly punished?" (477a5–6).

Now that the soul has entered the discussion, Socrates can proceed to identify the three distinct things that people have that might be in bad condition: (1) possessions, (2) the body, and (3) the soul. Of these, Socrates specifies the soul as the one whose bad condition is most shameful—and Polus agrees. But when Socrates attempts to infer that it is the bad condition of the soul that is then also the *worst* of the three, Polus balks (477c). He has not really yet come to accept a connection between shamefulness and badness. And so, Socrates explains it to him again: As we agreed, Socrates says, the thing that is more shameful is either more painful or more harmful or both (477c). Polus agrees. Employing now the same line of argument he used in the second argument (but not in the third), Socrates reasons that since injustice, intemperance, cowardice, and ignorance (jointly, *ponēria* of the soul) are more shameful than poverty (*ponēria* of possessions) or illness (*ponēria* of the body), and since what is more shameful is either more painful, more harmful or both, it follows that if injustice, intemperance, cowardice, and ignorance are not more painful than poverty and illness, they must be more harmful and hence worse. The argument then continues as follows.

1. The art of moneymaking frees possessions from their baseness; the art of medicine frees the body from its baseness; the art of justice (in the form of just punishment) frees the soul from its baseness.
2. Baseness of the soul surpasses baseness of possessions and of the body in harm and bad.
3. Baseness of soul is the worst condition of all.
4. The art that cures the worst condition is the most *kalon*.
5. Justice is the most *kalon*.
6. Whatever is most *kalon* is most pleasant or most beneficial or both.
7. Justice is not most pleasant.
8. Justice is most beneficial, hence best.
∴ 9. It is far better, despite the pain, to be justly punished than to escape punishment.

Of course, best of all is never to have bad in one's soul at any time—this is surely why Socrates had said at 469b that he who is killed unjustly is less wretched and pitiable than he who is killed justly—but second best is to have had bad in one's soul and to have been freed of it. In this fourth argument the painfulness of punishment is duly acknowledged but its importance minimized: since baseness of soul is the worst possible condition one can suffer, one who is afflicted with this condition should submit bravely to punishment, "not taking account of its pain" (480c).

How does punishment release a soul from baseness? First, it prevents the soul from continuing to fester as if with sores underneath to the point that it becomes incurable (478a–b). Second, it keeps the soul away from the things it desires, since feeding its base appetites will only make it worse (505b). Third, it brings benefit by way of the infliction of pains and griefs, the only way a soul can be freed of injustice (525b). And fourth, it "moderates men and makes them more just and comes to be the medicine for baseness" (478d).[57] A similar account is given in the *Republic* at 9.591a–b: "Or does not the man who gets away with it become still worse; while, as far the man who does not get away with it and is punished, is not the bestial part of him put to sleep and tamed, and the tame part freed, and does not his whole soul—brought to its best nature, acquiring moderation and justice accompanied by prudence—gain a habit more worthy of honor than the one a body gains with strength and beauty accompanied by health, in proportion as soul is more honorable than body?"

Punishment, then, works directly on the irrational elements of the soul, taming them and disciplining them so that injustice does not recur. Pain is inflicted so that the soul will recoil from repeating its crimes—indeed, so that it will become moderate, just, and prudent. Contrary to what is widely believed, punishment, as Socrates understands it, aims not at changing a person's beliefs; it aims at changing his character.

Even though Socrates uses the same strategies in his fourth argument against Polus that he used in the second, misleadingly linking pain and harm in both arguments to *aischron,* and pleasure and benefit to *kalon,* and deliberately switching in both from conventional to natural senses of pleasure and pain, he nevertheless achieves in his fourth argument something monumental: he drives a wedge between pain, on the one hand, and harm and bad, on the other.[58] And although it is likely that Polus has not quite absorbed this lesson, he is at long last been given a *reason* to think such a separation not unreasonable: if the soul is of greatest importance, and if committing injustice worsens its condition whereas being justly punished improves it, then it is worse to commit and avoid punishment than to commit injustice and be subjected to punishment, even if being punished is the more painful course. Indeed, just punishment, though painful, is beneficial and good—and *kalon:* a person must "pursue what is *agathon* and *kalon,* not taking into account what is painful" (480c).

---

57. See Aristotle, *EN* II.iii. 1104b: "Another indication is the fact that pain is the medium of punishment; for punishment is a sort of medicine and it is the nature of medicine to work by means of opposites."

58. At 475d Socrates urges Polus not to shrink from answering but to submit himself to the argument "as to a doctor," for he will "suffer no harm" (*ouden gar blabēsēi*). Socrates does not assure Polus that he will suffer no pain. If anything, the implication of the doctor analogy is that there will be pain: pain, but not harm; pain, but benefit.

One interesting feature of Socrates' fourth argument is that it "naturalizes" the conventional categories of *aischron* and *kalon*. The shamefulness or ugliness of committing injustice and not paying the penalty is attributed to the natural (*pephuken* [479d6]) badness of the real harm it brings to the soul.[59] And, by implication, the nobility or beauty of being just may be attributed to the natural goodness of the real benefit *it* brings to the soul. Socrates has no need for the conventional when he can speak of natural—that is, real—harm and benefit to the soul. Significantly, it is pain and pleasure that are now left out in the cold. Bodily pain is irrelevant to determinations of *aischron* and *kakon*. So, too, bodily pleasure with respect to *kalon* and *agathon*.

The discussion with Polus has had much to say about doing bad things and about injustice. In Socrates' first argument, it was contended (1) that bad things, repugnant things, are not wanted, so killing, confiscating, and banishing are not wanted; and (2) that people do not "do what they want" in doing these bad things for the sake of benefit if they fail by doing them to secure for themselves real benefit. In the second, third, and fourth arguments, Socrates sought to show that committing injustice is just about the worst thing there is, there being only one thing that is even worse—committing injustice without paying the penalty; and that for the sake of the benefits of being justly punished one should be willing to endure pain. Through the last of these lessons Socrates anticipates two of the important points that he will soon propose to Callicles: (1) that pleasure is not the same as good, and (2) that pleasure should be chosen for the sake of good, not good for the sake of pleasure. It is his acceptance of these two ideas that will make it impossible for Callicles to reject the conclusions that Socrates had reached with Polus, and that will make the Socratic paradox, as formulated at 509e, something to which, whether he likes it or not, he, too, and not just Polus, is logically committed.

Callicles

If Gorgias is a decent man who would like to see the powerful rhetoric he teaches used justly, and Polus a childish fool fascinated with doing wrong and getting away with it, who is Callicles? Is he perhaps, as Socrates says, a man

---

59. See *Rep.* 3.392c, where Socrates speaks of how justice "*by nature* profits the man who possesses it, whether he seems just or not."

who, unlike the others, possesses "knowledge, goodwill, and outspokenness" (487a)?

It is doubtful that Socrates is sincere in crediting Callicles with either knowledge or outspokenness.[60] For how can Socrates believe that Callicles has knowledge when Callicles' views oppose his, and he identifies his own views with those of philosophy (482a)? And how can Socrates believe that Callicles possesses outspokenness (*parrhēsia*) when, as he observes, Callicles says whatever his boyfriend Demos says and whatever the Athenian demos says (481d–482a)?[61] Although, as Socrates is quick to observe, Callicles talks tough, saying "clearly" (*saphōs*) in his conversation with Socrates "what others are thinking but are unwilling to say" (492d),[62] in his political life he is prepared to ingratiate himself with the powers that be by being like them, saying what they say and doing what they do (481d–482a; 510a–e).

What things does Callicles say that others are thinking but are unwilling to say? One such thing is that suffering injustice is more shameful than doing it.[63] Berating Polus for admitting out of shame that committing injustice is more shameful than suffering it, and shaken by what he regards as the sheer perverseness of Socrates' view that committing injustice is worse than suffering it[64]—he

60. Of the three characteristics that Socrates ascribes to Callicles, the only one he appears actually to have, if just initially, is goodwill (*eunoia*) toward Socrates: he claims to have it (at 486a), and Socrates seems to believe he does (487c, 487d).

61. See *Rep.* 6.493b, where Socrates observes that sophists take what everyone else says, organize it into an art, and teach it. Despite what Socrates says, it is clear from the outset that Callicles is no lover of the demos (see 483b–c, 490a, 492a–b). Indeed, as Socrates later points out, Callicles so prides himself on his nobility of birth that he would not give his daughter in marriage to the son of an engineer nor take for his son the daughter of an engineer (512c). But Callicles is afraid of the demos because it has the power to hurt him. Kahn (1983, 100) characterizes Callicles as "an ambitious politician in a democracy" who is "obliged to be a lover of the demos and an endorser of popular views." Protagoras, as we saw in chapter 2, finds himself in a similar predicament.

62. Callicles thinks that both Gorgias and Polus said out of shame, bowing to *ethos* (custom [482d2]) and to *nomos* (483a6), what they do not believe—Gorgias, that he would teach the just things to those who come to him without already knowing them, and Polus, that it is more shameful to commit injustice than to suffer it. Callicles will presumably not do the same.

63. See also 492c, where Socrates reacts to Callicles' contention that wantonness, lack of discipline, and freedom are virtue and happiness by exclaiming that Callicles is now saying what others are thinking but are unwilling to say.

64. Cf. *Crito* 49b, where Socrates says that "wrongdoing is in every way bad (*kakon*) and shameful (*aischron*) for the wrongdoer."

actually asks twice if Socrates is joking (481b7, 481c1; cf. Polus's similar in-
credulity at 461b3–4)—Callicles passionately defends the law of the jungle.[65] In
the jungle, nothing is more shameful than to suffer injustice; in the jungle, it is
the one who commits injustice who commands the greatest respect. Callicles,
then, agrees with Polus that doing injustice is better than suffering it. And for
him, too, the tyrant represents the highest human ideal.[66] Yet what distinguishes
Callicles from Polus is that whereas Polus admires the tyrant for the injustice he
can do and get away with, Callicles admires him for what he can get. Callicles,
unlike Polus, does not value injustice for its own sake. He envies powerfully unjust men not for their injustice but for their enormous appetites and their ability
to satisfy them. By nature, Callicles contends, the best man, the superior man,
is the man who has more and gets more. "Nature herself," he says, "reveals that
this very thing is just, for the better to have more than the worse and the more
powerful than the less powerful" (483c–d). Moreover, to have more and get
more is *kalon:* "No; *this* is the beautiful and just according to nature. . . . The
man who will live correctly must let his own desires be as great as possible and
not chasten them" (491e8–9). By nature (*phusei* [483a7]), or by natural beauty
and justice (*to kata phusin kalon kai dikaion* [491e7]), or by the law of nature (*kata
nomon ge ton tēs phuseōs* [483e3]), the strong man has more and gets more. The
weak many, Callicles argues, because they are unable to do what the strong do,
namely, let their own desires grow as great as possible and serve them with
courage and intelligence (491e–492a), make a virtue out of equality and call
seeking to have more than others doing injustice. According to Callicles, then,
nature and convention, *phusis* and *nomos,* are at odds, with nature defying the

---

65. Fussi (1996, 142, n14) argues that for Thrasymachus in *Rep.* 1 there is no natural standard
of justice: nothing is higher than *nomos.* She contrasts this view with that of Callicles, for whom,
as she points out, there is a natural standard of justice. The difference between Thrasymachus and
Callicles is, however, minimal. Thrasymachus defines "justice" as it is used conventionally, and
hence as the many do, in terms of obedience to law. What Callicles calls "natural justice" Thrasymachus calls "injustice" (as does Callicles by implication at 492b, where he excoriates [conven-
tional] justice and temperance). Insofar as natural justice is opposed for Callicles to conventional
justice, it is, from the point of view of convention, injustice. Where Thrasymachus and Callicles
differ is in their respective identifications of the source of conventional justice: Thrasymachus
thinks conventional justice is imposed by the strong on the weak to serve the interests of the
strong; Callicles thinks it is imposed by the weak on the strong to serve the interests of the weak.
Glaucon in *Rep.* 2 comes closer to Callicles than Thrasymachus does: he, too, thinks it is the weak
who make the laws.

66. What Archelaus is to Polus, on the one hand, Darius, Xerxes, and Heracles are to Callicles
(483d–484c), on the other.

many's artificial and self-protective *nomos* that calls unjust and intemperate those deeds of the naturally superior that deprive others of an equal portion. What Polus regarded as better but more shameful, namely, doing injustice, Callicles regards as both just and *kalon* by nature. But for Callicles, the injustice that is *kalon* by nature is not *kalon* in itself but only when it is done in the service of intemperance (483c–d).[67]

Callicles thus seeks to replace the distortive lens of *nomos* with the unclouded lens of *phusis*. He proposes nature as a better, clearer, and more accurate way of discerning the just and unjust, a way that is not compromised by the insecurities and fears of the weak. His preferred way of seeing dispenses with a category of *aischron* and *kalon* distinct from that of *kakon* and *agathon*. Like Socrates, then, but unlike Polus, Callicles brings together *aischron* and *kakon, kalon* and *agathon*. Whereas all three protagonists associate badness with harm, only Socrates and Callicles associate shame with harm, and they both do so taking nature as their standard: in nature it is when a man is harmed that he is shamed. Despite Socrates' and Callicles' common appeal to natural harm in assessing shamefulness, however, the gap between them is enormous: from Callicles' perspective, it is bodily harm to which shame attaches; from Socrates' perspective, shame attaches to harm to the soul. For as Socrates sees it, harm to the soul is as real, as natural (*pephuken* [479d6]), as independent of opinion and appearance, of convention and human invention, as is harm to the body.[68] Since, however, ordinary people, people like Polus, have no conception of harm to the soul, the notion of shameful by convention is

---

67. Callicles does not consistently admire all injustice or everyone who commits injustice. As early as 486b–c, he calls Socrates' imagined accuser "very lowly" (*panu phaulou*) and "degenerate" (*mochtherou*), and as late as 511b, he finds it most "infuriating" (*aganaktēton*) that a base man (*ponēros*) should be able to kill a noble and good one (see also 521c, where Callicles again characterizes as degenerate and lowly the person who would bring Socrates into court). Indeed, Callicles regards Socrates as having a good nature (486b; see also 485d) and as being a good and noble man (511b), and regards the accusation against him as one that charges him with "doing an injustice" that he did not do (486b). For the contrasting view that Callicles is a brutal man who has no regard for justice and decency, see Dilman 1979, 171; Shorey 1933, 154; Allen 1984, 210; Gentzler 1995, 30.

68. Antiphon the Sophist makes the distinction this way (*On Truth,* fr. A, col. 2). If one's actions oppose nature, the harm one suffers is not a matter of opinion (*dia doxan*) but a matter of truth (*di' alētheian*), and so it makes no difference whether one's actions are seen. But if one's actions oppose law, one suffers no harm unless one's actions are seen. Socrates regards committing injustice as causing harm to the soul *di' alētheian:* the harm is suffered whether anyone sees it or not.

often the only consideration besides fear of getting caught and punished that stands between them and doing wrong.

Callicles counts among the natural entitlements of the superior the right of rule. But he is far more impressed with their power to have more and get more.[69] It is telling that the terms *pleon echein* (to have more) and *pleonektein* (to get more) appear in the dialogue only in the exchange with Callicles. Indeed within fewer than ten Stephanus pages (483c–492c) these terms appear twenty-two times: 483c2, c3, c3–4, c4–5, c7; 483d1, d6; 488b5; 489a3; 490a3, a8; 490c1, c4, c5; 490d5, d8, d11; 490e7; 491a5, a5; 490d2; 492c2. (There is a twenty-third occurrence, of *pleonexia,* at 508a7.) Yet only three times does Callicles mention ruling over others, twice echoing Socrates (at 490a and 491d) and but once on his own (at 483d). Moreover, Callicles never mentions ruling without also mentioning having more; and the very first thing he mentions as a mark of the naturally superior is that they have the power to have more than others (483c). Why does Callicles admire most in the superior their ability and determination to get more and have more? Because it is not ruling that Callicles wants for himself, nor does he want, like Polus, to kill and banish at whim. All Callicles wants is to be safe and prosperous.

But what does Callicles mean by "having more"? Despite his protestations, he probably *does* think the superior man should have more food and more drink and more clothing and more shoes (if not more seeds) than others (490b–491b).[70] We see just a bit later on that he includes hunger and thirst, rather prominently, among the desires he thinks should be encouraged to grow as large as possible and be continuously replenished (494b–c). Similarly, his repeated emphasis on *pleon echein* and *pleonektein* suggest that Callicles thinks superior men should have more material goods. What irks him, then, is probably not so much Socrates' notion of what sorts of things the superior man should have more *of,* but his notion of who the superior man who should have more

---

69. Among scholars who think that Callicles has more refined aspirations are Nichols (1998, 133), who thinks that seeking pleasure is not what Callicles really aims at in his life, but that he is drawn to "nobler and more demanding goals" that he is unable to articulate; and Fussi (1996, 132): "once split from power and glory, life loses any value for him." See also Gentzler 1995, 37–38. Among those who see hedonism as central to Callicles' life plan are Irwin (1986, 69); Kahn (1983, 76); and Santas (1979, 256–57).

70. Socrates makes fun of Callicles' fascination with having more by suggesting that, according to Callicles, the weaver should have not only the most numerous and most beautiful cloaks but the biggest ones, and the cobbler not only the most numerous shoes but the biggest ones!

of these things *is*.[71] What he seems to object to is Socrates' idea that it is the doctor who, by virtue of being superior, stronger, and more intelligent about food, should have more food; that it is the weaver who, by virtue of being superior, stronger, and more intelligent about clothes, should have more clothes; that it is the cobbler who, by virtue of being superior, stronger, and more intelligent about shoes, should have more shoes. That is why Callicles exclaims at 491a: "By the gods, you simply always talk without stopping about cobblers, clothiers, cooks, and doctors, as if our speech were about these people!" It is not for Callicles *these* men who should have more of the things concerning which they are experts ("First, then, by those who are stronger, I mean neither cobblers nor cooks," he says at 491a), for the kind of superiority that entitles men to more goods of all kinds consists in intelligence with regard to the affairs of the city and courage (491a–b; 497e).[72] Why Callicles should think that the qualities of intelligence with regard to the affairs of the city and courage go hand-in-hand with getting more and having more is a mystery to Socrates.

Why, then, *does* Callicles think that superiority in intelligence and, as he now adds, courage (491b) are related to having more? Because for Callicles having more is the greatest good, and the greatest good, he thinks, is the natural entitlement of the greatest men. But it is not just that intelligence and courage entitle one to more. They are also what enable superior men to attain that to which they are entitled: intelligence and courage are deployed by such men in service of the all-important end of having more. Those who are both intelligent and courageous are able "to accomplish what they intend and not flinch through softness of soul" (491b).

It is hardly surprising, then, that in speaking with Callicles, Socrates steers the conversation around to the matter of self-rule, of *sōphrosunē*, temperance.[73] For unlike Polus, who gets his thrills at the prospect of killing, confiscating, and banishing as he pleases—and especially doing so unjustly and

71. It is probably not completely perspicuous to Callicles what it is that he means. Within the same complaint he whines about Socrates' talk of "food and drink" but also of "doctors and drivel" (490c)—that is, not just of what things a superior man ought to have more of (490d), namely, food, drink, cloaks, shoes, and seeds, but about who the stronger are: "By those who are stronger I mean neither cobblers nor cooks" (491a).

72. Thrasymachus, too, at *Rep.* 1.340e, endows the unjust man, the stronger man, with intelligence, and Glaucon, at *Rep.* 2.361b4, endows him with courage.

73. Pace Kahn (1983, 100), who speaks of "the suddenness of the shift in topic." Also Gentzler 1955, 36.

without reprisal—what impassions Callicles is the prospect of getting more and having more. If for Polus what makes tyrants enviable is their unrestrained injustice, what makes men superior in Callicles' eyes is their unrestrained pursuit of more, that is, their intemperance.

For Callicles, therefore, self-rule is foolishness. When Socrates explains that in speaking of those who are self-ruling what he has in mind are those who are temperate, Callicles predictably retorts: "What a pleasant fellow you are—you are saying that the temperate are the foolish!" (491e).[74] Justice and temperance, he thinks, are the surest path to wretchedness;[75] moreover, it would be *more shameful and worse* for those who are born to rule or whose nature destines them for tyranny or dynasty to enslave themselves to the law and concern themselves with the reproach of the many. Such men would be wretched if, under the sway of justice and temperance, they were to dole out no more to their own friends than to their enemies. Luxury, intemperance, and freedom, when they have sufficient support, are, according to Callicles, virtue and happiness (492b–c). Whereas Polus thinks that it is the unpunished unjust who are happy, Callicles thinks it is intemperance that guarantees happiness: no human being, he says, could "become happy while being a slave to anyone at all" (491e), that is, while subject even to his own control.[76] Just as Callicles does not see that the man who seeks to shield himself from injustice by placating those in power is not free but a slave,[77] so is he unaware that a man who is perpetually engaged in satisfying his appetites is not his own boss but is *their* servant: "he must be able to serve (*hupēretein*) them through courage and

---

74. Since Socrates thinks, of course, that the temperate are the wise, he responds: "There is nobody who would not understand that this is not what I am saying" (491e).

75. Note that Callicles uses justice here in its conventional sense (492b1, b5, c1).

76. For Callicles, those who rule themselves allow themselves to be governed by the conventions that would require that they suppress their appetites. For Callicles, self-rule "as the many understand it" (491d10) entails being enslaved to the *nomoi* of the many. "What would be more shameful and worse than moderation and justice for these human beings . . . who can enjoy the good things and with no one blocking their path . . . [than their] imposing a master on themselves, the law and speech and blame of the many human beings?" (492b). See *Rep.* 4.430e–431b, where Socrates remarks on the absurdity of the phrase "stronger than himself": is not he who is stronger than himself also, then, weaker than himself? Socrates goes on, however, to make sense of this puzzling phrase. It means, he says, that the element in the soul that is better by nature is master over the one that is worse.

77. See note 98.

intelligence, and to fill them up with the things for which desire arises on each occasion" (492a).[78]

In his dealings with Polus Socrates' goal was to divest Polus of his fascination with killing, confiscating, and banishing and, in particular, of his envy and admiration of those who commit injustice but do not pay the just penalty. Although Polus was unable to resist Socrates' conclusions, Callicles scoffs at them. Why is Callicles unpersuaded by Socrates' arguments against Polus? Because Callicles, unlike Polus, thinks he can identify that benefit, that truly good thing, that those who commit injustice achieve through their injustice. Callicles can say, as Polus could not, that those who commit injustice do indeed "do what they want" because he believes that they do attain, through their wrongdoing, real benefit. Since Polus could not see the need to posit any end beyond the wrongdoing itself to render it attractive—from his perspective there is nothing more attractive than wrongdoing itself—it falls to Callicles to suggest what such an end might be. The end he proposes is pleasure. For the sake of accumulating more and more pleasure, Callicles thinks, it is right even to do wrong. If Callicles is to be convinced that Socrates and Polus were not mistaken in agreeing that "no one does wrong willingly," that is, that no one who commits injustice does thereby "what he wants," Socrates must discredit Callicles' notion that pleasure is the good.

Socrates tries several approaches in an effort to divest Callicles of his view that the best way for a person to live, the way for a person to be happy, is to let his appetites grow as large as possible and to continue to satisfy them. First, he resorts to the rather shocking imagery of leaky jars, perpetual itch-scratching, stone-curlews, and catamites in hopes of showing Callicles "that the good is not this, to derive enjoyment (*chairein*) in all ways" (495b).[79] But Callicles is adamant. A person who is fully satisfied, whose appetites no longer

---

78. At 518a Socrates regards the "arts" that serve the body's desires as slavish, servile, and illiberal (*douloprepeis, diakonikas, aneleuterous*), echoing the terms "slavish" and "illiberal" that Callicles uses at 485b and 485c, respectively, for those who philosophize as adults and for those who do *not* philosophize in their youth.

79. In order to reconcile Socrates' alleged advocacy of hedonism in the *Protagoras* with his blatant antihedonism in the *Gorgias,* scholars maintain that the hedonism is different in the two dialogues. (See, e.g., Rudebusch 1989 and 1999.) But it is not. The formulations of hedonism in the *Gorgias* have their precise parallels in the *Protagoras*: "And if pleasantly, then happily" (*Gorg.* 494d7; cf. *Prot.* 351b6–7); "and who does not distinguish among the pleasures what sort are good and what sort bad" (*Gorg.* 495a1–2; cf. *Prot.* 351c2–6); "the pleasant and good are the same" (*Gorg.*

crave pleasure and are therefore no longer being fed, is, he thinks, like a stone or corpse (492e5–6; 494a8; 494b6–7): such a person might just as well be dead. For Callicles, the best men, those who are fully alive, are those who keep renewing the cycle of cravings and replenishment.

Socrates next tries argument. He produces for his obstinate interlocutor two arguments, both of which are intended to demonstrate that pleasure is distinct from good. The first of these (495e–497d) turns on the difference between the way, on the one hand, that pain (desires like hunger and thirst) and pleasure (desire-satisfactions like eating and drinking) are related to each other—they can be present simultaneously and can cease together—and the way, on the other, that bad (such things as illness) and good (such things as health) are related to each other: they are not present simultaneously and when the one begins the other ceases. This first argument contends that since good and bad function differently from pleasure and pain, these pairs cannot be the same.[80]

The second argument (497d–499b) turns on the idea that those who are courageous and intelligent and hence good, and those who are cowardly and foolish and hence bad, experience roughly comparable amounts of pleasure and pain when they undergo the same experience. Since in war cowardly and foolish bad men experience pleasure at the retreat of an enemy not less than and perhaps even more than courageous and intelligent good men do, and since the former experience pain at the advance of the enemy no less than and perhaps even more than courageous and intelligent good men do, it follows that if the good are good because of goods in them and the bad are bad because of bads in them, and if in addition pleasure and good are the same as pain and bad, then the courageous and intelligent are no better and no worse than the

---

495a3; cf. *Prot.* 355b4–c1); "there is [not] some one of the pleasant things that is not good" (*Gorg.* 495a3–4; cf. *Prot.* 355a3–5); pleasure is a good thing just because it brings enjoyment in whatever way or from whatever place (*Gorg.* 492d6–7, 494e10; *Prot.* 353d5–6).

80. This argument is reminiscent of the *Euthyphro*'s argument concerning whether the gods love something because it is holy or whether something is holy because the gods love it. In that argument Socrates shows that the logic of holiness and the logic of being loved (or being god-loved) are not the same. A loved (or god-loved) thing becomes a loved (or god-loved) thing because someone (the gods) loves it, but it is not the case that someone (the gods) loves it because it is a loved (god-loved) thing. (In the same way, a carried thing becomes a carried thing because someone carries it, but it is not the case that someone carries it because it is a carried thing.) But a holy thing does not become holy by virtue of someone's (the gods') loving it; rather, someone (the gods) loves it because it is holy. The holy, therefore, cannot be the same as the god-loved.

cowardly and foolish. There is, on the assumption that pleasure and good, pain and bad, are the same, little or no difference between good people and bad, between courageous and intelligent men, on the one hand, and cowardly and unintelligent ones, on the other.

There is a striking similarity between this second argument and the final argument concerning courage at the end of the *Protagoras*. Recall that, in the *Protagoras,* Socrates shows that if pleasure and good are the same, then, since everyone, both the courageous and the cowardly, go for what they think is more pleasant/best/less fearful, there is no difference between them other than that the courageous do know, and the cowardly do not, what is more pleasant. In both the *Gorgias* and the *Protagoras* Socrates builds his case on the idea that the courageous and cowardly are alike if pleasure is the same as good. The arguments diverge only in that whereas in the *Protagoras* Protagoras's belief that the courageous and cowardly go toward opposite things quickly gives way in the face of what is for him the more firmly established idea that pleasure and good are the same, in the *Gorgias* Socrates exploits Callicles' firm commitment to the superiority of the courageous man to discredit his identification of pleasure and good.

Like his arguments against Polus, Socrates' arguments against Callicles are also obviously deficient. Their greatest deficiency lies in that they teach nothing, explain nothing, and say nothing about why pleasure and good are not the same. Socrates' victory is, again, merely verbal: Callicles agrees that pleasure and good are not the same—but not because Socrates' arguments help him to appreciate the difference between them. He agrees because he is trapped and cannot see a way out.

Technically, too, the arguments leave much to be desired. It is not immediately evident that, for example, all desires are pains.[81] Nor is it obvious that pain and pleasure are present together and leave together. In the *Phaedo* (at 60b–c), for example, where there is no Callicles to contend with, Socrates makes precisely the opposite point about pain and pleasure. Although pain and pleasure are very closely linked, he says, "the pair of them refuse to visit a person together . . . anybody visited by one of them is *later* attended by the

---

81. The source for Socrates' characterization of desire as pain may well be Callicles' view that when a person no longer has needs, he is like a stone or corpse, feeling neither pleasure nor pain (494a–b). If pleasure is the satisfaction of need (or desire), then pain must be the need (or desire).

other as well . . . there was discomfort in my leg because of the fetter, and now the pleasant seems to have come to *succeed* it." Indeed, even in the *Gorgias* Socrates stops short of saying explicitly that pleasure cannot succeed pain as good does bad; his distinction between good and bad, on the one hand, and pleasure and pain, on the other, rests only on its being possible for the latter— but impossible for the former—to be things that a human being is released from, and experiences, at the same time (496c). In the case of desire for food and drink—when desire is conceived of as pain and its satisfaction as pleasure—even though the pleasure of drink might outlast the pain of thirst, it is certainly possible for the pleasure of drinking to cease when the pain of thirst ceases. But there are other cases, of course, in which pleasure follows pain— as, for example, when torture ends. In order to make his point plausible, then, Socrates must limit it to the claim that what is *possible* in the case of pleasure and pain, namely, their compresence and simultaneous cessation, is not possible with respect to good and bad. Socrates' claim, however weak and narrow, successfully targets the specific conception of desire and its satisfaction to which Callicles subscribes: if for Callicles pleasure did not cease when pain does, he would see no need to follow every satisfied desire with a new as yet unsatisfied one.

Through his argument Socrates challenges Callicles' notion that the best life, the right life, is the life in which one encourages one's appetites to grow larger and larger and is then occupied constantly with filling them. For if desire is pain, then it turns out that what Callicles is advocating is that one increase one's *pains* in order to increase one's pleasures. Callicles, then, does not simply advocate that one endure pain for the sake of pleasure, but actually that one create pain, increase pain, and enlarge pain for the sake of pleasure. What makes good and bad different from the pleasure and pain that drive Callicles' thinking is that good is not tied to bad. For example, health (good) can follow disease (bad) but (1) health need not be followed by yet more disease in order to persist, (2) one need not be diseased in the first place in order to be healthy, and (3) one's health is not greater if one gets sick and is restored to health or if one gets repeatedly sick. Yet, according to Callicles, one cannot enjoy eating (experience pleasure) unless one is hungry (in pain) and, unless one becomes hungry again (has more pain), one cannot enjoy eating again (experience more pleasure).

Socrates' second argument, too, fares far better when read as a response to Callicles rather than as a general argument to break the identification of pleasure with good. For it contains at least two questionable moves. First, it argues that if (1) things are beautiful because of beauty (*kallos*) (sing.) present in them, then (2) men are good because of the presence in them of goods (pl.). But what actually follows from (1) is not (2) but, if anything, (2′): men are good because of the presence of *goodness* (*aretē*) (sing.) in them. And second, it assumes, incorrectly, that experiencing pleasure and pain more or less intensely is the same thing as having more or fewer pleasures and pains present within one.[82]

What the argument lacks by the measure of logic, however, it more than makes up for rhetorically. It is precisely because Socrates is talking to Callicles that he speaks of goods rather than of goodness and that he speaks of more pleasures as if that were the same as greater intensity of pleasure. For Callicles thinks that the mark of superior people, those who are courageous and intelligent, is that they have more pleasures. What Socrates can then take this to mean is that for Callicles what makes good men good is that they have in them more goods—that is, more pleasures—than other men do. All he then has to do in order to discredit Callicles' position is to show that since superior people do not have more pleasures in them than others do, the goods by virtue of which superior people are superior cannot be pleasures.

Why do Socrates' arguments succeed in rattling Callicles? He is disturbed by the first argument simply because he is defeated.[83] The second argument, however, actually causes Callicles to change his mind—indeed, to say that what he had rather tenaciously insisted on earlier was meant only in jest (499b).[84] And that is because its conclusion is that if pleasure is good then "the

---

82. In the *Protagoras*'s hedonism section, recall that Socrates first converts the agent's desire for pleasure, which the many think of as a force that competes with the agent's knowledge, into amounts and sizes of goods or pleasures in the agent's options (355e, 356a), and then turns the attraction exerted by the nearness of pleasure into an illusion of greater size engendered by the pleasure's proximity.

83. After the first argument, Callicles tries to end the conversation and Gorgias's intervention is required to persuade him to continue (497b).

84. The aim of Socrates' second argument is to show that unrestricted hedonism is incompatible with Callicles' view of the superior man as courageous and intelligent. Although unrestricted hedonism is an embarrassing view, and one that embarrasses Callicles, it is nevertheless his view. Gentzler (1995) argues that Callicles' commitment to unrestricted hedonism follows from his concession that the itch-scratcher is happy, but in truth it is this concession that follows from Callicles' commitment to unrestricted hedonism. Although Gentzler maintains that "unrestricted hedonism is incompatible with Callicles' elitist contempt for anyone who does not meet his ideal of the strong, intelligent, and brave man of political action (497e–499b)," Cal-

bad man becomes good and bad equally with the good man, or even more good" (499a7–b1). Callicles is more committed to keeping the good man distinct from the bad than he is to equating pleasure with good.[85] Socrates' second argument, though no logical tour de force, is a strategic success. It compels Callicles to concede that some pleasures are bad, some pains good (499b–c),[86] and thus topples pleasure from its perch as the highest good.

To say that some pleasures are bad is not to deny, of course, that pleasure is in itself an attractive, hence good, thing: one could hardly classify it as either bad or intermediate. Socrates could not say with respect to pleasure, as he says with respect to bad and intermediate things, that no one could want it just like that, *haplōs houtōs.* If pain is one of the bad things, then pleasure, its opposite, is surely one of the good things. Not only is pleasure alluring; it is even, as Socrates says, thought to constitute a benefit (522b). But if, as Callicles reluctantly concedes, some pleasures are bad and some pains good, then pleasure and good are not the same, and pleasure is to be chosen for the sake of good,

---

licles in fact holds that courage and intelligence should serve the superior man's unrestrained desire for more (492a).

85. I accept H. Schmidt's emendation (1874) of *agathou* to *hēdeos* at 495d5. Socrates is repeating the things that Callicles *said,* which were that knowledge is different from pleasure and that courage is different from pleasure (495c–d). Dodds (1959, 308) vehemently opposes the emendation, since he takes Socrates to be declaring at 495e1 his disagreement with *all* the things that Callicles said, yet, as he argues, surely Socrates does not disagree with the proposition that knowledge and courage differ from pleasure. The fact is, however, that Socrates does not say that he disagrees with everything that Callicles said; all Socrates says referring to himself is, "He does not agree" (*Ouch homologei*)—indeed, even Callicles (495d5–6) uses only an indefinite "these things" (*tauta*). The only one of Callicles' assertions that we know Socrates disagrees with is the first, namely, that pleasant and good are the same (495d4, endorsed initially by Callicles at 495a5–6). It is only this proposition that Socrates argues against in what follows, and so concludes (500d6–8): "you and I have agreed that some good exists and some pleasant exists, and the pleasant is different from the good." Moreover, since Socrates' second argument depends for its success on Callicles' fervent endorsement of the proposition that knowledge and courage are good, it would be counterproductive for him to get Callicles to affirm that knowledge and courage are different from the good. I suspect that "good" crept into the manuscript precisely because others thought, like Dodds, that Socrates was proclaiming his disagreement with Callicles on all counts.

86. The *Gorgias*'s notion that some pleasures are bad and some pains good represents a significant departure from the *Protagoras,* in which pleasures are bad only because they lead to pains and pains are good only because they lead to pleasures (*Prot.* 353c–354b), so that pleasures and pains are measured against each other only in terms of size and amount. Whereas the expert in the *Protagoras* is skilled at weighing and measuring pleasures and pains (*Prot.* 356a–e), the expert in the *Gorgias* is skilled at distinguishing good pleasures from bad (500a).

not good for the sake of pleasure. That is to say, one should choose pleasure precisely as one should choose bad and intermediate things: for the sake of what is truly good. Pleasure, even though it is something wantable for its own sake, still stands with respect to what is truly good as bad and intermediate things do. And since pleasure is not "*the* good," those who do injustice (admittedly a very bad thing) for its sake surely do not "do what they want." To borrow an idiom from the *Protagoras,* they "take greater bads for lesser goods" (*Prot.* 355a).

Note that in concluding the discussion of the relationship between pleasure and good, Socrates no longer speaks of what one wants, or of what one does and pursues, as he did in the early discussion with Polus concerning bad and intermediate things. Instead, he speaks only of what is *to be* chosen and done (*haireteon* and *prakteon*) and of what should (*dein*) be done.[87] He reasons as follows: since (1) pleasure is not the same as good and some pleasures are actually bad, and (2) it is the beneficial pleasures that are good, the harmful ones bad (499d), it turns out that (3) the useful pleasures and pains are *to be* chosen and practiced (*haireteon estin kai prakteon* [499e4]).[88]

The verbal adjective *prakteon* also appears in Socrates' summary of the argument with Callicles at 506c7–8: "Is the pleasant to be done [*prakteon*] for the sake of the good or the good for the sake of the pleasant?" In saying at 499e6–7 that he and Polus had agreed that all things are to be done (*prakteon*) for the sake of good things, when in fact he and Polus had not actually spoken in just those terms,[89] Socrates takes himself to be drawing only the most obvious prescriptive implications of what they had agreed to:[90] Polus should not want

87. See also *chrē zēn* at 500c3–4, and *bioteon* at 500d4, referring to the life one *ought* to live. *Bioteon* appears too at 492d5 and at 512a7, both times with a prescriptive sense. Compare Socrates' use of *lēptea* and *praktea* in the *Protagoras* at 356b. See chapter 2, note 39.

88. The term for "useful" is *chrēstas* (499e3). As I argue in chapter 6, *Rep.* 4 distinguishes *agatha*, good things that are the subjects of thirst and hunger simpliciter, from *chrēsta,* good things that are the objects of thirst and hunger directed by reason.

89. Socrates is generally less than meticulous in referring back to putative previous agreements. At 508c, for instance, he says that Polus and Gorgias agreed in turn that he who is to be justly rhetorical must be just and a knower of just things, yet this is not something to which Polus agreed. Compare *Meno* 98a5, where Socrates says that he and Meno had earlier agreed—though in fact they did not—that recollection is a tethering of true opinion by "calculating the reason."

90. There is just a hint of the prescriptive in Socrates' conversation with Polus: early on, at 469a, Socrates admonishes Polus not to envy the unenviable or wretched but rather to pity them (he says *ou chrē*: it is not right); and toward the end of their exchange, at 480a2–4, Socrates advises that "a man *should* (*dei*) most of all guard himself so as not to do injustice."

what is not wantable, namely, the activities of killing, confiscating, and banishing "just like that"; those who must kill and confiscate should do so only if the benefits they derive from their actions are genuine; because of wrongdoing's detrimental effect on the soul, people should do anything to avoid committing injustice, and should even run to the courthouse to be punished in the event they do wrong. As Socrates says: "the end [*telos*] of all actions is the good [*ton agathon*],"[91] and "all other things [bad and intermediate things] should [*dein* (499e9)] be done for the sake of it [the good (*tou agathou*)] but not it for the sake of other things" (499e9–500a1). Bad things, then, as well as intermediate and even pleasant things, should be done for the sake of what is truly good. As Socrates says: "One should (*dei*) therefore do both other things [presumably, bad and intermediate things] and pleasant things for the sake of good things, but not good ones for the sake of pleasant" (500a2–3). Since pleasant things are neither bad nor intermediate, they are given separate consideration. But since they are also not necessarily good, at least not in the sense of beneficial, they are still *to be* done for the sake of those good things that are beneficial.

Socrates is at last in a position to claim that good is the orderly arrangement of things, of body and especially of soul,[92] and that therefore it is not intemperance and injustice but rather the whole gaggle of traditional virtues that are virtue and happiness—not just courage and wisdom but temperance, justice, and piety as well (507a–c). Whereas Callicles had thought the temperate foolish in that they do not know how to live correctly, Socrates shows the *intemperate* soul to be the foolish one. And whereas Callicles had thought that courage is to be used in service of desire, Socrates argues that courage is to be used in service of what is right: the moderate man is also the courageous one for he will flee from and pursue "what one ought" (*ha dei*), "abiding and being steadfast wherever one ought" (*hopou dei*) (507b–c).

On Callicles' picture of the superior soul, appetite reigns supreme, and it is the job of courage and intelligence to serve it. This Callicles-approved soul inverts the well-ordered and healthy soul of *Rep.* 4, in which reason (intelligence) rules, and spirit (courage) and appetite serve *it*. The very Callicles who

91. When Socrates says here that *to agathon* is the *telos* of all actions he means that it is that at which all actions *should* aim.

92. Socrates calls this orderly arrangement *nomimon te kai nomos*, "lawful and law" (504d2). Is this not Socrates' way of rejecting the lawless excesses of which Callicles is so enamored? *Phusis* itself, Socrates seems to be saying, is lawful and ordered; one cannot look to nature to justify appetites gone wild.

earlier accused Socrates of turning everything upside down (481c) is, from Socrates' perspective, the one more appropriately so charged. For, as Socrates argues, Callicles, in privileging appetite, neglects the geometrical or proportional equality (508a) that would keep the soul in proper balance. By advocating "taking more," Callicles' intention was only to scorn the arithmetical equality that would assign the same amount to each man and would thus satisfy the many. But insofar as "taking more," as Socrates points out, also encourages the disproportionate swelling of appetitive desire, it does violence to the geometrical equality in the soul as well.

Committing injustice has indeed turned out to be, as Socrates puts it, "both worse and more shameful for him who does injustice" than suffering injustice is for one "who suffers injustice" (508e). Even though it is something of an exaggeration to say that Socrates' views are supported by "arguments of iron and adamant," it is nevertheless true that it is not his position that has turned out "ridiculous" but rather the position of those who disagree with him. It is not the man who suffers injustice who is "ridiculous," but rather the man who commits injustice and foolishly avoids being duly punished.[93]

Now that committing injustice has emerged as both more shameful and worse than suffering it—though suffering it is still bad—the question arises as to how best to avoid each of these unwelcome conditions. It is easy to understand why a certain power is needed to avoid suffering injustice—one suffers injustice at someone else's pleasure. We must wonder, however, why Socrates would think that doing wrong, which is surely within the agent's control, is not easily avoided.

It is here—in seeking to bolster his contention that the man who wants to avoid committing injustice should (*dein*) cultivate a certain power and art (509e1)—that Socrates has recourse to his paradox. If Socrates can get Callicles to subscribe to the proposition to which Socrates and Polus already agreed, namely, that "no one does wrong willingly, but it is unwillingly that all

---

93. By using the word "ridiculous" twice in this passage (*katagelastos* [509a7, 509b4–5]) Socrates attempts to turn the charge back on Callicles. It was Callicles who four times called the philosopher "ridiculous"—at 484e1, 484e3, 485a7, and 485c1. Socrates indeed uses the term twice more—at 512d4 and 514e3—to even the score. Another such reversal is Socrates' claim at 515d and 516c that the great politicians made the citizens not better (tamer, gentler) but more unjust and worse (more savage), in reaction to Callicles' much earlier contention (in what is probably a quote from Euripides): "How can this [philosophy] be a wise thing, an art that took a man with a good nature and made him worse?" (486b).

who do wrong do wrong," he will have to concede as well, Socrates thinks, that the mere wish not to commit injustice is insufficient to keep one from doing wrong.

It is not immediately clear what Socrates is thinking here. He cannot be arguing (even though it does sound as if he is) that since no one wants to do wrong and yet people do in fact do wrong, it follows that merely wanting not to do wrong is insufficient to prevent wrongdoing. For, first, he does not think that no men want to do wrong; not wanting to do wrong is the distinguishing feature of just men (460c). Second, he does not straightforwardly say "no one wants to do wrong," though he surely could have. And third, he seems to be asking how those men who do not want to do wrong—rather than how all men—will avoid it. Nevertheless, Socrates certainly seems to be establishing a connection between the involuntariness of everyone's wrongdoing and the need for a power and art. As he says: "one must *therefore* (*ara*)"—that is, *because* no one does wrong willingly—"prepare a certain power and art" (510a3). How is this connection to be construed?[94] It is clearest in context.

Callicles is resistant to the idea that the man who does not want to do wrong will need a power and art to prevent his wrongdoing. His resistance is evident in two ways, first, from Socrates' demand at 509e2–3: "Why have you not answered me this very thing, Callicles?" and, second, from his response at 510a1–2 to Socrates' statement of his paradox at 509e5–7: "Let this be so *for you,* Socrates, so that you may bring the argument to a conclusion." Why is Callicles so reluctant to accept a notion that Socrates is so eager for him to embrace? And why is Socrates so eager for him to embrace it?

Callicles, as we know, thinks of the just man as a fool, a simpleton, a victim. Only a weak and inferior man does not commit injustice—any man who

---

94. I used to think (Weiss 1985c) that what Socrates means by "no one does wrong willingly" is that no one *would* want to do wrong if only he knew both that it was wrong and that wrongdoing is harmful to him. This is apparently Nietzsche's understanding of the paradox: "Nobody wants to do harm to himself, therefore all that is bad is done involuntarily. For the bad do harm to themselves: this they would not do if they knew that the bad is bad. Hence the bad are bad only because of an error; if one removes the error, one necessarily makes them—good!" (1992, §§190, 293). But first, "no one does wrong willingly" is not a counterfactual; it states that no one who does wrong does so willingly. And second, as is now clear to me, Socrates recognizes that people do want to do things they know will harm them in the long run—not because they want the harm, but because they desire pleasure or wish to avoid pain. He would have no reason then to think that simply knowing that injustice is harmful would suffice to make people not want to do it.

could, would. Callicles associates with such a man no cleverness, no power, and certainly no art. He is the man who, when dragged into court by an unscrupulous opponent, will "be dizzy and gaping without anything to say" (486b) and will be "unable to help himself or to save either himself or anyone else from the greatest dangers" (486b–c). From Callicles' perspective, it is the politician, the rhetorician, who is clever, powerful, and master of an art. And the great value of his art is that it enables its practitioner to avoid suffering injustice at the hands of others. For Callicles, the only reason a man would need *dunamis* and *technē* is in order to avoid suffering injustice. He cannot begin to imagine how power and art might be associated with not committing it.

Has nothing changed, however, since Callicles asserted with such assurance that the man who has more and gets more is the superior man? Has not everything by now indeed "been turned upside down" (481c)? Now that it has been demonstrated that "no one does wrong willingly," that is to say, that it is doing wrong that is most disadvantageous and harmful to the agent, and that it is by doing wrong and not paying the penalty that a man makes himself unhappy and wretched (507c4–5, d5–6), has it not become all-important to avoid *committing* injustice? Since committing injustice and not paying the penalty causes one "the greatest harm" (509b1–2), would not the man who does not wish to do wrong egregiously fail to "help himself" (*boēthēseien autōi* [509c8]) if he leaves matters to his wish alone?[95] Should he not rather equip himself, through learning and practice, with a power and art that will enable him to avoid the worst predicament of all? If the person who wishes to avoid suffering injustice would not rely for protection on his mere desire to be safe, how would the man who understands that "it is unwillingly that all who do wrong do wrong," and who consequently wishes not to do wrong, not secure himself by power and art against wrongdoing? If Callicles acknowledges, along with Socrates and Polus, that "no one does wrong willingly," he will have to concede that the man who wishes to avoid doing wrong would have even greater incentive to invest in power and art—and not depend on his wish

---

95. Since Callicles had said, at 486b, that the man who continues to philosophize past his youth would be "unable to help himself (*mēte auton hautōi dunamenon boēthein* [486b6]) or to save either himself or anyone else from the greatest dangers" (486b), Socrates counters now, at 509b–c, that the kind of "help" that one ought to be ashamed not to be able to provide for oneself or for one's friends and relatives is the "one which turns the greatest harm away from us," the greatest harm being that of doing wrong. The terms *boētheian* and *boēthein* appear five times from 509b4 to 509c3.

alone—than would the man who wishes to avoid suffering wrong. Indeed, as will become clear in what follows, the kind of power and art that saves one from suffering injustice merely keeps one alive, but the kind of power and art that saves one from doing wrong keeps one's life from being a wretched one.

The skill or art needed to avoid suffering injustice is quickly identified by Socrates as flattering those in power (this "art" is the rhetorical one) and imitating them (this "art" requires doing injustice). If rhetoric was thought to ensure, in Gorgias's words, "freedom for human beings themselves and rule over others" (*Gorg.* 452d), it has turned out to be a rather dismal failure: its "power" lies in that it enables one to enslave oneself effectively to *others* who rule. Moreover, insofar as what is required for the avoidance of suffering injustice is its commission, the rhetorician incurs a greater bad in order to avoid a lesser one. Rhetoricians are not, then, as Polus thinks, just like tyrants; the only thing the two have in common is that both are vicious.[96] If rhetoric is the power to avoid one bad thing but only at the cost of acquiring a much worse one, and if the rhetorician is powerless to avoid the worst of all bad things— namely, committing injustice without being punished—then rhetoric is hardly the great good that its admirers take it to be. All it is able to do is secure a man's physical safety.[97]

Physical safety, however, indeed life itself, is hardly the most important thing. "The true man," says Socrates at 512d–e, "ought not to concern himself with living a certain length of time, and ought not to be a lover of life (*ou philopsuchēteon* [512e2])." What matters is how one lives, that one live well. Knowing how to swim can save one's life; ferrying people safely from one place to another accomplishes the same for them; indeed, if staying alive were the most important thing, the engineer's art should be the most valued. Rhetoric is of little worth, Socrates contends, for the same reason that these *technai* are not held in the highest esteem: it is not sheer living that counts but living well, and all these arts do is preserve lives; they do nothing to improve

96. See Benardete 1991, 38: tyrants "overwhelm the rhetoricians and show up their weakness." As Benardete notes, tyrants often neither use nor need rhetoric at all.

97. Callicles' preoccupation with preserving his safety is closely related to his obsessive attachment to pleasure. Recall from chapter 2 that Protagoras, too, assigned the highest priority to his own safety. See also *Crito* 45d–46a, where Crito contends that a good and brave man can save himself and his friends, and that the "ridiculous" (*katagelōs* again [see note 93]) predicament in which Socrates now finds himself reflects "a certain badness and lack of courage on our own part, since we did not save you, nor did you save yourself."

them (511c–513a). In the final analysis, only the man who is not afraid to die is free. The man who will stop at nothing to save his own life is a slave.[98]

How bleak a picture Socrates paints: the only way a man can stay safe in a society whose government, whether tyranny or democracy, is vicious and unjust is to be himself vicious and unjust. Indeed, it would seem that the only way a man can stay just in such a society is at the cost of his safety. Socrates never does say what skill or art might be necessary for staying just. Might it not be, however, that the very intelligence and courage that Callicles thinks a man should mobilize to satisfy his appetites are those Socrates thinks a man should enlist to advance the cause of justice? Just as Callicles believes that only a wise man will recognize that pleasure is what he wants and will have the courage to pursue it, so does Socrates believe that only a wise man will know that it is more important to be just than to stay alive and will have the courage to stand firm in that judgment. As Socrates says: "No one fears dying itself who is not all in all most without reason (*alogistos*) and cowardly (*anandros*), but he fears doing injustice" (522e1–3).

---

98. See *Ap.* 38e: "But neither did I then suppose that I should do anything unsuitable to a free man because of the danger." See also *Crito* 53e, where the Laws warn Socrates that if he flees to a lawless place like Thessaly, "you will live by fawning upon all human beings and being their slave."

4

THE *HIPPIAS MINOR*: "IF THERE BE SUCH A MAN"

Lurking in this most puzzling of Plato's dialogues is the barest trace of the Socratic paradox "no one does wrong willingly."[1] Scarcely noticeable, and coming at the dialogue's very end, it is believed to hold the key to tempering the dialogue's outrageous conclusion—namely, that "the man who willingly errs, doing shameful and unjust things, is none other than the good man" (376b4–6). The paradox is thought to reside in the qualifying clause "if there be such a man" (*eiper tis estin houtos*), which Socrates deftly inserts into his conclusion. Does Socrates not mean to offer thereby the reassurance that since there is no such man, that is, no man who does wrong willingly, it is only counterfactually true that he is the good man?

Even if only counterfactually true, however, the conclusion remains alarming, especially coming as it does on the heels of two other quite shocking conclusions: (1) that there is no difference between the truthful man (*ho alēthēs*) and the liar (*ho pseudēs*), and (2) that the voluntary liar is better than the invol-

---

1. It is difficult to maintain, as only very few nineteenth-century scholars nevertheless have, that the *Hippias Minor* is spurious, particularly since Aristotle mentions and discusses it (*Met.* V. 29.1025a6–13). But it is likely, as Friendländer (1964, II, 146) remarks, that "without the explicit testimony of Aristotle, probably few critics would consider the *Hippias Minor* a genuine Platonic work."

untary.[2] What is common to all three conclusions is the alleged skill of the man in question: both the truthful man and the liar are skilled—they are able to tell the truth or to lie because they are experts in the art or science in which they tell the truth or lie; the voluntary liar is more skilled than the involuntary; and the good man, the man who, if there were such a one, does wrong willingly, is the man who has mastered the skill (power [*dunamis*]) or science (*epistēmē*) of justice.

Despite their startling conclusions, all three arguments are, as I shall show, technically valid inasmuch as their conclusions do follow from their premisses. And indeed Socrates appears unperturbed by the conclusions of the first and second arguments. Only the conclusion of the third argument troubles him (372d7–e6). Yet this conclusion—that the man who errs willingly, doing shameful and unjust things, is the good man—follows no less inexorably from its premiss that justice is a *dunamis* or *epistēmē*, or both, than the conclusions of the first two arguments do from theirs. Evidently, then, the premiss of the third argument is repugnant to Socrates in a way that the premisses of the first and second arguments are not. Socrates can abide the idea that a *pseudēs* might be skilled, and he actually encourages the idea that the voluntariness of action is an indicator of skill. What he cannot abide is the notion that justice is a *dunamis* or *epistēmē* or both.

The First Argument

The first argument appears at 365b7–369b7. It runs as follows:

1. *Polutropos* = *pseudēs*. (365b7–9)
2. *Ho pseudēs* and *ho alēthēs* are different. (365c3–7)
3. *Ho pseudēs* is the man most able (*dunatōtatos*) to speak falsely. (366e3–367a2)
4. *Ho alēthēs* is the man most able (*dunatōtatos*) to speak truthfully.[3] (367c1–2 with 367c6)

---

2. The dialogue has traditionally been thought to contain but two arguments. See, e.g., Hoerber 1962. But it contains three.

3. As we shall see, proposition (4) is the crucial move in the argument (367c6). It flatly contradicts Hippias's association of *alēthēs* with *haplous,* for here the true man and *ho dunatos,* the skilled man, are one and the same. See Sprague 1962, 68.

5. In any art or science, the man most able to speak truthfully is the wisest and ablest in that field.[4] (366d3–e1)

6. In any art or science, the man most able to speak falsely is the wisest and ablest in that field. (367ca8–b5)

7. In any art or science, the man most able to speak truthfully is the man most able to speak falsely, namely, the wisest and ablest man. (5, 6; 367c4–6)

8. The man most able to speak truthfully and the man most able to speak falsely are the same man, namely, the wisest and ablest man. (367d1)

∴ 9. The man who is *pseudēs* is the same man as the man who is *alēthēs*. (369b3–4)

∴ 10. If Odysseus is *pseudēs* he is also *alēthēs*. (369b4–5)

∴ 11. If Achilles is *alēthēs* he is also *pseudēs*. (369b5)

∴ 12. Achilles and Odysseus are not opposed to one another but are alike. (369b6–7)

The argument as it stands is valid. Nevertheless it generally strikes its readers as fallacious because they assume that *ho alēthēs* and *ho pseudēs* denote, respectively, the man who typically tells the truth and the man who typically lies. They think that the argument fails because, as Mulhern puts it (1968, 286), it uses *dunamis*-terms, terms that denote ability, in propositions (3) and (4), but switches to *tropos*-terms,[5] terms that denote typical behavior, in proposition (9).[6]

Is there, however, any reason to assume that in (9) Socrates introduces a standard, *tropos*-sense of *alēthēs* and *pseudēs*? The move at 366b4–5 that glosses

4. To illustrate this point Socrates refers to all the *technai* and *epistēmai* that Hippias himself has presumably mastered (366c–367a). There is palpable irony here as Socrates seeks Hippias's assurance that as an expert at calculation he is most able both to tell the truth and to lie about the product of 700 × 3.

5. The term *tropos* is found at 365b3–4, where Hippias says that the *tropos* of Achilles and Odysseus as set forth by Homer is such that Achilles is *alēthēs* and *haplous,* and Odysseus *polutropos* and *pseudēs.* Mulhern (1968, 287) rightly takes note of the Platonic pun in Hippias's specifying *polutropos* as Odysseus's *tropos.* As I understand the pun, it makes fun of a Hippias so entrenched in *dunamis* that the only *tropos* he can assign to Odysseus is the *dunamis, polutropos:* Odysseus's manner is to be many-mannered, multitalented.

6. Hoerber (1962) thinks the pairs of terms that are intentionally confused in this argument are *dunatoi/sophoi* and *panourgia/phronēsis.* Sprague (1962, 67–68) thinks Socrates deliberately uses the ambiguous terms *dunamis* and *panourgia,* the former of which denotes power that can be used either for good or for evil, and the latter of which denotes either the shiftiness of the false man or the intellectual ability that enables such a man to carry out his designs.

hoi pseudeis (liars) as *hoi sophoi te kai dunatoi pseudesthai* (those wise and able to lie) and so removes from *pseudēs* its standard connotation of one who habitually lies, investing it instead with a new and nonstandard connotation of one who has the power to lie is, in fact, never reversed. On the contrary, it is the *dunamis*-sense of these terms that Socrates uses in all his illustrations. With respect to arithmetic and calculation, Hippias, who is able to tell falsehoods *dunatōtata* (366d6), is thus the *pseudēs* concerning calculation (367c5); in geometry, the man who is not able to lie (*mē dunamenos pseudesthai*) is not *pseudēs* (367e5–6); in astronomy, the good astronomer will be a *pseudēs*, one who is skilled at lying (*ho dunatos pseudesthai* [368a4–5]). The first conclusion of the argument, proposition (9), is therefore best read as follows: the man able to speak falsely (lie) is the same man as the man who is able to speak truthfully. The alleged fallaciousness of the argument thus vanishes; and with it, at least to some degree, the paradoxical nature of its conclusion.[7]

Of course, were Socrates and Hippias both consciously using only *dunamis*-adjectives throughout the argument, the conclusion would strike neither of them as paradoxical or problematic. Yet Hippias balks at the suggestion that *ho alēthēs* and *ho pseudēs* are the same man. Why, we must wonder, is he resistant to the argument's conclusion? What does *he* mean by *alēthēs* and *pseudēs*?

In order to know what Hippias means by *alēthēs* and *pseudēs*, we must first know what he means by *polutropos*. For when, at the beginning of the dialogue, Socrates seeks to determine whether Hippias regards Achilles or Odysseus as the better man, Hippias asserts that Homer made Achilles the bravest (or best, *aristos*), Nestor the wisest, and Odysseus the *polutropōtatos* of the men who went to Troy.

For Hippias, *polutropos* is from the first a pejorative term. (Hence, Jowett's and Fowler's "wily" is a suitable translation of the term as Hippias uses it.)[8] Otherwise, it would be extremely difficult to see why Hippias regards it as obvious that Homer's characterization of Odysseus as *polutropos* makes him the lesser of the two heroes when compared with Achilles.[9] For Socrates, by

---

7. The conclusion continues to sound paradoxical because in standard usage *alēthēs* and *pseudēs* are not people merely *able* to tell the truth or lie.

8. "Wily" suggests the cleverness that is essential to *polutropia* and yet, despite its pejorative taint, is not so deprecatory a term as, say, "wicked" or "treacherous."

9. Hippias does not say directly that Homer means Achilles to be the better man until stage 2 (at 369c3–4). (When Hippias says at 364c that Homer has made Achilles the *aristos* of the three, he probably means "bravest.")

contrast, it seems that *polutropos,* at least initially, suggests having ability, and probably means something closer to Mulhern's "resourceful." That is why Socrates cannot understand why Hippias would say that Homer made Odysseus, but not Achilles, *polutropos* (364e5–6) until Hippias explains that since Achilles is *haplous* (simple) and *alēthēs,* he could not possibly be *polutropos,* for the terms *polutropos* and *pseudēs* distinguish Odysseus. At this point Socrates realizes that he and Hippias do not share the same conception of *polutropos,* and so, if the discussion is to proceed, he must adjust his conception of *polutropos* to match Hippias's.

Socrates asks first if Hippias means to identify *polutropos* with *pseudēs* (365b8). When Hippias answers that he does, Socrates continues to probe what Hippias has in mind: is *ho pseudēs* different from *ho alēthēs* (366c3–4)?; is he *dunatos* in what he does (365d6–7)?; is he *polutropos* and *dunatos* (365e1–2)?; does he deceive by *panourgia* (cunning) and *phronēsis* (prudence) (365e3–4)?; is he ignorant or wise (365e10)? And Hippias answers: *ho pseudēs* differs from *ho alēthēs* (365c1–2); he is *polutropos* and *dunatos* (365e2); he deceives by *panourgia* and *phronēsis* (365e4–5); he knows what he is doing (365e8); he is wise—not ignorant (365e10). But Hippias also adds a few unsolicited qualifications: he says of the *pseudeis* that they have the power to do many things, *and in particular to deceive people* (365d7–8), that it is on account of their knowing very well what they are doing *that they do bad* (*kakourgousin* [365e8–9]), and that they are wise *insofar as they deceive* (365e10–366a1).

Hippias's expansion of his answers beyond the simple yes or no required by Socrates' questions helps us see exactly where Hippias stands: whereas he readily affirms that his *pseudeis* are *dunatoi, phronimoi, sophoi,* and (even) *polutropoi,* thereby endorsing the *dunamis*-status of *pseudēs,* he insists that the *dunamis* of the *pseudēs* is an ability, a skill, a know-how, a proficiency, particularly at deceiving and doing wrong. Hippias provides not a *tropos* for Odysseus but a negatively charged *dunamis.*[10]

Hippias from the start associates lying and deceit and evil and wrongdoing with intelligence and power and prudence. Like Protagoras, who affirms, al-

---

10. Zembaty (1989, 54) cites the quotation from Homer in which Achilles refers to Odysseus as someone "who hides one thing in his mind but says something else" (365b1) to show that Hippias at first uses *polutropos* in a *tropos*-sense. Yet Hippias brings the quotation not to support his view that Homer depicts Odysseus as a *pseudēs,* but to support his view that Homer depicts Achilles as *haplous.* Moreover, that Odysseus "hides one thing in his mind but says something else" suggests that he is careful and calculating—not that he regularly lies.

beit with the worry that he might be saying something shameful, that a person can be acting temperately, prudently, sensibly, and wisely while acting unjustly (*Prot.* 333b–d); like Polus, who thinks tyrants are the most powerful of men (*Gorg.* 466b–e);[11] and like Thrasymachus, who thinks not only that "injustice is a thing that is stronger, more free, and more powerful than justice" (*Rep.* 1.344c4–6), but also that injustice is "good sense" (*euboulia*) and that the unjust are prudent (*phronimoi*) and good (348d2–6), Hippias, too, regards the deceitful and unjust as men most able, prudent, powerful, and wise.

Hippias, moreover, is a man who has nothing but the highest regard for skill. He is inordinately proud of his own multiple and varied skills and of his own purportedly superior intelligence. When Socrates remarks (364a3–6) that he would be amazed if any of the athletes who compete at the Olympic games were as confident about their bodies as Hippias says he is about his intellect (*tēi dianoiāi* [364a5–6]), Hippias boastfully proclaims: "Ever since I began to compete in the Olympic games, I have never come upon anyone superior (*kreittoni* [364a8–9]) to me in anything" (364a7–9). For Hippias, then, superiority, and hence human excellence itself, is measured by intelligence and ability.

When Hippias categorically rejects Socrates' suggestion (at 364e5–6) that Homer makes not just Odysseus but also Achilles *polutropos*, he rejects at the same time the possibility that Achilles is intelligent and wise. As the polar opposite of Odysseus, Achilles is characterized by Hippias as *haplous*, an interesting word with a range of meaning as broad as that of *polutropos:* frequently translated "simple," it can be taken to mean either something like "hapless," the opposite of *polutropos* as "resourceful," or something like "artless," the opposite of *polutropos* as "wily." For Hippias the difference between Odysseus and Achilles is the difference between being *polutropos* and being *haplous,* that is, between being cunning and being guileless: Hippias says of Achilles that Homer has certainly not made him *polutropos;* Homer has made him "exceedingly simple and truthful" (*haploustatos* and *alēthestatos* [364e7–8]).[12]

11. Polus also thinks it possible for a man who behaves unjustly and who is unjust to be happy, since he believes Archelaus to be both unjust and happy (*Gorg.* 472d). Socrates insists, however, that such a state of affairs is impossible.

12. The better manuscripts have only *haploustatos* and not *alēthestatos.* Burnet and Stephanus, following inferior manuscripts, insert *alēthestatos. Alēthēs* and *haplous* do appear together shortly, however, at 365b1, where Hippias says of Achilles that he is "both truthful and simple." See Leake 1987, 283, n4.

From the start Socrates is disturbed by Hippias's view that the *alēthēs* is *haplous*. Although he seizes on *polutropos* as the problematic term in Hippias's disquisition (364e1–4), Socrates never permits Hippias's alignment of *alēthēs* with *haplous* to fade from view. When seeking ostensibly to clarify what the characteristics of the false man are, Socrates consistently offers, along with each characterization of the false man that Hippias is likely to accept, the alternative, the opposite characterization, that Hippias is likely to reject. And since, for Hippias, the false man and the true man are opposites, the rejected characterization of the false man is, by implication, the characterization Hippias assigns to the true man. Thus, when Socrates asks if the false, like the sick, have no power to do things, and Hippias answers that, on the contrary, the false do indeed have the power, the unmistakable implication is that for him it is the *true* who are like the sick and have no power to do things. When Socrates asks if the false deceive by reason of their simplicity and folly or by reason of their cunning and a kind of *phronēsis,* and Hippias chooses the latter, the clear implication is that for him the true are the ones who lack cunning and are foolish. When Socrates asks about the false whether or not they know what they do, and the answer Hippias gives is that the false know, again the implication is that it is the true who do not. And when Socrates summarizes the things that Hippias has said about the false, namely, that they are *dunatoi, phronimoi, epistēmonai,* and *sophoi,* and the things he has said about the true, namely, that they differ from the false and are, indeed, their very opposite, what other conclusion can be drawn but that the true are for Hippias incapable, unintelligent, unknowing, and unwise?

Hippias, then, like Thrasymachus in *Rep.* 1 and like Glaucon in *Rep.* 2, associates honesty and goodness with simplicity and folly. Thrasymachus regards the just, including Socrates (*euēthestate Sōkrates* [*Rep.* 1.343d2]), as "truly simple-minded" (*hōs alēthōs euēthikōn* [*Rep.* 1.343c6; see also *Rep.* 1.349b5]), and justice not as a vice but as "genteel simplicity" (*gennaian euētheian* [348c12]). And Glaucon (*Rep.* 2.361b6–7) characterizes the just man as simple and genteel (*haploun kai gennaion*). If Hippias objects to the conclusion of the dialogue's first argument, that the *pseudēs* and the *alēthēs* are the same man, it is because he does not regard the *alēthēs* as skillful, able, powerful, or wise. For Hippias, the *alēthēs* lacks the capability, and is insufficiently wise and prudent and knowing, to lie, deceive, and do wrong.

Unlike Protagoras, Polus, Thrasymachus, and Glaucon, all four of whom openly admire those who are wise and skilled and prefer them to the simple and foolish, Hippias claims to favor the simple and truthful Achilles over the smart and skillful Odysseus, insisting that Achilles is the better man. This preference, however, is one to which Hippias is not entitled. What Socrates has every reason to expect from Hippias is an open admission that he admires Odysseus, the man *skilled* at lying, considerably more than he admires the simple and naïve and artless dupe Achilles. What he gets instead are Hippias's repeated disparagements of the *pseudēs* (in Homer's name) insofar as what the *pseudēs* is clever at is deceiving people and doing wrong.[13] The argument of stage 1, which concludes with the pronouncement that the truthful man and the liar are the same and that neither is better than the other, is designed to prevent Hippias from preferring Achilles to Odysseus on the grounds that Achilles is simple and truthful and Odysseus shifty and false. Both men, Socrates argues, are able, and it is for that reason that both are equally worthy of Hippias's adulation. If it is intelligence and skill that Hippias really admires, then he must admire Odysseus no less than Achilles and he must admire Achilles not for his simplicity but because he, too, has intelligence and skill.

What Socrates does by way of his first argument, then, is restore the dignity of the true man, the *alēthēs,* by locating his goodness not in his simplicity but, on the contrary, in his ability: far from being simple, *haplous,* Socrates argues, the *alēthēs* is as able—both to tell the truth and to lie—as the *pseudēs.* Indeed, it is because the *alēthēs* is just as capable and knowledgeable and wise as the *pseudēs* that the *alēthēs* is good. The *alēthēs* and the *pseudēs* are, then, both good, Socrates concludes, and for precisely the same reason. Throughout his argument Socrates looks away from Hippias's emphasis on the *pseudēs*'s propensity to use his skill to deceive and do wrong, focusing more broadly on his skill as a man who knows. Both the *pseudēs* and the *alēthēs* have skill, Socrates contends; in fact, they have the same skill because they are masters of the same arts and sciences.[14]

If the reason that the *pseudēs* and the *alēthēs* have the same skills is that they

---

13. Homer may not have thought ill of those who are clever at lying and deceit. In *Rep.* 1.334a–b, Socrates quotes the *Odyssey* (xix.392–98) to show that Homer held in esteem Odysseus's maternal grandfather, who was better than all others at lying and stealing. Apparently such cleverness runs in the family.

14. Socrates in effect erases all distinctions among the three heroes, Odysseus, Achilles, and Nestor, when he says that the same person (Hippias!) who is able to speak truthfully about the product of 700 × 3 is not only *polutropos* (Odysseus's quality) but is also *dunatos* and *sophos* (Nestor's qualities)—all because he is *aristos* (Achilles' quality) (366d3–5).

are masters of the same arts and sciences, however, there is interestingly more to Socrates' argument than just the claim that the *pseudēs* and the *alēthēs* are equally skilled. For even as he is engaged in setting the *pseudēs* and the *alēthēs* on a par with each other by showing that the same person who knows enough about a particular art or science to lie well also knows enough about that very art or science to tell the truth well, he is teaching that it is not lying per se that one has expertise in or, to put it somewhat differently, that lying itself does not qualify as an art or science. Whereas Hippias presents lying as the thing Odysseus is good at, as a kind of wisdom or prudence or expertise in itself, albeit one directed toward questionable ends, Socrates characterizes it as something one can be good at only derivatively, that is, by being good at or knowledgeable about something else, something that *is* a genuine art or science. What makes one able to lie well, that is to lie at will, Socrates will argue, is being good at such things as writing, geometry, calculation, or astronomy, that is, at some genuine art or science. But being good at some art or science makes one equally able to tell the truth well, that is, to tell the truth at will. If lying were an art or science as Hippias thinks it is, then, of course, the *pseudēs* would be skilled at it and the *alēthēs* hopelessly inept. What makes it possible for Socrates to put the *alēthēs* on an even footing with the *pseudēs* is his withholding from lying the status of art or science.[15]

In the early part of the *Hippias Minor,* then, what we witness is three ways in which Socrates challenges Hippias. First, Socrates questions Hippias's right to favor Achilles over Odysseus on the grounds of Achilles' greater truthfulness and simplicity, when he is so ardent an admirer of skill and intelligence. Second, Socrates wonders how the *pseudēs* can be *polutropos,* wise, prudent, and knowing but the *alēthēs* only *haplous,* unwise, foolish, and ignorant, if both are skilled at the same arts and sciences. Third, he disputes Hippias's assumption that lying is in itself an art or science at which one can be an expert. If

---

15. The strategy Socrates adopts in the *Hippias Minor* with respect to lying is the same strategy he adopts in the *Gorgias* with respect to clever speaking. (See also *Prot.* 312d–e.) One can be a clever speaker about a subject *x* if one has mastered it. Clever speaking is not itself, however, a *technē* or *epistēmē.* In both dialogues Socrates denies what he surely knows, namely, that it really is possible to be a clever speaker (in any ordinary sense) without mastering particular *epistēmai,* that it really is possible to be a good liar (in any ordinary sense) without mastering particular *epistēmai.* Whereas the *Gorgias* at least carves out a space for the clever but non-knowing speaker as a persuader of ignorant mobs, the *Hippias Minor* recognizes as a clever liar only a knower of particular *epistēmai* and *technai.*

Hippias values the *alēthēs,* Socrates contends, it can only be because the *alēthēs* is skilled. But if the *alēthēs* is skilled he is no different from the *pseudēs*—unless, of course, the *pseudēs* is skilled at the art or science of lying and deception. But since there is no art or science of lying and deception, the *alēthēs* and *pseudēs* are equally skilled at truth-telling and at lying: they are equally proficient in some particular art or science.

The Second Argument

The dialogue's second stage (369b8–373c6) marks the transition from the present topic, namely, whether Odysseus alone or both Odysseus and Achilles are *polutropoi,* hence skilled, hence able to tell lies, to the final topic, whether it is the intentional or the unintentional wrongdoer (*adikōn*) who is the better man. It once again considers which of the two heroes, Odysseus or Achilles, Homer himself favors. Although Socrates has argued that there are no grounds for preferring the one to the other—each was shown to be as skilled as the other at truth-telling and lying—nevertheless, Hippias continues to insist that Homer has made Achilles the better man, portraying him as no liar (*apseudē*), and has made Odysseus the inferior man, portraying him as crafty (*doleron* [369c5]) *and* as very deceitful (*polla pseudomenon* [369c5]).

Socrates disagrees: whereas Homer indeed calls Odysseus *polutropos* (in line 1 of the *Odyssey*),[16] the purportedly wily Odysseus is nevertheless never found to tell a lie. If anyone, therefore, really is *polutropos,* is it not Achilles? He, at any rate, does lie.[17] Although it is true, says Socrates, that Achilles accuses Odysseus of lying (*Iliad* 9.308 f.),[18] still, within just fifty lines of that passage, another passage is found (*Iliad* 9.357 f.) in which it is Achilles who actually lies. In response to Hippias's objection that Achilles speaks falsely only

16. Hoerber (1962), 124–25, points out that *polutropos* in the first line of the *Odyssey* probably means "much-traveled," "much-wandering." Hippias, however, understands by it "crafty," "shifty," "clever," or "versatile" when he equates it with *pseudēs.*

17. The *ge* ("at any rate") in Socrates' assertion that Achilles actually lies indicates his awareness that the mere fact that someone actually lies does not show that he is *polutropos,* because people may lie by mistake or out of ignorance or compulsion. The term *pseudēs* as it appears at 366b6–7 ("Therefore, a man who is not skilled at lying and is ignorant would not be a *pseudēs*") should be understood to denote not someone who lies but rather someone who is able to lie (at will).

18. Plato does not allow Hippias to cite those passages (particularly in the *Odyssey*) in which Odysseus does actually lie.

unintentionally (*akōn* [370e7]), and not by design (*ouk ex epiboulēs* [370e6]) but misled by naïveté (*hupo euētheias anapeistheis* [371e2]),[19] Socrates points out that, on the contrary, Homer makes Achilles lie by design (*ex epiboulēs* [371a2]) and makes him so much more clever (*phronein*) than Odysseus in dissembling that Odysseus does not even detect the deception—he, after all, does not accuse Achilles of lying (371a2–b1). Hippias insists that Socrates is mistaken: he thinks Odysseus speaks falsely willingly and by design (*hekōn te kai ex epiboulēs* [370e8–9]); indeed, he declares, Odysseus speaks by design (*epibouleusas* [371e3]) whether he speaks falsely or truly.

A most striking feature of this interlude is Hippias's persistent attachment to a *dunamis*-conception of *pseudēs*. Hippias distinguishes Achilles from Odysseus by asking not which of the two men actually tells the truth or actually lies but rather which of them displays guile or cunning whether he tells the truth or lies. Since for Hippias it is Odysseus who is the more cunning, the one who plans and plots and always acts with forethought, it is he who is the worse of the two. The simple Achilles once again gains ascendancy—not because he is more truthful but because he lies only unintentionally.

That Hippias still prefers the unintentional liar to the intentional one shows that the point of the first argument was lost on him. And Socrates registers his surprise: "Were not the intentional liars revealed just now to be better than the involuntary?" (371e7–8). If (1) the man ablest in calculation, geometry, astronomy, and all the arts and sciences is he who is able to speak falsely in these matters (366e1–367a5), (2) only the man who does what he wishes when he so wishes is able (366b7), and (3) the good man is the able one (367c5–6), it follows that (4) the intentional liar (that is, the liar who lies when he so wishes and only then) is better than the unintentional liar (who, as incapable, cannot of course be *agathos*).

Why, indeed, does Hippias fail to derive the superiority of the intentional liar to the unintentional from the points made in the first argument? Because Hippias apparently does not accept or even take seriously Socrates' conclusion in stage 1. As Hippias sees it, Socrates' argument in the first stage is but round one in a competition between himself and Socrates in interpreting Homer, a

19. Burnet, following the less reliable manuscript F, has *eunoias* (good will) in place of *euētheias* (naïveté), which is found in the more authoritative T and W. *Euētheias* also makes better sense given Hippias's characterization of Achilles as *haplous*.

competition whose ultimate aim is to determine "which of the two of us is the better speaker" (369c7–8). This first round has not ended well for Hippias. Nevertheless, he now has a second chance to prove that Homer makes Achilles superior to Odysseus. And then, as he says, Socrates will have another turn to prove that Odysseus is Homer's intended better man. Note that Socrates had not, of course, contended up to this point that Odysseus is the better man; he contended, on the contrary, that the false man and the true are the same, that neither Odysseus nor Achilles is superior to the other. But since Hippias sees what he and Socrates are engaged in as a competition, he barely notices what Socrates has actually claimed: if theirs is a contest in which Hippias takes Achilles' side, then Hippias can only presume that Socrates, as his opponent, takes Odysseus's side.

It is interesting that Socrates does end up taking Odysseus's side, explaining that if Odysseus is, as Hippias contends, really the one who, "when he speaks truthfully, does so by design (*epibouleusas* [371e3]), and so, too, when he speaks falsely" (371e2–3), then Odysseus does, after all, turn out to be better than Achilles.[20] Socrates registers no doubt concerning the proposition that the voluntary liar is better than the involuntary.

Although Hippias senses that something went terribly wrong in this exchange, his main, if not his sole, concern is to try again to establish himself as the better speaker. And so he seeks again to prove the superiority of the *alēthēs,* Achilles. Yet he makes the same unwitting assertions this time that got him into trouble in the first round. He admits that Achilles lies, but contends that the lies he tells are not expressions of his informed mastery of a situation; they are, instead, beyond his control or the result of error or miscalculation. Achilles, Hippias says, is "compelled" to remain and rescue the army in their misfortune; what he does he does *akōn,* against his will; he does not act according to a plan (*ex epiboulēs*) (370e).

---

20. As Gomperz (1905, II, 292) explains, Hippias thinks that since Achilles has no intention of deceiving, but "the force of external circumstances [the desperate position of the army] had brought his actions into disaccord with his words," Achilles is therefore the better man. (Gomperz regards Hippias's defense of Achilles as a "just" one.) Socrates maintains, however, that this is precisely what makes Achilles the inferior man: he is unable to tell the truth and to lie only when he means to. (The extenuating circumstances described by Socrates earlier [366b], namely, being prevented by disease or some such thing, are different from those that prevent Achilles from keeping his word.)

Hippias's intended defense of the well-intentioned but hapless Achilles is construed by Socrates as an indictment. Not only does Achilles, on Hippias's account, not always speak the truth, but his lies are unwitting. Yet Odysseus, as Hippias will say, whether he tells the truth or lies, knows exactly what he is about; he acts by design. When Socrates wonders how in that case the former can surpass the latter in Hippias's estimation, Hippias recasts the involuntary liar as the involuntary wrongdoer, and the voluntary liar as the voluntary wrongdoer, and wonders now how anyone could prefer the latter to the former.

Since Socrates cannot take Hippias's praise of the witless liar/wrongdoer Achilles at face value, he proceeds to do what he does best: he reduces Hippias's view to absurdity. If Hippias (1) sees the voluntary liar/wrongdoer Odysseus as smart, prudent, and skilled, and (2) sees the involuntary liar/wrongdoer Achilles as decidedly ignorant, foolish, and impotent, then Socrates will compel Hippias to acknowledge, to his chagrin, that (3) it is not the involuntary wrongdoer, Achilles, but the voluntary wrongdoer, Odysseus, who is the better man, and not only the better man but, indeed, the good man.

Socrates, it is likely, does not think very highly of either Homeric hero (though he pretends to think equally highly of both [370d6–e4]). Neither is truly wise, for neither puts justice above all other considerations.[21] Both indeed are equal in the sense that neither knows anything of importance. That Odysseus acts always by design does not make him a better man than the rudderless Achilles; for even if Odysseus has a rudder he has no worthy destination toward which to steer.

From the point of view of goodness as skill, however, the point of view that Socrates has been from the first urging Hippias to adopt, the voluntary always beats the involuntary. Whereas in the first argument, Achilles and Odysseus turned out to be equally good since the true man and the false were construed as being equally proficient at the various arts or sciences, in the middle and final arguments Odysseus must outstrip Achilles: if it is he who voluntarily lies and he who voluntarily does wrong, then it is he who is superior and only he who is good.

---

21. In the *Apology* Achilles is seen to value something above death, but not the right thing: revenge, but not true justice. Socrates' laudation of him (*Ap.* 28b–d) is, therefore, not fully sincere. See Weiss 1988, 8–10.

The Third Argument

Once Hippias replaces the proposition comparing voluntary with involuntary liars with the corresponding proposition comparing voluntary with involuntary *wrongdoers* (*adikountes* [371e9]), wondering how voluntary wrongdoers can be better than involuntary ones (371e9–372a2), Socrates for the first time claims to be greatly confused and confesses a tendency to change his mind (372d–e).[22] What Socrates had concluded without hesitation about voluntary liars, that they are better than the involuntary, he now concludes with a measure of skepticism with regard to voluntary wrongdoers. Yet, despite the horror engendered in Hippias by the very suggestion that voluntary wrongdoers might be better than involuntary, and despite his own professed uncertainty about the matter, Socrates states that at least for now it does seem to him that voluntary wrongdoers are superior.[23] Note that at 372e3–6 he attributes his present professed belief to the previous argument: the argument in stage 1 suggested that one who acts involuntarily is generally worse than one who acts voluntarily, so perhaps that rule applies as well to wrongdoers. Socrates now

22. Vlastos (1991, 279) thinks that since Socrates is an "honest arguer," he must really be in the muddle he professes to be in. But Socrates is not confused. He says twice that it is the conclusion about which he has doubts, and that the conclusion is compelled by the dialogue's—that is, by Hippias's—*logoi* (372e3–4, 376b8–c1). Kraut (1984, 311) cites besides the *Hippias Minor* two other passages in which Socrates confesses his "intellectual limitations": one at the very end of the *Protagoras* (*Prot.* 361a–c), the other at the very end of the *Gorgias* (*Gorg.* 527d7–e1). But Socrates is confused in neither of these places. In fact, in the *Gorgias* he asseverates (482a–b) that he faithfully follows his adored philosophy which never wavers—indeed, at 491b Socrates notes that what Callicles accuses him of and criticizes him for is his always saying the same thing. When, then, he remarks at the dialogue's very end that "*we* never think the same things about the same things" (527d7), he is just being polite. And lest one think otherwise, he quickly sets the record straight, saying rather bluntly of Callicles' position: "for it is worth nothing, Callicles" (*Gorg.* 527e6–7). Plato scholars cite also *Euthyph.* 11e and *Meno* 81a as places where Socrates admits confusion. But in the *Euthyphro,* the confusion that arises is attributed directly to suppositions that are Euthyphro's. And in the *Meno,* it is clearly Meno who is confused. Socrates may accept Meno's characterization of him as a "perplexed man who perplexes others"—but, as he understands his own perplexity, it amounts to no more than his rather clear-sighted recognition that he lacks moral knowledge.

23. Zembaty (1989, 59) points out that the view opposite to Socrates' professed view, namely, Hippias's purported view that those who commit injustice involuntarily are better than those who do so voluntarily, is simply "nonsensical" if "better" is taken to mean "more skilled." And indeed it is. It is because, as we have seen, Hippias has not fully grasped or accepted the *dunamis*-sense of "better" that he stands by his absurd view. More importantly, however, *unless* "better" is taken to mean "more skilled," it is Socrates' professed view that would be the nonsensical one.

resumes the argument in order to consider whether intentional wrongdoers (*adikountes*), like all other intentional "doers," are better than unintentional.

The argument of the final stage of the *Hippias Minor* invites Hippias to compare (1) one who intentionally does poorly with one who does poorly unintentionally in all forms of bodily exercise requiring strength or grace, for example, running and wrestling; (2) organs that perform defectively intentionally with organs that do so unintentionally[24]—voices, feet, eyes, ears, and so on; (3) instruments with which one does poorly intentionally with those with which one does poorly unintentionally, for example, rudders and musical instruments; and (4) souls that intentionally exercise their skills badly with those that exercise their skills badly unintentionally,[25] such as the souls of horses, dogs, archers, users of the bow, physicians, flute-players, lute-players,

---

24. Socrates speaks of these as doing the actions themselves, except in the case of eyes, *with* which one is dim-sighted voluntarily. Aristotle criticizes Socrates' argument by pointing out that one who willingly *imitates* limping might be better than one who does so unwillingly, but that one who is actually willingly lame is surely worse than one who is unwillingly so—and so, too, in the moral case. (See Blundell 1992, 161.) Aristotle, however, misunderstands and distorts Socrates' example. Socrates readily admits that lameness is a bad condition of the feet (374d1–2), one that therefore no one would want. His point is that what makes lameness bad is precisely that it does not permit one to limp willingly but indeed compels one to limp unwillingly. No one therefore is lame willingly. What we prefer, Socrates maintains, is feet that are *not* lame, for only with such feet, with good feet, can we limp willingly rather than unwillingly. What makes bodily organs, instruments, bodily conditions, and souls good is that they enable a person to do poorly willingly or, as Aristotle might put it, to be actually only "imitating" the man who does badly. It must be added that Aristotle (if his text of the *Hippias Minor* is the same as ours) is careless in reproducing Socrates' argument. He claims that the identity of the false man and the true is derived from the two assumptions that (1) the man who is more skilled at lying is the false man, and (2) he who is voluntarily bad (*phaulon*) is the better man. Aside from the just-mentioned point that for Socrates the good man is not someone who is "voluntarily bad" in the sense that he voluntarily takes on a bad condition, but only someone who does bad things or does poorly voluntarily because the *good* condition he is in enables him to do so, there is the additional factor that Socrates determines that the false man and the true are said to be the same *before* the question arises of whether the voluntary or involuntary *adikōn* is the better man.

25. The verb *kakourgeō* (do to bad) appears in only three places in the dialogue: (1) at 365e8–9, where Hippias says that *hoi pseudeis* have knowledge and therefore *kakourgousin;* (2) at 373b4–5, where Hippias, accusing Socrates of being troublesome in argument, says that Socrates "seems like one who does wrong" (*eoiken hōsper kakourgounti*); and (3) here, at 375c5 and d1, where the soul that intentionally *kakourgē* is seen to compare favorably with the soul that does so unintentionally. This word is found then in each of the dialogue's three parts: once in the discussion of *ho pseudēs,* once in the discussion of the voluntary versus involuntary deceiver, and once in the discussion of voluntarily versus involuntarily wrongdoing souls (here).

and slaves.[26] In each instance, Hippias agrees that the first in the pair is preferable to the second. With this granted, Socrates proceeds to ask Hippias about "our" souls: are they analogous to the other souls discussed? Are those that do wrong voluntarily superior to those that do wrong involuntarily? Anticipating the conclusion that those who do wrong intentionally will turn out to be better than those who do so unintentionally, Hippias jumps the gun and denies it. But Socrates goes on with the argument:

1. Justice is either a power or skill (*dunamis tis*), knowledge (*epistēmē*), or both. (375d8–9)
2. If justice is a skill (of the soul), the more skilled the soul, the more just. (375e1–3)
3. If justice is knowledge, the wiser soul is the more just. (375e3–4)
4. If justice is both skill and knowledge, then the wiser and more skilled soul will be the more just, the more ignorant soul the more unjust. (375e6–8)
5. The soul that is more powerful and wiser is the better. (375e9)
6. The better soul is better able to do both noble and shameful things (since it is more skilled and wiser). (375e10–376a1)
7. The soul that does shameful things (*aischra*) intentionally does them by skill and art (*technē*).[27] (376a2–3)
8. Acting unjustly (*adikein*) is doing bad things (*kaka*). (376a4–5)
9. The abler and better soul acts unjustly intentionally. (376a6–7)
10. The bad soul acts unjustly unintentionally. (376a7)
11. The good man[28] has the good soul. (376b1)
12. The bad man has the bad soul. (376b1–2)
13. The good man acts unjustly intentionally. (9, 11; 376b2–3)
14. The bad man acts unjustly unintentionally. (10, 12; 376b3)
∴ 15. He who willingly errs (*hamartanōn*), doing shameful and unjust things (*aischra kai adika poiōn*), is the good man (*ho agathos*). (13; 376b4–6)

26. Though not specified, the skill of slaves is presumably to carry out their masters' wishes well. Even if it is unlikely that a master would really prefer a slave who errs and does wrong intentionally to one who does so unintentionally, it is perhaps not as unlikely that he would prefer a slave who had that sort of soul—the more skilled one.

27. *Technē* substitutes for *epistēmē* here. Throughout the dialogue Socrates uses the two terms interchangeably, calling Hippias's crafts *epistēmai*.

28. In stage 3 it is only in the case of the runner and wrestler and other masters of bodily exercise that it is the man himself who is considered rather than the things a man has—voices, feet, rudders, musical instruments, horses, dogs, and all sorts of souls.

There are two important ways in which this argument takes the argument of stage 1 to the next level. First, whereas in stage 1 Socrates steers the argument away from a concern with the goodness or badness of telling the truth or lying, concentrating instead on the *ability* to tell the truth or to lie, the current argument does not shy away from affirming the badness in each case of the action being done. The runner who runs slowly intentionally is not doing something good, but rather something bad and shameful (*kakon kai aischron* [373e1]) in the race. Similarly, he who is better does bad things (*ponēra* [374b2]) with his body intentionally. In terms of grace, the better man assumes shameful and bad postures (*schēmata* [374b6]). Seeing dimly is a defect (*ponēria*) of the eyes (374d3), senses act *kaka* (374e1), a man steers *kakōs* (374e4), one rides horses *kakōs* (375a2), one produces bad actions (*erga ta ponēra* [375a4–5]) with horses, and so, in all the arts and sciences, the soul "does bad things and shameful things and errs" (375c1–2). Furthermore, the argument never suggests that there is anything good about doing these admittedly bad things intentionally; nor does it contend that it is better to do them intentionally than to do them unintentionally.[29] Acts that are bad remain bad, and doing them intentionally does not purge them of their badness.[30] All stage 3 argues is that that *person or bodily organ or instrument or soul* is better, in the sense of more skilled, that does these bad acts voluntarily rather than involuntarily.

To be sure, one might wish that Socrates had defined the good man as the man who does *kala* and *dikaia,* noble and just acts. Yet, although he does not explicitly provide such a definition, it is nevertheless clear that he does endorse it. For such a definition of the good man is implicit in the corresponding definition of a good runner, who is defined both as (1) he who runs slowly (*bradeōs*) intentionally (373e4–5), where running *bradeōs* is running badly

29. Confusing voluntary wrongdoing with the voluntary wrongdoer is perhaps what causes Hamilton and Cairns (1961, 200) to regard the *Hippias Minor* as a dialogue "inferior to all the others." "It turns," they say, "upon voluntary and involuntary wrongdoing, Hippias maintaining that it is better to do wrong unintentionally than intentionally and Socrates taking the opposite side." Shorey (1933, 86–87) makes the same mistake, assuming that the *Hippias Minor* argues that "it is better to do wrong knowingly than without knowing it" since "the good artist is the one who can most skillfully and most certainly do wrong if he chooses." As does Leake (1987, 306): "Why does Socrates argue that to commit a wicked or unjust act voluntarily is better than to do so involuntarily?"

30. In Xenophon, at *Mem.* IV.iii.19–20, Socrates also speaks of voluntary deceivers' being better than involuntary, rather than of voluntary deception's being better.

(*kakōs* [373d3]), and as (2) he who runs well, that is, fast (*tacheōs*) (373d3). If the good runner, besides being the one who runs slowly intentionally, is also one who runs well, that is, fast, then, by the same token, the good man, besides being the one who does shameful and wrong things intentionally, is also the one who does noble and just things. A definition of the good man as one who does noble and just things, however, would not help to determine which *adikōn,* the intentional or the unintentional, is the better man.[31]

Second, whereas stage 1 concludes that there is no difference between the *alēthēs* and the *pseudēs,* and that the former is not any better than the latter (367c8–d1), our current argument contends that not only is the unintentional bad-doer and wrongdoer worse than the intentional, but the former is actually bad and the latter good (373e4, 374e1, 374e2, 376b6). The current argument underscores, then, the reason that the *alēthēs* and *pseudēs* of stage 1 were equivalent: since they are equally skilled, lying done by either one would be done intentionally. The very skill that made these two men equal in stage 1 now makes the intentional bad-doer and wrongdoer better than the unintentional, and makes the former good and the latter bad.

Is the current argument valid? The equivocations most commonly alleged with respect to this argument are on (1) *agathos,* which may mean either good at something or morally good, (2) *ameinōn,* which may mean either better at something or morally better, and (3) *hekōn,* which may refer either to one's ability or to what one desires. If there is equivocation, one must consider (as commentators have) whether it is intentional on Plato's part and, if so, what purpose it serves and if it is justified. Some accuse Plato of sophistry, regard-

---

31. Zembaty (1989, 58), relying on the *Laches* (192b1–9) and on the *Protagoras* (esp. 329d3–333b6), argues that a virtue-term "necessarily functions as both a *tropos* and a *dunamis* term. . . . A *dunamis* which *defines* a human excellence or its opposite cannot be a *dunamis* for the opposite of that which it defines" (emphasis in original). The point of Socrates' argument in the *Hippias Minor,* however, is that if a virtue is defined by a *dunamis,* its practitioner, like the practitioner of any other *dunamis,* will be a better one and indeed a good one if he either (1) performs well or (2) performs poorly on purpose and only on purpose. The implication in the *Hippias Minor* that since justice is a *dunamis* it is a *dunamis* not only for doing justice but also for doing-injustice-only-deliberately is not discounted by anything in the *Laches* or *Protagoras.* Whereas in the *Laches,* for example, foolish endurance does not count as courage, the possibility is not excluded that the wise and courageous man is the one who, whenever he fails to endure, does so only deliberately and not because he cannot help himself. It is the case in all three dialogues that the virtuous man typically does what is good and honorable. But in the *Hippias Minor* it is also the case that the virtuous man, however atypically, does what is bad and dishonorable only on purpose, only when he wishes to.

ing the equivocation as deliberate but unjustified;[32] others excuse it on the grounds that Hippias deserves no better;[33] some think it a device to trap opponents;[34] still others, a challenge to the reader.[35]

As in stage 1, however, it seems most likely that the words are used in just one, albeit nonstandard, sense consistently. The sense of *agathos* as morally good, for example, is not supported by anything in the argument; the argument generally uses *agathos* to mean "good at/for something." For this reason, *ho agathos* himself need not be the morally good man, except in the sense that he is good *at* morality (or justice).[36] To say that one person is better than another is to say that he is more skilled. To say that something is done *hekōn* means throughout this section that it is done when and only when the agent wishes.

Socrates, despite having qualms about the conclusion (372d7–8; 376b8), is quite sure that it is compelled by the argument (*anankaion . . . ek tou logou* [376b8–c1]; cf. 372e3–4: "I blame the previous arguments as causes of my present experience"). It seems fair to say as well that Hippias seems quite comfortable with the progress of the argument—at least, that is, until he grasps its implications (375d3–6). If we simply hold constant the *dunamis*-sense of *agathos, ameinōn,* and *hekōn* to the bitter end, rejecting the charge of equivocation, we, too, would have to concede that although the conclusion sounds wrong, it is nevertheless formally legitimate. We would just have to remind ourselves that the conclusion's claim is limited: it says only that the man who willingly errs, doing shameful and unjust things intentionally, that is, when and only when he so wishes (since he has complete mastery of the skill or science of justice), is the good, that is, the able, man.[37]

The arguments in the *Hippias Minor,* then, need not be, although they frequently are, thought guilty of patent equivocation and flagrant abuses of language. They make perfectly good sense if the terms *alēthēs, pseudēs, agathos,*

32. Grote 1875, I, 394, following Steinhart.

33. Mulhern 1968, 286.

34. Apelt 1912, 205.

35. Hoerber 1962, 128.

36. Sprague (1962, 75) sees equivocation in stage 3 since "no other activity than the activity of being a man has been specified for him [the good man] to be skillful at." Yet the argument specifies *justice* as the science or skill at which the good man is skillful.

37. Socrates' conclusion is reminiscent of the opening definition in Donald Ogden Stewart's burlesque of Emily Post (1922, 1): "The perfect gentleman is he who never unintentionally causes pain."

ameinōn, and *hekōn* are all taken throughout in the *dunamis*-sense stipulated. The truthful man and the liar are the same, both equally able to tell the truth or to lie at will because they are skilled in the various arts or sciences; he who has the ability to do badly in a particular art or science only when he so wishes is better, that is, more skilled, than he who lacks that ability and therefore does badly against his will; the man who has this ability in any art or science, including justice, is the good, that is, the able, man.

"If There Be Such a Man"

Still and all, the conclusion of the argument is shocking. And because it is shocking Plato's readers look to the four-word qualification, *eiper tis estin houtos* (if there be such a man [376b5–6]), to save the day.[38] If Socrates holds, they reason, that there is no man who willingly errs, doing shameful and unjust things, then such a man can hardly be the good man.[39] Does this solution work?

One thing that those who pin their hopes on this solution fail to realize is that what Socrates means in the *Hippias Minor* by the intentional wrongdoer is a man so proficient at justice that he does wrong when and only when he so wishes. To say in the *Hippias Minor* that "the man who willingly errs, doing shameful and unjust things, if there be such a man, is the good man" is to say that if only there actually were a man so skilled at justice that he does wrong when and only when he means to and never simply because he is unable to do right, that man would be the good man.[40]

Moreover, the qualifier "if there be such a man" in no way suggests that the

---

38. It is worth noting that the first time the conclusion appears, at 376b2–4, it appears without this qualification: "Well, then, it is characteristic of a good man to do injustice voluntarily, while it is characteristic of a bad man to do so involuntarily, if, that is, the good man has a good soul."

39. Proponents of this interpretation of the dialogue's end include O'Brien (1967, 165–6); Sprague (1962, 76); Gomperz (1905, II, 294); Irwin (1977, 77, 299, n48); Penner (1973, 133–51); Shorey (1933, 89); A. E. Taylor (1937, 37–38); Blundell (1992, 161–62); Waterfield (1987, 269); Kahn (1996, 132).

40. Blundell (1992, 161, n133) thinks that "the proviso would be pointless here if Socrates accepted the conventional view that such people abound." The conventional view, however, is the view that people who deliberately do wrong abound—not the view that people who do wrong *only* deliberately, that is, when and only when they so wish, abound. The proviso, then, is not pointless.

difficulty or even the impossibility of finding so skilled a man nullifies Socrates' point that if he were found he would indeed be the good man, that is, the able one. Indeed, regardless of whether there are runners so skilled that they run slowly only intentionally, eyes so good that one sees dimly with them only intentionally, feet so reliable that they limp only intentionally, or bodies so graceful that they are graceless only intentionally, it would nevertheless be true that, if there were, they would be better than their counterparts who (or which) did any of these things unintentionally. The qualifier "if there be such a man" suggests, then, no more than that in the case of wrongdoing it might be difficult or even impossible to find a man so skilled at justice that he does wrong only intentionally. The same limited role is assigned to the very similar qualifier found at *Crito* 47d1–2: "if there be such an expert" (*ei tis estin epaiōn*). Here is the passage in which this qualifier appears (*Crito* 47c–d):

> And in particular, concerning the just and unjust and shameful and noble and good and bad things, about which we are now taking counsel, must we follow the opinion of the many and fear it rather than that of the one—if there be such an expert (*eiper tis estin epaiōn* [*Crito* 47d1–2])—before whom we must be ashamed and whom we must fear more than all the others?

In this passage, Socrates certainly registers his doubts about the existence of the moral expert he describes. Nevertheless, he shows no sign of having any comparable doubt that, were such a man to be found, *his* opinion—and not that of the many—would be the one to be followed and feared. If in the *Crito* the extreme improbability—indeed, even the impossibility—of finding a moral expert does not in the least undermine the truth of Socrates' claim that, *if* such a man were found, he would be the man whose opinion is to be feared and followed, why should it be the case in the *Hippias Minor* that the extreme improbability—indeed, even the impossibility—of finding a man who does wrong only intentionally nullifies Socrates' claim that, *if* such a man were found, he would be the good man?[41]

---

41. Cf. *Gorg.* 520d6–7, where the man who benefits another by relieving him of his injustice has no reason to fear injustice at his beneficiary's hand—"if indeed someone is in truth able to make men good" (*eiper tōi onti dunaito tis agathous poiein*). Here, too, the point would hold theoretically even if it were to turn out to be not actually possible for someone to make others good. See also *Gorg.* 484a2 and *Meno* 100a1.

Like the intentional wrongdoer who is not the same man each time he appears in the Platonic corpus, so, too, the Socratic paradox does not mean the same thing each time it appears in the dialogues. Whereas its core meaning, expounded most forcefully in the *Gorgias,* is that one who does wrong fails, in so doing, to do the single most important thing he wants to do, namely, live well really and have things that are truly good, what "no one does wrong willingly" signifies in the *Hippias Minor* is that there is no one sufficiently skilled at justice as to do injustice when and only when he so wishes.

Socrates' Rejection of the Argument's Conclusion

Why, then, is Socrates unhappy with the conclusion that the man who errs willingly, doing shameful and unjust things, is the good man?[42] After all, he argues for it. He painstakingly builds the case for it. He believes it is compelled by the case he has built. And he seems to thrust it on Hippias rather than the other way around.[43] Perhaps what Socrates finds truly alarming about the notion that the man who does wrong intentionally is the good man is that it violates his own most deeply held conviction that it is precisely the man who does wrong unintentionally, that is, only unintentionally, who is the good man. The good man is, to be sure, the man with the good soul, but this is the man whose soul is so ordered that what he wants is to do right (see esp. *Gorg.* 460c; also *Rep.* 1.335d–e).[44]

42. Here the *Hippias Minor* departs from the *Crito:* in the *Hippias Minor*—but not in the *Crito*—Socrates disapproves of his argument's conclusion. See Gomperz 1905, II, 294: "Socrates does not disguise his dissatisfaction with the conclusion, in spite of the necessity with which it appears to flow from the discussion leading up to it." Note, however, that Aristotle quotes the *Hippias Minor*'s paradoxes without giving any indication that Plato or Socrates did not believe them. Xenophon, too, has Socrates bring up the identical point in *Mem.* 4.2.19–20, with respect to liars and deceivers. Many modern scholars as well have taken as Socratic the view that intentional wrongdoers are better than unintentional. Grote (1875, I, 303), for instance, considers this view to be one of Plato's and Socrates' "startling novelties in ethical doctrine." See note 51.

43. Grote (1875, I, 393) suggests that the *Hippias Minor* would have been more acceptable had the roles of Hippias and Socrates been reversed. In the *Protagoras,* too, Socrates seems to foist the hedonistic credo on a skeptical Protagoras.

44. It is evident that Socrates harps on souls, asking which is the better horse's soul, dog's soul, other animals' soul, archer's soul, doctor's soul, musician's soul, and slave's soul, in order to ask finally about the better human soul itself. By defining the good man as the man who has the good soul, Socrates makes his conclusion—that the good man is the man who commits injustice only voluntarily—even more startling and unacceptable than it would otherwise have been. Is it even thinkable that Socrates regards the man with the good soul as the man who does wrong only intentionally?

For Socrates, it seems, it is the man who will not do anything that he himself regards as unjust, the man whose every wrong deed is quite literally done by mistake, who is the good man. This is the sort of man whom the gods do not neglect. This is the sort of man whom it is wrong to punish. And those who would punish a man of this sort are bad men doing wrong to a good man.

Socrates is, in his own view, just such a man—a good man who does wrong only unintentionally (see *Ap.* 37a5–6; *Gorg.* 488a2–3). He is a man who has no wish to do wrong. To be sure, Socrates can imagine a better man, a man who not only does no wrong intentionally but a man who does no wrong. If there were such a man, this man would be the moral expert. Like the good man, like Socrates, the moral expert would never deliberately do wrong. But he would surpass the good man, he would surpass Socrates, in having the kind of clarity concerning matters of right and wrong that would enable him successfully to avoid all wrongdoing. The proficiency of the true moral expert would be such as to make it possible for him always and only to do right; it would not be such as to make it possible for him to do wrong when and only when he wanted to.

If, then, Socrates in fact cannot but reject the conclusion of his argument, holding not that if only there were a person so skilled at justice as to do wrong exclusively voluntarily he would be the good man, but maintaining instead that the good man is the man who does wrong exclusively *in*voluntarily and that the moral expert is the man who simply never does wrong, why, indeed, does he argue for it? Why does he force justice into the mold of all other arts and sciences so that, even if there is technically no fallacy in his argument, he ends up praising the man who does shameful and wrong things voluntarily? And why does he then say, "if there be such a man"? The answer to all these questions is to be found in the views of the character Hippias. What charts the course of the arguments in the *Hippias Minor* is something amiss in the views of its protagonist.

Hippias

The shift that Hippias introduces in the dialogue's third stage, where the comparison between voluntary and involuntary liars gives way to a comparison between voluntary and involuntary wrongdoers (371e9–372a2), radically alters the course of the argument. For so long as Socrates could proceed on the assumption that the liar is just someone who is wise or proficient in the various arts or sciences, he could conclude that the voluntariness of the liar's lying only confirms his expertise in the given art or science and hence his goodness. Indeed, as we saw, Socrates does not shrink from the idea that the voluntary liar is better than the involuntary; he might well believe that lying and deceit are necessary—even beneficial—on occasion.[45] Yet, once the liar is conceived of as a wrongdoer, the voluntariness with which he lies seems to threaten his goodness. For wrongdoing, unlike lying, is not, and cannot be construed as, an ability one has by virtue of one's proficiency in the various arts or sciences: although knowing geometry or astronomy is presumably what enables one to tell the truth or to lie about geometrical and astronomical matters at will, knowing geometry or astronomy surely is not what enables one to do justice or injustice at will. If knowing geometry or astronomy does not confer the ability to do justice or injustice at will, then it cannot be geometry or astronomy at which the intentional wrongdoer (unlike the intentional liar) is skilled.

What, then, *is* the art or science at which the voluntary wrongdoer is skilled? Speaking for himself Socrates might simply have declared that the voluntary wrongdoer is not skilled at all. Yet, since on Hippias's account, the voluntary liar, now the voluntary wrongdoer, *is* skilled—it is he who acts wisely, prudently, and intelligently—Socrates must find for him an area of expertise. Might not the art or science at which the voluntary wrongdoer is skilled be injustice or wrongdoing? No; for to do wrong is to do badly at something, to perform poorly: it is like running slowly or being ungraceful. It seems then that, however paradoxically, the only art or science that might qualify as that at which the voluntary wrongdoer excels is justice.

If justice is a skill or science or both, it follows, of course, that the more *un*just a man is, the more ignorant he is. And so Socrates says explicitly at 375e7–8. But the link between injustice and ignorance holds, as Socrates sees, only for *un*intentional injustice. For, on Hippias's account, it is the voluntary wrongdoer Odysseus who is intelligent and skilled. If Socrates is to accommodate Hippias's belief that the voluntary wrongdoer is wise, prudent, and

---

45. See, e.g., *Rep.* 1.331e–332a, where withholding "what is due" from someone who is out of his mind at the time he asks for it is seen not to be unjust because it spares him harm. See also *Gorg.* 469b, where the man who kills another justly is not enviable—because he kills—but, because he does so justly, is not pitiable and wretched either. Perhaps the expert at the art of politics would be the one who is able to judge when it is appropriate to lie and to do other things that are normally considered wrong. But even the expert at politics could not know when it is right to be unjust: there is no such time.

able, then he will have to recognize not one but two indicators of mastery of the science of justice: not only will one's doing right be a sign of one's having mastered the science of justice, but so will one's doing wrong intentionally. Just as the slow runner is a bad runner who has failed to master the art of running, so the unjust man is a bad man who has failed to master the art of justice. But just as the runner who runs slowly deliberately, when and only when he wishes to and never because he is unable to run fast, is on that account a good runner, so the man who does injustice deliberately, when and only when he wishes to and never because he is unable to do right, is on that account a good man.[46]

The final argument of the *Hippias Minor* thus takes its fateful turn when Socrates asks "Is justice a skill, or knowledge, or both?"—a question to which Hippias responds, with no hesitation whatsoever, in the affirmative. Why does Hippias so readily endorse the notion that justice is a skill or knowledge or both? Has he not been insisting all along that the better man, Achilles, is the one who is *haplous* and that the worse man, Odysseus, is the skilled and knowing one?

Hippias is a sophist; he is a teacher of *aretē*. Although Socrates does not list *aretē* among the many skills that Hippias boasts of having mastered, he does make it clear (368d5; 368de1) that Hippias has other skills, many others, besides the ones Socrates does name. Moreover, the question Socrates directs at Hippias—who is the better man?—shows that Socrates assumes that human goodness is one of Hippias's purported areas of expertise. Note that Socrates does not at first ask Hippias what Homer thinks of Achilles and Odysseus; he asks Hippias what *he* thinks of them (364b3–5). At one point Socrates even asks that Homer be set aside since he cannot be questioned and since Hippias apparently shares his view (365c8–d4). Hippias, however, hides behind Homer (like Protagoras hides behind Simonides, and Meno, as we shall see, behind Gorgias): "what I say about these men and others, too" quickly becomes "I say that Homer made . . ." (364c3–5). Hippias teaches virtue, then, without having given any thought to who *he* thinks the good man is. Whereas

---

46. There is an interesting disanalogy between the unjust man, on the one hand, and at least some of the doers to which he is compared. The slow runner cannot run fast; bad feet cannot but limp; graceless people cannot be graceful—even by mistake. But the unjust man certainly can do just things—by mistake or on purpose. Part of being an unjust man is not wanting to do right. The bad runner presumably wants to run fast.

Socrates seeks illumination from this preeminent teacher of virtue concerning who is the better man, Achilles or Odysseus, the only question that concerns Hippias is who is the better speaker, Hippias or Socrates (369c7–8).[47]

Hippias is the celebrated master and teacher of a wide array of *technai*. Yet at 366c–368e Socrates mocks, gently, Hippias's presumed proficiency in all things technical. Unlike Protagoras, who prides himself on teaching only *aretē,* Hippias takes pride in teaching everything—including *aretē*. But *technai* can be put to uses both good and bad. The same egregious fault that Socrates finds in Protagoras and Gorgias, namely, that they teach a skill concerned with justice without concerning themselves with the state of their pupils' souls—indeed that they lure young people away from those who are concerned with nurturing them and substitute their skills for that nurture, applies no less to Hippias. If justice is a skill like others, then the just man, the good man, cannot be, as Hippias had sought to maintain, the simple man who means well. The good man will be instead the man who does precisely what he intends, whether he means well or not.[48] Indeed, if justice is a skill like others, then the

---

47. As we saw in chapter 2, Protagoras's preference was to engage Socrates in a poetry-interpreting contest (*Prot.* 338e–339a).

48. Irwin (1977) and Penner (1973) argue that justice in the *Hippias Minor* is indeed a *technē,* but that it differs from other *technai* in that only in the case of the *technē* justice is there no higher end that the agent could prefer to the *technē*'s own proper end. Irwin and Penner appeal to what they regard as the psychological necessity (in Socrates' view) of a man's choosing what he thinks conduces to his own happiness, and since happiness is, they argue, the proper end of the *technē* justice, it follows that the man who has this *technē* will not choose anything but the just, insofar as he will know that the just will make him happy. As I have argued in previous chapters, however, Socrates does not recognize in human beings any psychological necessity to choose what they believe will yield their own happiness.

Irwin and Penner regard as pointless Plato's selection of "technical man personified," as O'Brien (1967, 104) calls Hippias, to be Socrates' interlocutor in this dialogue. As O'Brien puts it, it is an "anachronism" to say that Plato is showing the breakdown of the analogy between justice and *technē* in the face of the biggest technician of them all; to say this is, he says, "the indulging of modern preconceptions at the expense of Socrates' and Plato's known acceptance of the craft-analogy." See also Guthrie 1975, IV, 199; Waterfield 1987, 269; A. E. Taylor 1937, 37. Indeed, all Irwin (1977, 26) can say in response to the question "Why Hippias?" is that the dialogue reveals that "Hippias has no more than a layman's understanding of morality." Far more reasonable than the Irwin-Penner view is the view that the *Hippias Minor* teaches that justice is not a skill at all. Among the supporters of this idea are Ritter (1933, 38) and Hall (1963, 100). See also Kahn (1996, 118): "The one thing that is unmistakably clear . . . is that moral virtue and vice are *not* to be understood simply as a trained capacity or skill. Being good as a human being is not like being good at running or good at arithmetic." On this view it makes perfectly good sense that Plato would choose "technical man personified" to be Socrates' interlocutor.

simple, well-intentioned, but inept goodness of Achilles cannot be the *aretē* that Hippias teaches. The kind of student that Hippias, like all professional teachers of *aretē,* will turn out will be wily like Odysseus—equally adept at lying as at truth-telling, at cheating as at playing it straight.

Hippias is not like Thrasymachus, who brazenly assigns *in*justice to the camp of virtue and wisdom and assigns justice to the camp of "genteel simplicity" (*Rep.* 1.348c–e).[49] What Hippias does is assign justice to both camps. Thrasymachus's unyielding but consistent stance makes it hard for Socrates to know what to say to him (*Rep.* 1.348e), but Hippias's nod to convention (like Polus's in the *Gorgias*) and his defensiveness with respect to his profession (like Protagoras's in the *Protagoras*) make him an easy mark. For at the same time that Hippias affirms the goodness of the simple Achilles he assigns to justice the status of *dunamis/epistēmē/technē.* The justice that the conventional Hippias associates with guilelessness and innocence is clearly no *technē.* But Hippias, qua teacher of *aretē,* feels constrained to call justice a *technē.* And once he concedes that justice is a *technē,* it follows that the man who does wrong voluntarily is the good man.

Hippias is not happy with this conclusion. It violates, as he points out, law and convention, and Hippias does not wish to offend, to say or do anything that might be construed either as strange or terrible (*deinon* [363c7, 365c7, 375d3]), as shameful (*aischron* [364d3]), or as contrary to law (372a3–5). Socrates, too, is unhappy with this conclusion. But, then again, it is not *his* premises that compel it.[50] For Socrates, justice is not an art or science. It is not a skill that

---

49. Nor is Hippias like Glaucon, who in *Rep.* 2 characterizes *in*justice as a *technē*: "So, first, let the unjust man act like the clever craftsmen (*hoi deinoi dēmiourgoi*). An outstanding pilot or doctor is aware of what is impossible and possible in his craft" (*Rep.* 2.360e6–8).

50. At *Rep.* 1.334a, the just man turns out to be a man who is good at stealing money as well as at guarding it, and eventually emerges as some kind of thief. Here, too, the argument is spurred by the view espoused by Socrates' interlocutor—in this case, Polemarchus: "Justice, then, seems, *according to you* and Homer and Simonides, to be a certain art of stealing, for the benefit, to be sure, of friends and the harm of enemies." As in the *Hippias Minor,* justice in *Rep.* 1 is treated as an ability, a skill, a *dunamis,* as well as an art, a *technē.* Once Polemarchus suggests that the just man is a man who is *skilled at* guarding money, Socrates can then make the point that a man skilled at guarding money is equally skilled at stealing it, and therefore that "justice is a certain art of stealing" (1.334b4). Unlike in the case of the *Hippias Minor,* no one, as far as I know, doubts the authenticity of *Rep.* 1 on the grounds that it contains an argument so obviously unworthy of Plato. That Plato has Socrates reach an even more absurd conclusion in the *Republic* than in the *Hippias Minor* (supported by an arguably far weaker argument), but allows him to abandon it as soon as he suggests it (by 1.334d3 Socrates is seen to take it for granted that "the good are just and not the sort to do

permits of deliberate wrongdoing.[51] It is Hippias who is quite certain that a man can be wise, skilled, prudent—and unjust; it is he who pronounces the truthful and good man simple, foolish, and incompetent. Yet it is also Hippias who cannot deny that justice is a *technē*. As Socrates sees it, it would no doubt be difficult or impossible to find a man who could do good or bad at will, but even if such a man were found, he would *not* be the good man.[52] For Socrates, the good man is neither master of a skill called justice nor a simpleton. He is wise, but his wisdom resides in his desire to harm no one. The man who does desire to harm others is a bad man. Only the good man, the just man, never does wrong intentionally.[53] Other men, bad men, surely do.[54]

---

injustice"), ought to give commentators an additional reason to doubt his endorsement of the conclusion in the *Hippias Minor*.

51. It is argued in the *Gorgias* (460a–c) that the man who has learned justice is a just man, just as the man who has learned medicine is a doctor. But it is then made clear that if one has learned justice and has thus become a just man, one will not—indeed one cannot—use *any* skill unjustly. The just man, the man who has learned justice, is a man whose desires have been perfected—he no longer wishes to do wrong—and, as a consequence, he is a man who is not able ever to do wrong intentionally. As Socrates says, if the orator has learned justice he "is incapable of using oratory unjustly and of being willing to do what is unjust" (*Gorg.* 461a–b). See also *Gorg.* 520d, where Socrates argues that the one benefaction that it is perfectly safe to confer is relieving someone of injustice, for once a man becomes just or good he can no longer do anyone injustice.

52. One might cite in this connection *Crito* 44d, where Socrates suggests that those who can produce the greatest evils can also produce the greatest goods. Socrates may well think that those who can corrupt others are in a better position to improve others because at least they know what is bad and what is good and so are different from the many who "act by chance" (*poiousi . . . tuchōsi* [44d9–10]). But, even if those who can make others imprudent are the very ones who can make others prudent, it does not follow that they are just or good men. Just or good men are men who do good—not men who *can* do good. As the *Republic* tells us (*Rep.* 1.335d–e), it is not the function (*ergon*) of the just man to harm friends or anyone else; to harm is the function of his opposite, the unjust man.

53. The third character in the *Hippias Minor* is Eudikos—the conjunction of good and just. See Friedländer 1964, II, 145.

54. It is unlikely that there are men who do wrong *only* intentionally, never failing to do right through weakness or ignorance. The qualifier "if there be such a man," as was explained earlier, signals this unlikelihood. The *Hippias Minor* never intimates, however, that there are no men who ever do wrong intentionally—that is, deliberately. Men who frequently do wrong intentionally are bad men.

5

THE *MENO:*
DESIRING BAD THINGS
AND GETTING THEM

Is there reason to believe that in his argument at *Meno* 77b–79a Socrates endorses the idea that no one does bad things, that is, things that one regards as harmful to oneself, willingly? Does Socrates hold here that those who do things that are in fact bad (harmful to themselves) do so believing those things to be good, that had they but recognized the harmfulness to themselves of these bad things they would have neither desired nor pursued them?

If this is Socrates' view, how odd it is, then, that this very passage characterizes as wretched those who *desire bad things believing them to be bad.* Whereas, to be sure, the *Meno* firmly maintains that no one wants (*bouletai*) to be wretched and that, therefore, all people want good—and not bad— things, it asserts, too, that there are those who desire (*epithumei*) the very things they regard as bad. It seems, then, that what the *Meno* offers is the innovative idea that people can desire things they do not want. Although the *Meno* does not contain in so many words the paradox "no one does bad things willingly" (and certainly not the paradox "no one does *wrong* willingly"),[1] it does preserve something of the paradox's spirit: it contends that those who

---

1. Santas (1964) observes that whereas the *Gorgias* promotes at 509e the moral paradox "no one does wrong (or injustice) willingly," the *Meno* advances at 77b–78b the prudential paradox "no one does bad (imprudent) things willingly."

desire and successfully pursue things they recognize as harmful to themselves do not do what they want.

What Is Virtue? Meno vs. Socrates

Meno is a young man, around twenty years old,[2] from Thessaly, a place that, according to the *Crito,* is known for corruption (*Crito* 53d). He is of aristocratic birth, a man of means, and quite handsome. The *Meno* takes note of his association with Aristippus, whom the dialogue identifies as his lover (70b); with Gorgias, whose views he is depicted as adopting seemingly uncritically; and with Anytus, notorious for his participation —along with Meletus and Lycon—in prosecuting Socrates and seeking his execution.

The *Meno* opens abruptly, with Meno soliciting Socrates' answer to a practical and pressing question: how does a person come to possess virtue? Socrates counters Meno's practical question with a theoretical one: what is virtue? For Socrates, the question of what virtue is logically precedes the question of how one comes to have it.

Meno and Socrates disagree utterly and fundamentally on what virtue is. At the heart of their disagreement is not simply that Meno enumerates different virtues for men, women, slaves, children, and old men, but the implication of this enumeration—namely, that virtue is a function of *what* is done and not of the manner in which it is done. Whereas Meno specifies the roles that different types of people play, what Socrates wants to know is whether these various types play their respective roles justly and temperately.

The virtue of a man, Meno (or Meno quoting his teacher Gorgias) says, consists in taking part in the affairs of the city, helping friends and harming enemies, and protecting oneself; the virtue of a woman consists in managing the household well, looking after its contents, and being subject to one's hus-

---

2. Bluck (1961, 123) places Meno's age at twenty. Other scholars, however, such as Morrison (1942, 157–58), Ryle (1976, 3), and Stokes (1963, 294), think Meno must have been older. he is in charge of a company of mercenaries, has a household of his own, including slaves, is of high military rank, and has been long acquainted with Aristippus and Gorgias. Moreover, the dialogue says of him at 76b that he is *still* handsome enough to have lovers, the implication of which, it is thought, is that he is no longer young. If Meno is said to be *still* handsome enough to have lovers, however, does that not suggest that he is at the tail end of his youth? Cf. *Prot.* 309a, where a similar expression is used of Alcibiades who is probably in his late teens: "and he is certainly *still* a handsome man—and just between the two of us, 'man' is the proper word, Socrates: his beard is already filling out."

band (71e). But, Socrates wants to know, what is the virtue that is common to all its instances? What is the form that the various virtues share (72c)?

In trying to help Meno find, even among the disparate virtues he lists, some common ground, Socrates proposes that he consider the possibility that "managing well," *eu dioikein,* might be something that all those who are virtuous share: the virtuous woman manages a household well, the virtuous man, a city (73a6–7). Interestingly, however, the aspect of "managing well" that Socrates regards as essential to virtue is not the "managing" but the "well," not the activity performed but that it is performed temperately and justly. Indeed, by 73b3, the "managing" element has completely dropped out of Socrates' account of what the virtuous man and woman have in common, and Socrates speaks only of what both a man and a woman need "if they are going to be good." Moreover, since children and old men who do no managing at all also need to be good, how could managing constitute virtue? As Socrates argues, children and old men need the very same qualities as men and women do if they are to be good: "all human beings are thus good in the same way" (73c1–2).

When Meno makes another attempt to identify what it is that is common to all instances of virtue, he is drawn, despite Socrates' efforts, not to the "well" but to the "managing" in "managing well." Thus, when he casts about for a single common virtue, what he looks for is a single form of managing. Disappointingly, however, he comes up not with a form of managing *more* inclusive than the previous one, but with one less so: the form of managing on which he settles is one that excludes not only children, slaves, and old men, as the previous one did, but women, too; he so narrows his definition of virtue that it applies to no one but men in their prime. Virtue is, Meno says, ruling others (73c9).[3]

Is Meno's failing in this early part of the dialogue intellectual or moral? Is it that he does not know how to formulate an adequate definition or that he is unable to appreciate the "moral" dimension of virtue, its being tied to such things as justice and temperance? There can be no doubt that Meno is no whiz at definition. Instead of a single virtue common to all kinds of virtue, he cites the various kinds; he cannot see (as Socrates can [73d2–4]) that his "ruling others" definition is technically inferior to the earlier definition of "managing well"; and he fails to articulate why health and strength are the same for

---

3. See *Gorg.* 452d, where Gorgias boasts that the rhetorical craft secures for those who master it the greatest good: rulership over others and freedom for oneself.

everyone (72e2–3; 72e9) but virtue is not (73a4–5).[4] Nevertheless, his more disturbing and more serious defect is a moral one: he fails to appreciate the relevance of justice, temperance, and the other virtues or parts of virtue to virtue. Indeed, no matter how many times Socrates points out that virtue requires justice and temperance, Meno's definitions of virtue continue to omit them.

Were Meno's problem primarily intellectual or logical rather than moral, he would surely have had just as much trouble recognizing that health and strength are the same in men and women as he does in recognizing that virtue is. The reason he has considerably more trouble in the latter case is, no doubt, because what he really believes is that only men have real virtue, and that real virtue, manly virtue, the virtue he craves, has little or nothing in common with what women and children and slaves and old men have that goes by the same name. When Socrates insists, then, that virtue, like health and strength, *is* the same for everyone, Socrates makes more than just a logical point. In effect, he democratizes *aretē*. If virtue is something that can mark the excellence of an old man, a child, a slave, and a woman, no less than a man in his prime, then virtue cannot be tied to one's position in the world. On the contrary, since virtue is the same for everyone, since it has to do only with how "well" one does whatever it is one does, then virtue belongs to anyone who comports himself justly and temperately.

That Socrates singles out justice and temperance is no accident. These are the undistinguished virtues that the aristocratic Meno would never on his own associate with the virtue to which he aspires. Meno repeatedly pulls virtue in the direction of managing and ruling, and Socrates stubbornly pulls it back in the direction of justice and temperance. So, even when Meno obtusely proposes "ruling men" as that virtue which is common to all, Socrates continues to drive his moral point home: "Shall we not add to that justly and not unjustly?" (73d7–8). Meno concurs, asserting that "justice is virtue" (73d9–10). Justice, however, as Meno will soon agree (73e7–74a6), is but one virtue among many.[5]

---

4. Interlocutors in other dialogues occasionally challenge Socrates as well when he contends that a certain case is just like others. See, for example, *Charm.* 165e; *Rep.* 1.337c; *Euthyd.* 298c; *Cra.* 429a–b.

5. The plurality problem arises here, as Socrates says, "in a different way from that in which it happened just now" (74a8), that is, differently from how it arose in Meno's first definition. One important difference is that the swarm of virtues that Meno identifies for man, woman, slave, child, and old man, respectively, are not virtues at all. Justice, temperance, and piety, however, are.

What Is a Good Definition?

Since Meno is having difficulty producing an adequate definition of virtue, Socrates provides him with a definition of shape (*schēma*) to use as a model. Meno, it is clear, prides himself on his proficiency in geometry. Since Empedocles, who is himself a student of Pythagoras's, is Meno's teacher, it is likely that Meno has learned from Empedocles not only physics but Pythagorean geometry as well.

The definition of shape that Socrates offers is as follows. Shape is the only thing, among the things that are, that always accompanies color (75b9–11). Note that Socrates proposes this definition not as the unique or even as an especially good definition of shape, but rather as one that suffices for his present purposes: he introduces it with the words "Let shape be *for us* (*hēmin*)" (75b9–10). All Socrates needs is a definition on which Meno can pattern his definition of virtue: "For," says Socrates, "I would certainly be satisfied if you spoke similarly to me about virtue" (75b11–c1). Thus, unless Meno finds fault with the definition, it will stand.

Alas, Meno does find fault with the definition. His immediate response to Socrates' definition of shape is to call it *euēthes,* simple or simpleminded (75c2). What does that mean? When asked by Socrates to say what it means, Meno responds—probably reproducing an eristic quibble he had encountered somewhere, perhaps through his association with Gorgias[6]—that the definition is useless to "someone" who does not know color.[7] But who, after all, is unfamiliar with color? Socrates had tried to offer a straightforward, nontechnical definition that could serve as a model for defining virtue. Why does Meno reject Socrates' definition out of hand?

Note that Meno's complaint that the definition Socrates proposes will fail for someone who does not know color is but his second thought on the matter, uttered in an attempt to assign content and substance to his first, more visceral, objection. The very first thing that Meno says is that Socrates' definition is *euēthes,* simple or simpleminded. Unlike the gloss of it that follows, which implies that for Meno the problem with Socrates' definition is that it might

---

6. That Socrates suspects Meno of relying on a sophistic source might well underlie his speaking of the objector as "eristic." It is likely that Socrates suspects a similar source for "Meno's paradox," which he also calls "eristic" (80e2). The term also appears at 81d6.

7. Meno does not mean himself, of course.

prove too difficult or too obscure for "someone," Meno's immediate objection, the *euēthes* objection, implies, on the contrary, that the fault of the definition lies in its containing nothing esoteric or technical or sophisticated—indeed, nothing that the man in the street would not understand, nothing, that is, to distinguish the educated and cultured man from the boor. We may assume that Meno's first response to Socrates' definition—and not his subsequent commentary on it—betrays his true feelings: what he really finds repugnant is just how plain, how unpretentious, the definition is; what is distasteful to him is not that the definition *does* use terms that someone might not understand, but that it does not.

Meno, as Socrates quickly realizes, prefers the high-flown, the *tragikē* (76e3). The definition Meno favors is, therefore, the one that contains the more technical term "effluences," *aporroai*. We note that Meno expresses with respect to "effluences" no worry such as the one he expressed with respect to "color"; yet, is it not far more likely that someone might fail to know "effluences" than that someone might fail to know "color"?[8] Moreover, Meno is surprisingly unperturbed by the fact that if, as in his preferred definition, color is defined as an effluence from shapes (*aporroē schēmatōn* [76d4]), the definition might be useless to someone who does not know shape.[9] By offering a definition of color that commits the same offense as the initial definition of shape, Socrates is able to expose the disingenuousness and shallowness of Meno's objection to the definition of shape: whereas Meno peremptorily rejects the simpleminded definition of shape with its humble reference to color, he enthusiastically endorses the *tragikē* definition of color with its fancy, technical, effluences-talk. Meno, we see, is not really bothered by the use of unknown terms; what offends him is the use of known terms, that is, of terms known to everyone. Meno does not like Socrates' definition because Meno is a snob. Socrates, however, clearly does like the original definition of shape that he

8. Although the word *aporroē* is a perfectly ordinary Greek word, it takes on a technical and specialized meaning in Empedoclean perception theory, a meaning with which an ordinary Greek speaker would most likely be unfamiliar. "Effluence" is, in our context, technical jargon.

9. Like me, Davis (1988, 113) finds it significant that the third definition defines color in terms of shape. Bluck (1961, 243), however, dismisses the matter, saying that by this time an adequate definition of shape has been arrived at, presumably the definition of shape as the limit of a solid. Yet, one may reasonably doubt that the terms in "limit of a solid" are more known than "color." They may be known to Meno, but are they more generally known than color?

offered, for it has one merit that surely counts for much in his eyes: it is, as he says, true (75c8).[10]

Meno's response to Socrates' proposed definition of shape represents a turning point in the dialogue, the point at which Socrates sours on his interlocutor. Once Meno objects to Socrates' definition of shape as the only thing that always accompanies color (75b9–11), Socrates sees Meno for "the clever and disputatious (*eristikōn*) and contentious sort" (75c9) that he—and not just an anonymous "someone"—is. From now on, Socrates can only *pretend* that he and Meno are friends: "But if people were willing to converse with one another as friends, like you and I now" (75d2–3). Socrates clearly finds Meno's reaction to his unpretentious and easily understood definition both needlessly obstructive and deplorably arrogant.[11]

We may note that Socrates' second definition of shape—"the limit of a solid"—is more acceptable to Meno than the first one was: its terms are at least technical, that is, they are not "simple" ones that everyone can understand.[12] They do not, however, begin to approach in degree of ostentation a term like "effluences" and, for that reason, Meno's reception of the second definition of shape is tepid as compared with the enthusiastic reception he will soon accord to the definition of color: "But, I would stay, Socrates," Meno says with respect to the "effluences" definition alone, "if you were to give me many answers like this" (77a1–2). Not only does the arcane terminology of the definition of color greatly please Meno, but he has yet another cause for being pleased. Socrates' very act of providing a definition of color represents his yielding to Meno's authority: "Yes, gratify me," Meno commands (76c3)— and Socrates complies. Meno is, as Socrates says, the handsome, spoiled bully who dares to issue commands to an old man, exploiting his weakness for good looks. Socrates complies with Meno's order not only by formulating the de-

---

10. It might be thought that the notion that shape is the only thing that always accompanies color is not even true, let alone an adequate definition of shape. Yet Socrates' definition has merit, at least when confined to perceptible shape and color: if one sees something colored, one sees something shaped in some way.

11. See Klein 1965, 62.

12. Davis (1988, 112) asks: "in what sense is solid more known than color? Meno accepts it [the second definition] because its mathematical form is familiar to him." It is likely, however, that what recommends the second definition to Meno, even more than his familiarity with its terms, is their technicality. Significantly, Socrates checks to see that Meno is familiar with the terms "surface" and "solid" "*as in geometrical matters*" (76a2).

sired definition but by doing so "in the style of Gorgias, in the way that you would most easily follow" (76c4–5).

Which definition is Socrates' favorite? There should be no doubt that Socrates prefers the first one, his definition of shape as the only thing that always accompanies color: (1) if he prefers some other, one must explain why this is the one he proposes; indeed, he is prepared to have this definition stand unless Meno objects to it; (2) he says it is true; (3) it is intended to serve as the model for an acceptable definition of virtue; and (4) it follows a pattern Socrates had established earlier in seeking with Meno a definition of virtue, a pattern according to which what accompanies an activity determines its character: an activity is sure to be virtuous if done justly and temperately or, in other words, if accompanied by justice and temperance. When Socrates says, then, at 76e6: "The other one was better," he surely refers to the original definition of 75b9–11.[13]

The features of this definition that recommend it to Socrates—besides that it is true—are, first, that it uses familiar terms, terms that are not needlessly technical and grandiose; and second, that, unlike the definition of color that, as Socrates points out, works equally well for sound, smell, and many other things of that sort (76d9–e1), Socrates' first definition of shape identifies shape uniquely: shape is the *only* thing that always accompanies color. (Meno, ever careless of such things, misses, in his paraphrase at 75c4–5 of Socrates' definition of shape, the uniqueness of shape's role vis-à-vis color: he omits the word "only" [*monon*].) We shall see in the next section how these admirable features of the first definition of shape, when reproduced in the dialogue's last definition of virtue, go quite a long way toward providing an adequate definition for virtue.

A long way, but certainly not the whole way—not even in the matter of shape. Socrates' favored definition of shape, despite exhibiting the three strengths mentioned, fails to get to the essence, to the *ousia,* of what shape is;

13. Klein (1965, 70) believes, as I do, that Socrates' preferred definition is "the first sober—one which, correlating 'surface' and 'color,' hinted at a possibly satisfactory answer about 'human excellence,'" rather than "the geometrical—narrow—one which was given in Meno's own terms." Bluck (1961, 254) and Guthrie (1975, IV, 249, n1), however, think Socrates prefers the second definition: they do not say why. If their reason is that insofar as the second definition comes later it is the more likely referent of "the other one" that Socrates at 76e6 says is better, their reason is unconvincing because, even much later, at 79d1–2, the expression "the answer I just now gave you about shape" refers—this time unambiguously—to Socrates' first definition of shape, the one in terms of color.

at most, it picks out a trait that shape alone always instantiates. It seeks to understand shape not as it is in itself but as it relates to something else: shape is, after all, on Socrates' "definition," no more than the only thing for which the presence of color is a sufficient condition.

Defining shape has been a simpler task by far for Socrates than has defining virtue. In no time at all Socrates produces two acceptable definitions of shape; he could, perhaps, produce others as well.

What Is Virtue? Trying Again

Now that Socrates has given Meno a definition of which he approves (77a1–2), it is Meno's turn, in accordance with his and Socrates' agreement (75b4–5), to venture once more to define virtue.

It is only now that Socrates introduces his paradox into the discussion. In the early part of the dialogue, Socrates' aim was to deflect Meno's attention away from the activity or the role that to him in itself embodies virtue—ultimately, that of a man who rules other men—and to help him focus instead on the indispensability to virtue of *how* an activity or role is executed: an activity or role will not count as virtue unless it is executed "well," that is, justly and temperately. Having provided a model on which a suitable definition of virtue might be constructed, Socrates has reason to hope that Meno will define virtue in terms of the justice and temperance that he has agreed are its constant companions. Since Meno's final definition makes no mention of justice and temperance but instead posits a connection between virtue and something like social class, Socrates must not only once again insist on the indispensability of justice, temperance, and, now, also piety to virtue, but he must work, too, to reduce Meno to the size of every man.

Meno's new definition exhibits, not surprisingly, the very arrogance that just emerged in his reaction to Socrates' first definition of shape. Interestingly, however, it also reflects in certain respects the perhaps unwitting progress Meno has made in defining—for this latest definition neither breaks virtue into pieces nor uses unknown or technical terms; moreover, it picks out virtue uniquely.[14] Nevertheless, this final definition is as morally bankrupt as

---

14. As we saw, the definition of color in terms of effluences does not pick out color uniquely. A definition along these lines would, as Socrates notes, also serve to say "what sound is, and smell, and many other things of that sort" (76d9–e1).

all the others. Meno draws his new definition of virtue from an unnamed poet, for whom virtue is "to rejoice in fine things and to have power." In Meno's paraphrase, the poet's definition becomes: "Virtue is to desire fine things (*kala*) and to have the power to acquire them" (77b2–5).

According to Meno's definition, there are then two marks that distinguish the man of virtue, two criteria by which one man may be judged superior to his fellow: (1) a penchant for the fine, and (2) power. Socrates considers each of these in turn—first discounting the former, and then proceeding to discount the latter. Let us begin by considering Socrates' response to Meno's first proposed indicator of virtue, "desiring fine things."

Socrates is occupied with this first part of Meno's new definition from 77b6 to 78b2. It is his aim in this stretch of text to level all people with respect to what they want—note his concluding words: "and in this respect [in respect of what people want], no one is better than another" (78b5–6)—thereby discrediting the foolish and groundless elitism manifest in the first component of Meno's latest definition.

In order to accomplish his goal of having all people turn out to be the same with respect to their wants, Socrates employs two strategic moves: first, he reduces fine things (*kala*) to good things (*agatha*) and, second, he replaces desiring (*epithumein*) with wanting (*boulesthai*).[15] In order to understand Socrates' strategy, it is best first to try to determine how he understands Meno's definition: what does Meno mean by proposing that those with virtue desire fine things? Meno's intention is to elevate those with refined tastes above those whose pedestrian tastes mark them as hopelessly ordinary. Socrates' immediate substitution of *agatha* for *kala*—"Do you say that the one who desires fine things desires good things?" (77b6–7)—is the first step toward eliminating such specious class distinctions: "good things" lacks the highbrow air of "fine things." Meno, unaware of the implications of this substitution, readily assents to it;[16] he now finds himself committed to the proposition that some people, those who lack virtue, desire bad things (*kaka*).

---

15. Similar moves occur in the *Gorgias.* For the move from fine to good, see the notorious argument at *Gorg.* 474–475; for a move reminiscent of the one here from *epithumein* to *boulesthai*, see the argument at *Gorg.* 466–468, where the shift is, however, from *ha dokei,* what one pleases or what seems good to one, to *ha bouletai,* what one wants.

16. Guthrie (1975, 247 n1) notes: "M. was really beaten when he lightly agreed to the substitution of *agatha* for *kala* at 77b7." Thompson (1901, 102) points out that, as a result of the substitution, "any poetic tinsel attaching to the word *kala* is removed." It seems unlikely that what

From Socrates' perspective, the claim that people desire bad things is a most problematic one. He presses Meno further: do those who desire bad things think those things are good or do they desire bad things recognizing them as bad? Meno insists that some people, probably those he disdains as crude or vulgar, desire bad things recognizing them as bad. Meno is no doubt thinking not of *kaka,* bad things, but of *aischra,* base or crass things, things that are the opposites not of *agatha,* good things, but of his original *kala,* fine things. Thus, what Meno must mean is that even though the masses recognize their tastes as lowbrow, they persist in desiring what they desire: crab cakes, not caviar. But Socrates goes on: do such people desire to possess these things? And if they do, can they be thinking that bad things benefit their possessors or do they recognize that bad things harm their possessors? Meno, no doubt still thinking of *aischra* rather than of *kaka,* declares that some people (presumably, those without "class") desire to possess bad things (by which he means vulgar or crass or base things), thinking they are beneficial: what harm is there in crab cakes? As long as Meno has not yet, in his own mind, made the transition from the pair fine/crass to the pair good/bad, he sees no absurdity in the claim that some people desire to possess bad things thinking they are beneficial. But Socrates forces the point: if someone thinks bad things are beneficial, must he not fail to recognize that they are bad? In other words, whereas it is possible to say about *aischra* that they are beneficial, it is not possible to say that about *kaka:* no one who understands what "bad things" means can think that bad things are beneficial. Once Socrates gets Meno to see that if a thing is thought bad, it cannot, then, be thought beneficial, Meno must concede that those who desire to possess bad things thinking they are beneficial do not think the things they desire are bad: insofar as they think these things beneficial they think them good,[17] and whereas they may desire things that are in fact bad, they desire them—since they are ignorant of these things' badness—as good. Hence, those who desire bad things thinking they are beneficial actually desire (to possess) good things.

Socrates is determined to banish in urging the replacement of *kala* with *agatha* is the "moral flavor" (Guthrie's phrase) of *kala;* for it is difficult to see, on the one hand, what Socrates stands to gain by substituting a nonmoral term for a moral one or, on the other, what investment Meno has in the moral one. It is far more plausible to maintain that Socrates wishes to suppress that nuance of *kalon* that is important to Meno, the one that gives it snob appeal. As Sharples (1985, 138) says: "the contrast Meno has in mind is that between those who have the correct, splendid ambitions for themselves and those who lack, as it were, proper aristocratic taste in matters of behaviour."

17. As we saw in chapter 3, good (*agathon*) and beneficial (*ōphelimon*) go together.

Thus far Socrates has considered but the first of two sets of people identified by Meno as desiring bad things: those who believe that the bad things they desire are beneficial. And what he has shown with respect to this set is that they do not desire bad things after all: although the things they desire may be in fact bad, they desire (to possess) good things. The second set of people who desire bad things consists, according to Meno, of those who desire bad things recognizing them as harmful. Socrates contends—and Meno agrees—that there is no one who wants (*bouletai*) to be harmed because there is no one who wants (*bouletai*) to be wretched and unfortunate. Since bad things harm their possessor, there can be no one who wants (*bouletai*) bad things. Socrates concludes, therefore, that those who desire bad things thinking them harmful actually do not want (since no one wants) bad things.

If we attend carefully (as Meno does not) to this Socratic argument, we note that, although Socrates denies that anyone can *want* (*boulesthai*) bad things, he does not deny that someone can desire (*epithumein*) them. One *can*, then, as far as Socrates is concerned, desire bad things, even recognizing them as bad; what one cannot do is *want* them. Desire, brute appetitive craving (*epithumein*), for bad things is able to persist even in the face of one's recognition that the objects of one's desire can cause one harm; desire can remain unaffected by judgment. It is only wanting, *boulesthai,* whose objects are restricted to things one judges to be good or beneficial.[18] Since Socrates allows in the *Meno* that an agent might *desire* (and pursue) bad things even while judging them harmful, he ought not be charged, as he so often is, with overintellectualizing human choice, of making it always a function of one's rational determination of one's own good.[19]

---

18. We note that *epithumein* as used in our passage is broad enough to take as its objects both things judged beneficial and those judged harmful. In the first part of the argument, the part that concerns those who desire bad things thinking them good, its objects are things judged beneficial. In the second part, the part that concerns those who desire bad things thinking them bad, its objects are things judged harmful. *Boulesthai*'s objects in this argument, however, are exclusively things judged beneficial.

19. Devereux (1995, 398–403) recognizes that Socrates not only intends to distinguish in this passage between what people want and what they desire but holds, too, that people can desire things they believe are bad and harmful to them. Devereux is not, however, prepared to say that Socrates acknowledges in the *Meno* the possibility of *akrasia*. He attributes to Socrates the view that strong desires cloud people's judgment temporarily, so that when they choose things they themselves think are bad, they still believe them at the moment of decision to be good. The *Meno* text, however, in no way supports this reading.

There is considerable scholarly disagreement concerning how careful Socrates is to preserve fine distinctions between terms close in meaning—in this case, between *epithumein* and *boulesthai*. In the *Protagoras,* Socrates derides Prodicus for being obsessively fond of fine distinctions, making reference at *Prot.* 340a8–b1 specifically to his distinction between *epithumein* and *boulesthai*. And in the *Lysis,* Socrates unmistakably uses *boulēsis* indistinguishably from *epithumia*. He says of Lysis's parents, who love their son, that they surely would want (*boulointo* [*Lys.* 207d7]) or desire (*epithumoi* [*Lys.* 207e2]) that he be happy, and therefore would presumably allow him to do whatever he wants (*ha boulei* [*Lys.* 207e6]) or whatever he desires (*hōn an epithumēis* [*Lys.* 207e7]).[20] Yet in the *Charmides,* at 167e4–5, Socrates appears to distinguish sharply between the two terms, saying fairly explicitly that the objects of *epithumein* are pleasures but the objects of *boulesthai,* goods. The truth of the matter, though perhaps it is an unsettling truth, is that Socrates is at times careless and at times fastidious about such distinctions. It depends on what the situation calls for.[21] In our *Meno* passage, it is clear that Socrates recognizes a distinction between *epithumein* and *boulesthai:*[22] he shifts quite deliberately from *epithumein* to *boulesthai* in order to make the claim that no people want what they recognize as harmful, a claim that would hardly be plausible if it spoke instead of what people *desire*. And although it may seem paradoxical to say that one may desire but cannot want what one judges to be bad in the sense of harmful, it is actually a point well taken: despite one's recognition that certain things are harmful, one may still be drawn to those things; yet, insofar as no one wants to suffer and be wretched, there is one sense in which no one really "wants" the bad things that one finds oneself powerfully attracted to or craving. To be wretched, then, Socrates concludes (in a "playful inversion"

20. Also see *Rep.* 4.445b2, where *boulesthai* is used broadly to encompass doing whatever one wants, and specifically those things that will *not* rid one of vice and injustice; and *Rep.* 7.520a3, where the law is said to produce philosophers "not in order to let them turn in whatever way each wants (*bouletai*)." See chapter 6 for other examples of this less restrictive use of *boulesthai* in the *Republic.*

21. Such inconsistency in the dialogues is not unusual. As we saw in chapter 3, flute-playing, which quite frequently serves as a paradigmatic case of *technē,* is relegated in the *Gorgias* (at 501e) to a knack, an *empeiria,* something that aims at gratification rather than at some genuine good. For further discussion of *epithumein/boulesthai,* see McTighe 1984, 198 and n17, 215, 216, n53; and the discussion in chapter 6.

22. Among those who think that *epithumia* and *boulēsis* are used interchangeably at *Meno* 77–78 are Gosling (1973, 236), and Irwin (1979, 141–42).

of Meno's definition of virtue),[23] is to desire, *epithumein,* bad things (which, as has been argued, remains possible), and to get them. The desire is itself an important source of wretchedness because it is desire that impels one to pursue even things that one recognizes as being bad for oneself.

Meno, of course, fails to notice the shift from *epithumein* to *boulesthai.* He thinks, therefore, that by agreeing that "no one wants bad things" (78b1–2), he has in effect admitted defeat: "You probably speak truly, Socrates" (78a8–b1). Once it becomes clear that Meno has missed the distinction between "desire" and "want," Socrates can, without fear of detection, replace the "desire" in Meno's original definition with "want"—just as he earlier replaced "fine things" (*kala*) with "good things" (*agatha*)—so that Meno's definition now reads: "Virtue is to *want good things* and to have the power to get them" (78b3–4). Since, however, it has been shown that everyone wants good things—those who desire bad things thinking them beneficial desire good things, for they do not know that bad things are bad if they think them beneficial; and those who *desire* bad things thinking them harmful nevertheless do not *want* them, since no one wishes to be harmed, wretched, and unfortunate—it follows that no person can be said to be superior to others with respect to his wants. Yet, since Socrates does not make the claim that all men *desire* good things, things they judge to be good or beneficial, the possibility remains open that men might be distinguished from one another in terms of their respective desires, that is, in terms of the kinds of things that attract them and in terms of how able they are to resist the harmful things that attract them. The *Meno* strongly suggests that a man's desires can mark him as more wretched than his fellow; for the wretched are identified as being not only those who get (things they regard as) bad things but also as those who desire them. Thus, even if with respect to their wants all men are equal, it need not be so with respect to their desires.

It is noteworthy that Socrates does not argue here, as one would perhaps expect him to, that what sets the virtuous apart is that they know what is worthy of pursuit and so pursue what is *in fact* good. Since Socrates' urgent concern here is to eliminate or at least greatly to reduce Meno's groundless sense of his own superiority, what is important is that he prevent Meno from seeing in what men want the distinguishing mark of virtue: with respect to what they want, he argues, all men are the same.

23. Sharples 1985, 139. Cf. Nakhnikian (1973, 5), who argues (too heavy-handedly) that there is a logical flaw here.

At the same time, however, that Socrates levels all people with respect to their wants, he implies something that is strikingly at odds with the view that is usually attributed to him, namely, the view that all people act on their wants, that is, on their assessment of what is best for them. Sharples (1985, 139) lodges the typical charge: "However, Socrates might justly be criticised, here as in the *Protagoras* (356ab), for simply assuming that human behaviour is too rational; it may be illogical to want something while knowing that it is bad for oneself, but that it is illogical does not mean it cannot happen." What is true of the *Protagoras*, however, is hardly true of the *Meno*. For whereas it is true that the *Protagoras* portrays men as rational calculators of pleasure and pain who will always choose the most pleasure and the least pain, in the *Meno* people are portrayed as desiring and choosing the bad things that they do not want, things that they fully expect will harm them. These wretched people display the classic symptoms of incontinent and irrational action: despite not wanting the things they judge to be bad (after all, no one does), they nevertheless do desire them and act, on that desire, to acquire them.[24] The case of cigarette smoking, which is so frequently invoked to discredit the Socratic denial of incontinence,[25] in fact fits perfectly the model of wretchedness as set forth in the *Meno*. It could certainly be said, on the *Meno*'s model, that a person is wretched if he (1) recognizes smoking's harmful effects, (2) does not want to be harmed, (3) does not, therefore, want to smoke, but nevertheless (4) desires to smoke, and (5) consequently smokes. Of these five features of the wretched person, none but (3) sounds at all odd. And if (3) does sound a bit odd it is only because while *epithumein* is permitted to take as objects the vast array of things to which people are drawn, the objects of *boulesthai*, here taken in its restrictive technical sense, can only be things judged beneficial.[26]

Let us turn now, as Socrates does, to the second element in Meno's definition, namely, the power to get what one wants. If virtue, as has been shown,

24. One might even say that if no one wants to be wretched, and if being wretched is desiring bad things and acquiring them, it follows then that no one wants to desire bad things and acquire them.

25. See, for example, Nakhnikian 1973, 10.

26. Since Aristotle has occasion to distinguish *boulesthai* from *epithumein* in much the same way as Socrates does in our *Meno* passage, he, too, says (*EN* ix.4.1166b): "For such persons [the inferior, *phauloi*] are at variance with themselves, desiring (*epithumousin*) things other than what they want (*boulontai*). These are the incontinent (*akrateis*). They choose (*hairontai*) instead of what they themselves think is good the pleasant but harmful."

cannot be found in men's wants, might it be found in their power to get what they want? (It is likely that Gorgias taught Meno or at least reinforced for him the importance of power; see *Gorg.* 452d). And, if so, what are the good things that men want? Socrates proposes as the likely candidates for "good things" such things as health and wealth (78c6–7). Meno says, however, that what he calls good things is the acquiring both of gold and silver and of political honors and offices; indeed, the good things are all and only such things as these (78d1).[27] What is Socrates to think but that these things—gold, silver, political honors and offices—are the *kala,* the finer things, that Meno had in mind earlier when he defined virtue as desiring fine things? Indeed, what else is Socrates to think but that it is on account of his desire for such things that Meno thinks himself superior to the common run of men? We may note the derisive sarcasm in Socrates' proclamation: "Well, so procuring gold and silver is virtue, as Meno, the hereditary guest friend of the great king of Persia, says" (78d1–3).[28] Has it come to this?

The struggle between Meno and Socrates over the definition of virtue now resumes, with Meno and Socrates assuming once again the now familiar stances they had assumed at the dialogue's beginning. Meno sees virtue as a type of activity; Socrates thinks virtue is a matter of how activities are done. Is it, Socrates asks, the acquisition itself of gold and silver that is virtue, or does it matter whether the acquisition is accomplished justly and piously? Meno, not one to spurn conventional virtue outright, concedes to Socrates that it does matter, that if the acquisition is accomplished unjustly, it ceases to be virtue and becomes badness (*kakia* [78d7]). But Socrates goes further—

27. Meno does not actually say whether he agrees that health is a good thing. Speaking for himself (*legō* [78c6]), he says that the good things are the acquisition of gold, silver, and political office. Might health be too commonplace a good, such that one's wanting it does not strike Meno as a mark of distinction? Perhaps Meno thinks that, whereas undistinguished men do want health, they do not aspire to such *kala* as wealth and political office. Recall that in the *Hippias Major,* Hippias defines the beautiful, *to kalon,* as nothing other than gold (*HMa.* 289a 4).

28. Whereas Meno brushes past health as a "good thing" but adds political honor and rule (see note 27), Socrates ignores political honor and rule, leaving only the acquisition of gold and silver as what constitutes *aretē* for Meno. Why does Socrates drop political honor and rule? One possibility is that the definition of virtue as ruling others has already been discounted. A second possibility is that the pun on *aporia* (which means both nonacquisition and poverty [71e6]) works best when the nonacquisition that is virtue is the nonacquisition of gold and silver. Yet a third possibility might be that the emphasis on the acquisition of gold and silver makes Meno look foolish in insisting that virtuous men, men of distinction, desire *kala.*

much further. He secures Meno's endorsement not only of the idea that if an act of acquisition is performed without justice, temperance, and piety it cannot be virtue, but of the far more radical notion that, on those occasions when acquisition cannot be accomplished without injustice, then nonacquisition (or poverty), *aporia,* is virtue (78e6).[29] This concession on Meno's part represents Socrates' crowning achievement. He has moved Meno from associating virtue with political rule and wealth to the recognition that under certain circumstances it is the forgoing of wealth that will count as virtue. He has moved Meno from locating virtue in what one does to locating it in how one does *whatever* one does: "So, the acquisition of good things will no more be virtue than their nonacquisition, but, as it seems, *whatever* comes to be with justice is virtue and whatever comes to be without all such things is badness (*kakia*)" (78e6–79a1).[30] And he has moved virtue itself closer to the particular virtues of justice, temperance, and piety that are its parts. Rather than see these virtues as potential obstacles to the attainment of virtue as political dominance and wealth, Meno now sees them as the sine qua non of *aretē:* he says—even if he does not quite believe—that there can be no *aretē* in the *absence* of

---

29. Bluck (1961, 263) notes the word-play on *aporia*. Although in this context *aporia* means nonacquisition, an alpha-privative having been annexed to *poros,* acquisition, *aporia* also means poverty. Amazingly, then, what Socrates gets Meno to admit is that poverty can be virtue. Sharples (1985, 140) points out that besides these two meanings of *aporia,* namely, nonacquisition and poverty, there is yet a third, perplexity, which is just what Meno is about to be reduced to.

Wealth and poverty are an important theme in the *Meno* from its inception: the Thessalians who were renowned for horsemanship and wealth are also now reputed to be wise, wisdom (in the person of Gorgias) having departed from Athens to Thessaly; the Athenians, including Socrates, are, therefore, in dire poverty with respect to knowledge of virtue; there is also the matter of Meno's wealth and his desire to be richer; in addition, Socrates describes himself as being *aporōn,* without means, as opposed to *euporōn,* well-supplied or rich, with respect to being able to answer the questions he asks (80c–d). Also discussed in the dialogue (at 90a) is the wealth of Anthemion, Anytus's father.

30. See Adkins 1960, 228–29: Meno "is prepared to admit that justice and self-restraint are necessary to this desired end [of running his city and having his house run well, in the sense of efficiently], and hence that those qualities are desirable in a derivative sense . . . but . . . there is no doubt in Meno's mind which is the end and which is the means." In light of Adkins' insight, let us take due measure of Socrates' extraordinary accomplishment at 78c4–79a2: Socrates gets Meno to be less sure about which is the end and which is the means. See also Bluck 1961, 202: "Plato (and his Socrates) sought to attach the co-operative, 'quiet' virtues to the concept of *aretē* inseparably—to combine the two sets of values. But the Meno of our dialogue holds the usual view of *aretē* as practical efficiency in public and private life." It is precisely this usual view from which Socrates is able to wrench him, at least for the moment.

the *aretai*. Socrates can only be delighted that Meno has now defined virtue in terms of its parts.[31] For once Meno acknowledges that it is specifically the cooperative virtues of justice, temperance, and piety that are the necessary conditions for virtue, he is constrained to regard virtue as something that is, in the final analysis, not the province of the elite but something accessible to all.

We may note that the *Meno* passage, 78b3–79a2, with which we have just dealt, actually tends to undermine rather than to support the stock characterization of Socrates as either a psychological or an ethical egoist.[32] (A psychological egoist affirms that it is psychologically impossible for one to act in opposition to what one determines to be in one's own self-interest; an ethical egoist affirms that one *ought* to pursue, that it is morally right to pursue, only what one determines to be in one's own self-interest.) For in this passage Meno is helped to see that the acquisition of good things, that is, of things one judges to be good for oneself, is not virtue—that, indeed, on those occasions when acquisition of good things requires that one act unjustly, intemperately, or impiously, then it is the nonacquisition of good things rather than their acquisition that is virtue. To generalize: according to this passage, if one judges *x* to be good for oneself, that is, to be beneficial and happiness-producing for oneself, but one recognizes that *x* cannot be attained without injustice, intemperance, or impiety, then, if one is virtuous, one will forgo *x*, choosing just, temperate, or pious conduct over the acquisition of *x*. This passage implies both that one *can*, psychologically speaking, make choices that oppose one's determination that *x* is good/best for one, and that, on occasion, one *ought*, morally speaking, to make such choices. There is, let us note, no trace

---

31. Of course, it is not Meno but Socrates who includes justice, temperance, and piety in the definition of virtue. It is Socrates who does not permit *aretē* to be defined without reference to its "parts." Meno's own definitions make no mention of the *aretai*; he defines *aretē*, as it were, amorally. It comes, then, as something of a surprise that Socrates vigorously objects to the final definition of virtue: has he not been working from the very start toward a definition of virtue in terms of its parts, temperance and justice? One possible explanation for Socrates' objection is that the new definition fails to recognize the special relationship between *aretē* and its parts. For the *aretai* are not "parts" of *aretē* in quite the same way as, say, the "parts" of shape are its parts: a single shaped thing is not round, square, oval, and oblong, but every good man is just, temperate, pious, wise, and courageous.

32. There are many reasons to think that Socrates is not an egoist of either kind: see chapter 1. Kahn (1983, 11, n48) is one scholar who disputes the prevalent view that Socrates is an ethical egoist: "self interest can be used to justify or motivate, but not to define, the pursuit of what is good."

or hint in our passage of the idea that justice, temperance, and piety are in one's best interest. On the contrary, this passage recognizes that virtuous people are prepared to relinquish the things they regard as profitable whenever there is no just way to attain them. They can do so; they ought to do so; and this is what they do in fact do.[33]

Socrates takes in the *Meno*, then, a position diametrically opposed to the one he appears to endorse in the *Protagoras*. For in the *Protagoras* it is agreed that there is nothing good, nothing noble, other than pleasure. Under this condition, how indeed could one choose what is right over what one thinks most advantageous or most pleasant; how, that is, could one be virtuous? The superior skill at calculation that passes for virtue in the *Protagoras* is replaced in the *Meno* by the only real virtue, the kind that reflects strength of character.

The *Meno* also opposes the *Protagoras*'s stance regarding those who choose what is bad. From the point of view of the *Protagoras*, since everyone desires— and wants—what is most pleasant, the wretched are those who miscalculate. The *Meno* repudiates such foolishness. Through its distinction between *epithumein* and *boulesthai* it keeps all men the same with respect to what they want without absurdly making them all the same with respect to their desires. In the *Meno*, the wretched are those who desire what they themselves recognize as harmful.

At *Meno* 77b–79a, then, Socrates sees two ways in which a person might act in opposition to what he wants, that is, in opposition to his judgment of what is most advantageous to himself. A person might, on the one hand, yield to his desires for bad things even in the face of his recognition that they are bad for him (such a person is wretched: he desires bad things and gets them); or a person might, on the other hand, neglect the course that he regards as serving his interests for the sake of justice, temperance, and piety, that is, for the sake of the noble and right. At either end of the spectrum, then, whether to satisfy what is most base in oneself or what is most noble, one may act against what one determines is to one's advantage. In both cases, of course, one indeed chooses something that appeals to one—to one's appetites in the one case, to one's dignity in the other; otherwise, one would not choose it. But in neither case does one simply and automatically and necessarily choose what one

---

33. Socrates is not unaware of the difficulties of living justly, especially for those who have the freedom to do wrong with impunity. See *Gorg.* 526b, where he praises those among the powerful, like Aristides, who choose to live justly though they could easily live unjustly.

judges to be in one's best interest: in the first case, one does instead what one "desires"; in the second, one chooses instead what is just, temperate, or pious.

In the *Meno* Socrates makes the case that needs to be made against Meno. In order to undercut Meno's elitism Socrates elicits Meno's assent to the proposition that all people want the same things, that is, the things they think are beneficial. Socrates need not argue against Meno, as he does against Polus in the *Gorgias,* that unless people get what is truly in their interest they have not done what they want. Polus, whose deepest admiration is reserved for tyrants who ruthlessly pursue their own ends, has to be shown that no matter what they achieve, tyrants, insofar as they mistake their true advantage, do not do what they want. As for Meno, who is no champion of injustice despite his fondness for gold, silver, and power, and whose main flaw lies in his aristocratic sense of superiority, what he needs to be shown is only that all people want the same thing. But in neither the *Gorgias* nor the *Meno* is there any suggestion that all men of necessity pursue their advantage as they see it, so that those who do injustice in order to advance their interest could not have done otherwise. On the contrary, Socrates teaches Polus that *when* men pursue their advantage as they see it, but lack the intelligence to discern correctly wherein their true advantage lies, they fail to do what they want. And Socrates teaches Meno that what makes some people different from, and superior to, others is not the wealth and power they amass, and certainly not their wish to acquire such things, but their ability to forgo wealth and power when these cannot be obtained without resorting to injustice and intemperance. Virtue, then, is not the province of powerful men. All people can be virtuous simply by being just and temperate. Whereas justice and temperance promise no other rewards—not money, fame, or power—they do absolutely guarantee virtue. As shape is the only thing that is always present where there is color, so virtue is the only thing that is always present wherever justice and temperance are found.

6

REPUBLIC 4:
"EVERYONE DESIRES
GOOD THINGS"

Republic 4, unlike the dialogues we have considered thus far and unlike *Laws* 9, which we shall consider next, does not contain the "no one does wrong willingly" paradox. Nevertheless, since it is widely believed that this text confirms a particular conception of Socratic moral psychology frequently associated with the paradox—a conception to which the present work takes exception—a careful and fresh evaluation of it is needed.

According to what has become a fairly common reading of *Rep.* 4,[1] it marks the precise place at which Plato departs from the Socrates of earlier dialogues regarding the psychology of choice or how a person chooses from among the various alternatives open to him.[2] On this reading—I shall refer to it as "the standard view"—what the early Socrates believes is that in the final analysis a man cannot but choose in accordance with his rational assessment of what is best. Relying heavily on *Prot.* 358c–d, where Socrates says that human nature

1. Proponents of this view include Irwin (1995, 209); Reeve (1992, 113, n9, and 1988), 134–35); Brickhouse and Smith (1994, 90, n25 and 98, n35); Parry (1996, 93–94); Penner (1992, 129); Vlastos (1988, 99, 105); C. C. W. Taylor (1991, 203); Davidson (1980, 35); Watson (1977, 320).

2. Many scholars unflinchingly identify the Socrates of the *Republic* with Plato and the Socrates of the "early" dialogues with Socrates. See, e.g., Reeve (1992, x); Klosko (1986, 70); Pohlenz (1913, 156–57); Walsh (1963, chap. 11); Cooper (1984, 31); Shields (2001, 137–39); Bobonich (1994, 3).

does not permit a man to choose an option that he knows or believes to be worse than another, the standard view ascribes to Socrates an "intellectualism" that precludes the possibility that a person might act on his emotions and appetites rather than on his reasoned judgment. *Akrasia* is denied. But, the standard view maintains, all this changes in *Rep.* 4, where Plato introduces into the soul three parts or powers. Here, presumably, intellectualism ends as *akrasia* is affirmed. In Book 4 of the *Republic* the reasoning part or element of the soul (the *logistikon*) is said to override at times the clamorings of appetite and emotion—this is what happens for the most part in a man who has a healthy and ordered soul—but at other times appetite (the *epithumētikon*) or the spirited or emotional part (the *thumoeides*) prevails. On this conception of human choice, it is indeed possible for someone to believe that alternative *x* is better for him than alternative *y,* yet choose alternative *y* because his desire for food, drink, or sex, or the craving for prestige or power, or the feeling of fear or hope overcomes his reason, his deliberation, his calculation.[3]

It is not just on the new division of the soul into three parts, however, that the standard view relies. It draws support, too, from the following passage in the text, *Rep.* 4.438a:

> Now let no one catch us unprepared, I said, and cause a disturbance, alleging that no one desires drink, but good (*chrēston*) drink, nor food, but good (*chrēston*) food; for everyone, after all, desires good things (*tōn agathōn*). If, then, thirst is a desire, it would be for good (*chrēston*) drink or for good whatever it is, and similarly with the other desires.[4]

According to the standard view, when Socrates in this passage alerts Glaucon to an irksome objector who might try to confuse them, he is referring to himself, or to an earlier version of himself, that is, to the Socrates of the *Protagoras, Gorgias,* and *Meno.*[5] It is this Socrates who, it is believed, thinks every-

3. Ironically, the view expressed by Socrates in the *Republic,* a view that many scholars regard as a great advance in moral psychology over the primitive intellectualism of the "early" Socrates (see, e.g., Grube 1958, 131; Cooper 1984, 31) is not substantially different from the view Socrates attributes to the many in the *Protagoras.*

4. Translations of passages in the *Republic* are taken from Bloom 1968, and are occasionally modified slightly.

5. See, e.g., Penner 1971, 96; Vlastos 1991, 86 n22; Siewert 2001, 338; Murphy 1951, 28–29; Penner 1992, 129; Irwin 1995, 206; Shields 2001, 138–39, with reservations.

one desires that which he regards as good, or best, for himself. Thus, according to the standard view, what Socrates cautions his new self and Glaucon to be on guard against is a view that he had formerly held but now regards as illegitimate despite its superficial plausibility. His current view is that thirst is desire for drink rather than for drink believed to be good.

This chapter challenges the standard view. It considers, first, what it is that Socrates finds unacceptable in the hypothetical objector's objection; second, whether the so-called early Socrates qualifies as the putative objector with whom Socrates now finds fault; and third, whether and in what sense Socrates holds in the *Protagoras, Gorgias,* and *Meno,* dialogues commonly presumed to be earlier than the *Republic,* that all men desire good things.

The Objection

According to the standard view, Socrates maintains in *Rep.* 4, contrary to what he had maintained in earlier dialogues, that thirsty people desire drink but not necessarily good drink. Moreover, the standard view asserts, Socrates now, in order to hold this new view, disavows his own earlier view that everyone desires good things.

Three considerations, however, tell against the idea that Socrates means to discredit in *Rep.* 4 the view that everyone desires good things. First, he neither challenges it nor devotes any effort to disproving it. The notion to which he does take exception and that he does work to discredit is a different one, namely, "no one desires drink, but only good drink, or food, but only good food."

Second, one might think, along with the standard view, that if Socrates rejects the conclusion that thirst is for good drink, hunger for good food, then he must similarly reject the notion from which this conclusion derives, namely, that everyone desires good things. But there is another alternative. For the notion that thirst is for drink simpliciter—and not necessarily for good drink—might be compatible with the notion that everyone desires good things. Socrates might believe *both* that everyone desires good things and that thirst is for drink simpliciter and not for good drink.

There is in fact a rather conspicuous textual indication that Socrates sees no incompatibility between the proposition that everyone desires good things and the proposition that thirst is for drink simpliciter rather than specifically for good drink. Within the syllogism (1) everyone desires good things;

(2) thirst is a form of desire; hence (3) thirst is for good drink (rather than for drink simpliciter), the Greek term used for "good" changes. In premiss (1), good things are *agatha*. In the conclusion, however, good drink is not *poton* (or *pōma*) *agathon* but *poton chrēston*.[6] The distinction between *agathon* and *chrēston* is lost in the translation of both as "good," but the shift in terms is significant.[7] For things can be appealing or attractive in themselves, and hence be good things, *agatha,* regardless of whether they are also beneficial, and hence *chrēsta*. If thirst is for drink alone, drink alone is the good thing (*agathon*) that is its object. When the soul that desires food or drink nods assent to itself on seeing its desired object (437b), it sees that food or drink as a good thing, that is, as something desirable, but not necessarily as something good *for* itself, that is, as something beneficial. In other words, what Socrates finds objectionable in the hypothetical objection is not its insistence that everyone desires *agatha,* but its assumption that *if* everyone desires *agatha,* then everyone desires *chrēsta.*

We have thus far noted two reasons for thinking that it is not the proposition "everyone desires good things (*agatha*)" to which Socrates objects, but rather the inference from the proposition "everyone desires good things" to the conclusion that thirst or hunger is for beneficial drink or food. The first was that Socrates expends no effort at all on discrediting "everyone desires good things"; the proposition he attacks is "thirst is for beneficial drink." The second is that the shift from *agathon* in premiss (1) to *chrēston* in the conclusion suggests that what Socrates finds problematic is not premiss (1) but rather the illegitimate transition from that premiss to the conclusion.

There is, however, yet a third reason to think that what Socrates finds objectionable is not "everyone desires good things" but rather the inference from that proposition to the conclusion that "thirst is for beneficial drink." In the related passage that immediately precedes the one currently under discussion,[8] Socrates

---

6. See *Gorg.* 499e3–4, where it is *chrēstai* pleasures that are *to be* chosen and done.

7. Allen (1991) renders *chrēston* "wholesome," as does Cornford (1945). Cf. *Rep.* 1.334b d, where Socrates subtly, but deliberately, shifts from *chrēstoi* to *agathoi* in order to facilitate the transition from "friends" (who are *chrēstoi* to oneself) to "just men" (who are simply *agathoi*). Only in this way is he able to transform Polemarchus's definition of justice—"helping friends and harming enemies"—into "harming the just and helping the unjust" (in the case where one is mistaken regarding who are actually friends and enemies).

8. The earlier passage establishes that the soul has parts that make intelligible the conflicts it experiences. It thus lays the foundation for the claim in our passage that while one part of the soul thirsts for drink simpliciter, another protests if the drink in question is harmful.

also imagines a possible objector to watch out for, and in that instance there can be no doubt that it is not the objector's premiss that Socrates rejects but the conclusion that the hypothetical objector derives from it. The structure of the earlier passage parallels precisely the structure of our own. In both passages Socrates begins with a declaration of his own view (436b, corresponding to 437d–e). He then goes on to warn about a hypothetical objector (436c–d, corresponding to 438a). Next he explains why the objector's conclusion is incorrect (436c–e, corresponding to 438a–439a). And finally Socrates reaffirms the position with which he began (436e–437a, corresponding to 439a–b).

Let us look at the earlier passage. Socrates begins by announcing his position (436b):

> It is plain that the same thing will not be willing at the same time to do or to suffer opposites with respect to the same part and in relation to the same thing. So if we should ever find that happening in these things, we will know that they were not the same but many.

After Socrates states his view, he warns that someone might object that if a man stands in one place and also moves his arms and his head, does he not stand and move at the same time? Or if a top spins and at the same time stays in one place, is not the top simultaneously both at rest and in motion?

Socrates immediately responds to the imagined objector by showing him the error in his thinking. Socrates readily admits that a man can stand in one place and move his arms and head, and that a top can spin yet remain in place. What he is not prepared to concede is that this state of affairs entails that a man or a top can do two opposite things at the same time *with respect to the same part of himself or itself.* He accepts the objector's premiss but rejects his conclusion. And so Socrates concludes (436e–437a):

> Then the saying of such things will not scare us, or any the more persuade us, that something that is the same, at the same time, with respect to the same part and in relation to the same thing, could ever suffer, be, or do opposites.

If we turn now to our passage, we see precisely the same progression as we have just seen concerning the earlier one. At 437d–e, Socrates states his position:

Insofar as it is thirst, would it be a desire in the soul for something more than that of which we say it is a desire? For example, is thirst thirst for hot drink or cold, or much or little, or, in a word, for any particular kind of drink? Or is it not rather that in the case where heat is present in addition to the thirst, the heat would cause the desire to be also for something cold as well; and where coldness, something hot; and where the thirst is much on account of the presence of muchness, it will cause the desire to be for much, and where it is little, for little? But, thirsting itself will never be a desire for anything other than that of which it naturally is a desire—for drink alone—and, similarly, hungering will be a desire for food?

Socrates immediately goes on to express the objection of the putative objector who takes exception to the principle Socrates just established. The objector objects that since everyone desires good things, must not thirst, which is a desire, be for beneficial drink?

If the course of this passage duplicates that of the earlier one, we may presume that what Socrates means to say to the objector in our passage parallels what he says to the objector in the earlier one—namely, that though his premiss is true in some sense, his conclusion does not follow from it. In our case, what Socrates would be saying is that even if it is true that everyone desires good things, it still does not follow that thirst, which is a desire, is for *beneficial* drink. In the earlier passage there was no doubt about the veracity of the premiss that a man can stand still but move his arms and head, yet that premiss was insufficient to discredit the principle that a thing cannot do two opposite things at the same time with respect to the same part of itself. Here, too, the premiss that everyone desires good things (*agatha*) is certainly true, but this true premiss is insufficient to discredit the principle that thirst and hunger are for drink and food simpliciter, rather than for beneficial drink or food.

Indeed, just as Socrates in the earlier passage had returned to restate his original position, so, too, does Socrates here reaffirm the position with which he began (439a–b):

So a particular sort of thirst is for a particular kind of drink, but thirst itself is neither for much nor little, good nor bad, nor, in a word, for any particular kind, but thirst itself is naturally only for drink. . . . Therefore, the soul of the man who is thirsty, insofar as it thirsts, wants nothing other than to drink, and strives for this and is impelled toward it.[9]

It has been argued up to this point that Socrates finds objectionable the derivation of the conclusion that thirst is for beneficial drink from the premiss that desire always takes good things as its object. The premiss itself, however, I have argued, is not one Socrates rejects: he says nothing derogatory about it at all; he shifts from *agathon* to *chrēston,* showing thereby that the fault lies in the transition from premiss to conclusion rather than in the premiss itself; and just as Socrates in the passage that directly precedes this one does not reject the hypothetical objector's premiss but only takes exception to the objector's misguided and brazen supposition that his premiss necessitates the negation of Socrates' principle, so, too, here.

Why does Socrates accept the premiss of the objector in the first passage? He accepts it because it is simply and obviously true that a man who is standing still can move his feet and head; it is simply and obviously true that a top that is in one place can spin at the same time. But not much of import follows from these simple facts. What Socrates sees and shows is that this phenomenon has no bearing on the principle that he established, that this phenomenon poses no threat to it. Even though a man who is standing still can move his limbs and head, and even though a stationary top can spin, nevertheless one thing cannot do two opposite things with the same part of itself at the same time, from the same perspective, and with respect to the same thing.

Why does Socrates accept the premiss of the objector in our passage? Because it, too, is simply and obviously true: everyone does desire good things—when, at any rate, anything that attracts or appeals in any way counts as a "good thing." To say, then, that everyone desires good things is to say little more than that it is not possible to desire something that in no way appeals but, on the contrary, either repels or has no effect at all.[10] But this trivial

---

9. Even if thirst pure and simple is, logically speaking, for drink pure and simple, there may very well not be an actual thirst that is not qualified in some way. Socrates compares thirst to knowledge, saying of knowledge that it itself is of the knowable or learnable, though any particular kind of knowledge is of a particular kind of knowable or learnable thing (438c). It is unclear whether there can be such a thing as unqualified knowledge, knowledge that is of no particular kind because it is of no particular subject, or whether it is simply a logical point that knowledge simpliciter is for the knowable simpliciter.

10. As in *Gorg.* 466–468, where the only things that cannot be desired in themselves are bad and intermediate things, that is, things that exert no attraction.

truth, like the truth in the previous passage that a man who stands in one place can move his arms and head, poses no danger to Socrates' principle. Even if it is impossible for someone to desire something that does not appeal, it does not follow that just plain thirst is for anything but just plain drink: to a man who is just plain thirsty just plain drink appeals. Nor does it follow that just plain thirst is for beneficial drink, that is, for drink that the agent determines to be something that is useful and profitable for him: the desire for beneficial drink is a specific kind of desire, like the desire for cold drink or much drink.

Is Socrates the Objector?

Because those who endorse the standard view think that Socrates now regards as false the premiss of the objection, they do not regard that premiss as trivial but rather take it to make a controversial claim. Since they fail to distinguish between *agathon* and *chrēston*, reading *agathon* as *chrēston*, they take the claim that everyone desires good things to mean that everyone desires beneficial things. And since they believe that the Socrates who appears in the dialogues that Plato wrote before the *Republic* in fact endorses the premiss in its controversial sense, they believe, too, that it is Socrates who, having come to recognize in the *Republic* that he was previously mistaken, is the perspicacious objector to it.

Generally speaking, however, on those occasions when Socrates introduces an objector into a discussion, the objector is not Socrates himself.[11] Indeed, the objector in the passage immediately preceding our own, *Rep.* 4.436–437, is quite evidently not Socrates himself. Since the parallels between the two passages are, as we have seen, quite striking, it is hardly credible that the objector in the first passage would not be Socrates himself but the objector in the second passage would be.

But if the objector is not Socrates, why does Socrates introduce him into the discussion? At least three reasons suggest themselves. First, there are many people who do indeed think that food, drink, sex, and so forth are the "good things"—and not in the trivial sense of "good" as attractive that we previously stipulated, but in the more significant sense of beneficial and good *for* one.

---

11. See *Ap.* 20c4–d1, 28b3–5; *Crito* 48a10–b2; and *Prot.* 356a, 361a. There are many other examples that could be cited.

(Callicles holds such a view in the *Gorgias*.) By flagging the point, Socrates seizes the opportunity to dispute it: the food desired by a hungry man need not be thought beneficial.

Second, if all desiring involves the assessment that something is good in the sense of being beneficial and useful, then reason loses its distinctive role. What Socrates wants to make understood in *Rep.* 4 is that attraction is hardly the same as, and is often at odds with, calculation of benefit and harm. The objector's syllogism is unsuccessful because it confuses desire with considered judgment.

Third—and most important—it is likely that the objector is not just anyone but is actually Glaucon, Socrates' interlocutor. Indeed, Glaucon responds approvingly when presented with the objection: "Perhaps," he says, "the man who says that would seem to make sense" (*Isōs gar an . . . dokoi ti legein ho tauta legōn* [*Rep.* 4.438a6]).[12] Glaucon's response is reminiscent of Crito's when Crito finds himself in a similar situation in the *Crito*. When Socrates in the *Crito* at 48a puts into the mouth of some imagined objector the objection that there is good reason to attend to the view of the many because the many can kill us, Crito quickly agrees that there is something to be said for this objection. Socrates exploits the opportunity to explain to Crito—for the second time—that what the many think is not important because it is not death but the committing of injustice that is the worst thing for a man. Socrates raises the objection because he knows that Crito supports the objector's point of view: Crito had already said at 44d1–5 that one must be concerned about the views of the many because the many can do one the greatest harm. Is there, however, anything in what Glaucon has said earlier in the *Republic* that would cause Socrates to raise this objection on his behalf?

If we think back to *Rep.* 2 where Glaucon enumerates three classes of goods,[13] we note that in setting forth even the goods of the first category, which are the pleasures that we desire only for their own sake and not for their consequences, Glaucon cannot resist appending the following qualification: "which are harmless and leave no aftereffects" (*hosai ablabeis kai mēden eis ton*

---

12. In the earlier passage, by contrast, Glaucon immediately rejects the objector's objection (437a3).

13. The "good things" that are contained in Glaucon's third class, things that are desired not for themselves at all but for their consequences alone (*Rep.* 2.357c–d), are the equivalents of the "bad things" in the *Gorgias* that cannot be wanted in themselves (*Gorg.* 467–468). There is even some overlap in the examples given: medical treatment and the various ways of making money. (See Heinaman 2002, 311–14.)

epeita chronon dia tautas gignetai [*Rep.* 2.357b7–8]).[14] If Glaucon excludes from his three classes of good things anything that brings harm in its wake, then, it seems, he is unable to recognize as good things things that are objects of rash desire.[15] For that reason Socrates is obliged to explain to Glaucon in *Rep.* 4 that it is possible for a man to desire even something harmful, for not all desiring takes into account benefit and harm. Thirst is for drink—not exclusively for drink that is not harmful.

In the *Crito* Socrates does not disagree with the objector that the many can kill us. Nevertheless, it does not therefore follow for him that the many's views ought to be accorded any weight. Similarly, in *Rep.* 4 Socrates does not disagree with the objector that all people desire good things. Nevertheless, it does not follow for him that all the good things that men desire are things they judge beneficial.

Desire in the *Protagoras, Gorgias,* and *Meno*

Hunger and thirst in *Rep.* 4, then, are in themselves nonintellectualized desires. They are primitive, irrational (*alogiston* [439d7]) cravings for food and drink respectively. Thirst is what leads the soul "like a beast" to drink; such a soul wants nothing but to drink (439b).[16] Drink—not beneficial drink—is the good thing that thirst craves.[17]

14. One might say that what distinguishes Glaucon's first class of goods from the other two is that the goods in it have no *good* consequences: they involve enjoyment and nothing more. But, for Glaucon, nothing with bad consequences could qualify as any kind of good at all.

15. Ferrari (2003, 16) takes note of what he calls Glaucon's "hauteur," and attributes to that hauteur Glaucon's desire to keep the goodness of justice pure, confined to the soul and untainted by the worldly goods to which it might lead. It might well be, too, that Glaucon's hauteur keeps him from giving desire for things that are pleasant but harmful its due and recognizing its objects as constituting a class of "goods." Glaucon is no ascetic—he protests mightily at *Rep.* 2.372d against Socrates' austere "city of pigs"—but pleasures that bring harm are for him unworthy of the name "good."

16. Thirst can, of course, be qualified (see 437d–e). There is no reason, then, in principle, why there cannot be a kind of thirst whose object is beneficial drink. There is indeed no reason why there cannot be all sorts of desires whose objects are beneficial things. (The "necessary desires" of Book 8 might be desires qualified in just this way.) All Socrates wishes to contend is that it is a mistake to think that even *unqualified* drink is for beneficial drink or, more generally, that all desire, qua desire, is exclusively for things thought beneficial. Were desire in itself only for things beneficial, reason would not oppose appetite and would not emerge as a distinct part of the soul.

17. For an opposing view, see Carone 2001, 107–48. Carone argues that even in the *Republic* synchronic *akrasia* is impossible. For her, all desire remains for good as benefit; choices are al-

Unlike at *Meno* 77e–78b, where, as we saw in chapter 5, Socrates is careful to distinguish between *epithumein* and *boulesthai,* arguing that one can desire but one cannot want bad things, things one deems harmful to oneself, in neither the *Gorgias* nor *Rep.* 4 is *epithumein* distinguished from *boulesthai.* The *Gorgias* uses *boulesthai* throughout the early part of the dialogue, understanding it broadly enough to comprehend all the ways in which one can be drawn to something. Thus, when Socrates says to Polus in the *Gorgias* that no one can want (*boulesthai*) bad things or intermediate ones (468c6–7), he does not mean that no one can regard these things as beneficial. On the contrary, it is when (and only when) one does regard such things as beneficial that one can choose them, despite their intrinsic unattractiveness, for the sake of their perceived benefits. And when Socrates tells Gorgias that a just man is one who does not want (*boulesthai*) to commit injustice (460c3), he does not mean that the just man has assessed the commission of injustice as harmful to himself, but that he has no desire to commit injustice, that wrongdoing holds no appeal for him.

In *Rep.* 4 *epithumein* encompasses *ethelein* and *boulesthai,* along with *ephiesthai* (longing): "Will you not say," Socrates asks Glaucon, "that the soul of a man who desires (*epithumountas*) either longs for (*ephiesthai*) what it desires (*epithumēi*) or embraces that which it wants (*boulētai*) to become its own; or again, that insofar as the soul wills (*ethelei*) that something be supplied to it, it nods assent to itself as though it had posed a question and reaches out toward the fulfillment [of what it wills]?" (437c1–6). Moreover, *boulesthai* replaces *epithumein* at 439b, where the soul of a man who is thirsty is said to "want"

---

ways directed toward what is judged good, toward what reason approves, however momentarily. But surely in order for the principle of noncontradiction to work, the irrational desire to drink and the rational unwillingness to do so must be simultaneous: one part bids and the other forbids at the same time. In the struggle, sometimes reason wins, but at other times it loses. Appetite wins not, as Carone would have it (140), when it succeeds in persuading reason that it ought to follow appetite's dictates. On the contrary, appetite wins when it overpowers reason. Carone misconstrues the Leontius case when she argues that in it reason does not oppose appetite. It does. Leontius is drawn by appetite to act in a way that reason regards as reprehensible, and spirit rushes to the side of reason to chastise appetite, here in the form of Leontius's eyes. It is surely not the case that Leontius's reason had determined, in a moment of weakness, that it was indeed best to look at the corpses. (Even in Book 8 where Socrates describes what happens when the lowest part of the soul comes to dominate it, what he says is that reason is coerced into doing appetite's bidding. What he does not say is that reason acquiesces in appetite's conception of the good.)

(*bouletai*) nothing other than to drink. (See also *Rep.* 3.390c, where Socrates speaks of Zeus who, being so full of desire for Hera, wants [*boulomenon*] to have intercourse right there on the ground; and 4.426c, where Socrates speaks of the ruler who gratifies the citizens by flattering and knowing their wants [*tas bouleseis*] beforehand; similarly, 4.445b2 and 7.520a3.)

Although *Rep.* 4 includes within *epithumein* all forms of desiring, both un-reflective and reasoned, nevertheless it does call the appetitive part of the soul the *epithumetikon* (*Rep.* 4.439d8 and passim) and does single out certain desires (*epithumiai*), thirst and hunger in particular, as primitive drives (437d–e). The good things that hunger and thirst desire are food and drink, the things that look good to a hungry and thirsty soul.[18]

There is nothing in Socrates' stand in the *Gorgias* or the *Meno* that is incon-sistent with his stand in *Rep.* 4. In all three places people can desire—and choose—anything that strikes them as good in some way. And so, in neither the *Gorgias* nor the *Meno* is there any suggestion that people can desire—and choose—only what they consider beneficial. The *Gorgias* contends at 467–468 only that one cannot want in and for itself what is bad or intermediate, making it clear that what one can want in and for itself is anything good.[19] And when Socrates later on in the *Gorgias* contends against Callicles that the pleas-ant is to be chosen for the sake of good and not good for the sake of pleasant, it is clear that pleasant things are nevertheless indeed wanted in and for them-selves, and are thus unlike the earlier bad and intermediate things that are wanted only for the sake of the benefit they bring. In the *Meno*, even bad things, that is, things that are bad in the sense that they are judged harmful, can be desired. Indeed, it is because they desire bad things that some people are wretched. Yet even these bad things must, apart from the harm they are thought to bring, seem otherwise good—if they did not, why would they be desired at all? It must be presumed, then, that at the same time that these "bad

18. At *Rep.* 4.436a10, Socrates makes the point that we desire (*epithumoumen*) the pleasures of nourishment and generation and all their kin with a third part of the soul, distinct from the one with which we learn and from the one with which we become spirited. But he also recognizes desire (*epithumeten einai*) for learning (*Rep.* 5.475b7–8), and it is unclear whether this desire em-anates from the appetitive part or the reasoning part of the soul. Cf. *Phaedo* 66e, where Socrates says that we desire (*epithumoumen*) wisdom and are its lovers (*erastai*); and 67e7–8, where philoso-phers are said to desire (*epithumousi*) to possess their soul alone by itself.

19. It is fair to say, then, that not only is the *Gorgias* not inconsistent with *Rep.* 4 but both dia-logues make precisely the same point. In contending that bad and intermediate things cannot be wanted, the *Gorgias* affirms in effect that everyone desires good things.

things" are judged harmful they are also perceived as pleasureful and, in that sense, as good.

Republic 4, then, insofar as it allows that people can desire anything that they regard as good in some way—even food and drink simpliciter—is in complete accord with the *Gorgias* and the *Meno.* The reason it is perhaps difficult to see that accord is because "good things" sometimes means things judged beneficial and sometimes things that appeal, and "bad things" sometimes means things judged harmful and sometimes things that repel. The "good things" (*agatha*) in *Rep.* 4—things that are attractive in some way—are the opposites of the *Gorgias*'s "bad things" (*kaka*), which are not attractive in any way. But the *Meno*'s "bad things"—things regarded as harmful—are the opposites of *Rep.* 4's "beneficial drink and beneficial food." Moreover, *epithumein* and *boulesthai,* as we have seen, can be used broadly or narrowly. No one can want (*boulesthai*) the *Meno*'s bad things (= things judged harmful) because *boulesthai* is restricted in the *Meno* and can apply only to things that are believed to be beneficial and not harmful. In the *Gorgias,* where *boulesthai* is not similarly restricted, no one can want (*boulesthai*) in themselves bad things (= repugnant things) no matter how beneficial they are judged to be: at most one can want to do them (*prattein auta* [468c4]) for the sake of the benefit they bring. *Rep.* 4's "beneficial drink and beneficial food" would qualify as things that can be wanted even on *boulesthai*'s restrictive sense; but drink and food that is not beneficial, and therefore cannot be wanted on *boulesthai*'s restrictive sense, can nevertheless be wanted on *boulesthai*'s less restrictive sense under the name "good things" (*agatha*) in *Rep.* 4, just as they can be desired (*epithumein*) but not wanted (*boulesthai*) in the *Meno* under the name "bad things" (*kaka*).

It is only in the *Protagoras,* where the distinction between pleasure and good is dissolved and where people are transformed into rational pleasure- and pain-calculators, that no one can choose anything that is not deemed the most beneficial of the available options. In the *Protagoras,* the "good things" are pleasures, the "bad things" pains. People count, weigh, and measure pleasures and pains. Any special attractiveness or repugnance that might attach to them on account of their proximity is discounted and reinterpreted as calculable amounts, sizes, or weights. Not surprisingly, then, it is in the *Protagoras* that the possibility of *akrasia* is denied. *Rep.* 4 is indeed out of step with the *Protagoras.* But, then again, so are the *Gorgias* and *Meno,* which like *Rep.* 4 take it for granted that *akrasia* is a rather common and familiar occurrence.[20] That is why Callicles is told in the *Gorgias* that pleasures must be controlled and disciplined and not given free rein if one is to live well. And that is why Meno is told in the *Meno* that when gold and silver can be acquired only unjustly, virtue requires that they not be acquired at all, and that those who desire and pursue bad things are wretched. The *Gorgias, Meno,* and *Republic* all recognize the need for self-control. The only need the *Protagoras* recognizes is skill at weighing and measuring pleasures and pains. It is the *Protagoras,* then, and not *Rep.* 4, that is the odd man out: only in the *Protagoras* does Socrates contend that no one pursues the worse of two courses when he might pursue the better.

20. The scholarly preoccupation with the presumed reversal in the *Republic* of the alleged Socratic denial of *akrasia* has led to such views as the following one by Bobonich (1994, 27): "my fundamental point still holds firm: they [the parts of the soul] are no longer [in the *Laws*] thought by Plato to be necessary for framing or solving the philosophical problems surrounding akratic action." Bobonich here implies that in the *Republic* the soul is divided into parts in order to make *akrasia* possible. But surely it is the other way around: the very argument for the soul's having parts rests on the fact of *akrasia*.

7

LAWS 9:
ALL JUST THINGS
ARE BEAUTIFUL

In several places in the *Laws*,[1] particularly in Books 5 and 9, the Socratic paradox "no one does wrong willingly" appears. Yet Socrates does not appear anywhere in the dialogue. Unlike the *Republic,* in which it is Socrates who constructs the best polis in speech, in the *Laws* the task of designing a model polis is left to the Athenian Stranger.[2] It is in the *Laws,* therefore, if anywhere, and not in the *Republic* as is widely believed (see chapter 6), that Socratic ideals are abandoned. Despite the frequent echoes heard in the *Laws* of Socratic ideas, the Socratic paradox among them, the *Laws* promotes a practical compromise that is inconsistent with Socratic idealism. For there are only two ways of life that

1. Except where noted, translations are mine, although I have frequently consulted and benefited from the translations of Pangle (1980), Bury (1926), and A. E. Taylor (1934). References to passages in Book 9 of the *Laws* omit both the dialogue's name and the book number. Almost all references to other passages in the *Laws* contain the book number but not the dialogue's name.

2. Strauss (1975, 3–4) suggests that the Athenian Stranger is indeed Socrates who, had he escaped execution by fleeing to Sparta or Crete, would have arrived there as the Athenian Stranger. Strauss attributes the omission of Socrates' name from the *Laws* to Socrates' having been prevented by his *daimonion* from participating in politics. The *Laws,* Strauss thinks, is Plato's only political work. (Although the *Laws,* like the *Republic,* devises its policies "in speech," the *Laws,* unlike the *Republic,* proceeds to determine how to effect its policies in deed. See 5.736b5–6 along with 5.737d6.) My view is not incompatible with this one.

Socrates recommends. One way is the examined life, a life to be undertaken by each individual, a life in which a man is asked to think and then to follow the course that his best thinking dictates. This is the life that Socrates advocates in the *Apology*, where it is said that that man is wisest who recognizes his own ignorance with respect to the most important things. The second way is the one Socrates envisions in the *Republic*, where the possibility is entertained that a philosopher, one who has not only longed for but has actually attained wisdom about the most important things, might rule. Under such rule, the right life is one of obedience to the authority of the rulers' near-divine wisdom. What makes the *Laws* un-Socratic is that it gives *law* absolute authority, that it substitutes man-made law for both private individual reasoning, on the one hand,[3] and the rule of god-like philosopher-kings, on the other.

Just as it is not Socrates who expresses his eponymous paradox in the *Laws*, so, too, it is not the sophists against whom the paradox is directed. The Athenian directs the paradox against the many. As we saw in chapter 1, however, the many are hardly invulnerable or unreceptive to sophistic ideas. Sophists play on—and prey on—the popular regard for pleasure and material success and for the avoidance of pain and material deprivation.[4] They lay bare the powerful attraction to pleasure that traditional pieties and conventional tributes to justice rather thinly conceal. Yet many people, despite their desire for pleasure, believe that justice is noble and good. What they find difficult—and what sophists make even more difficult—is choosing the noble and good over the pleasant.

In framing a constitution, the Athenian confronts head on the views of the many that have been fanned by sophistic rhetoric—specifically, that injustice is advantageous and that punishment, even when just, is harmful to the man punished and therefore bad. In *Laws* 9 the Athenian challenges these popular views, constructing a system of justice consistent with the Socratic idea, prominent in the *Gorgias* and the *Republic*, that all just things are beautiful.

The Athenian begins by taking note of two contradictions. The first, which is found at 859d–860c and which he attributes to the many, may be formulated as follows: since (1) all just things are beautiful, but (2) just sufferings are ugly, it follows that (3) not all just things are beautiful. The second, which is found

---

3. See Weiss 1998. I argue that Socrates' law-abidingness and his advocacy of law-abidingness end at the moment that the law requires of an agent that he do what his own reason determines to be unjust.

4. See 5.733b.

at 860d–861a and which the Athenian attributes to himself, may be formulated thus to parallel the first: since (1′) all injustices are involuntary, but (2′) penalties for voluntary injustices are (rightly) more severe than for involuntary ones, it follows that (3′) not all injustices are involuntary.[5]

At first glance, these two contradictions seem unrelated. The first appears to address the question of whether all just things, including just sufferings, are beautiful; the second, the question of whether all injustices (*adikēmata*) can be involuntary if legislators are right to punish voluntary injustices more severely than involuntary ones. Yet, the Athenian suggests that the second has a bearing on the first or, more precisely, that the harmony he has with respect to the second somehow makes it possible for him also to have a harmony with respect to the first. As he says, whereas the many speak discordantly (*asumphōnōs* [860c1–2]),[6] "we [the Athenian and Cleinias][7] have a harmony about these same matters" (*peri auta tauta echei tēs sumphōnias* [860c5]).[8] The Athenian believes that once he resolves the merely *apparent* contradiction in his position on punishment, he will be able to replace the many's discordant view about justice and beauty with his own harmonious one. In other words, once he shows how the second contradiction is no contradiction at all, he will be able to discredit proposition (2) of the many's view, the proposition that just sufferings are ugly, and so dispel the disharmony in their view.[9]

5. The Athenian recognizes that if all injustice is committed unwillingly, there actually might be no place for punishment at all: "Should we legislate or not?" (860e6–7), he asks. (2′) could equally well, then, be put as follows: penalties are (rightly) imposed for, and only for, voluntary injustices.

6. The Athenian, having set as his goal to see "to what extent we [he and Cleinias] now agree and to what extent we disagree with ourselves" (*hopēi pote homologoumen nun kai hopēi dipherometha hēmeis te hēmin autois* [859c7–8]), wishes also to see with respect to the many the extent to which they agree and disagree "with themselves" (*autoi pros hautous au* [859d1]). Oddly, Bury, A. E. Taylor, and Pangle, all mistranslate this *pros hautous* at 859d1 as "among themselves."

7. Although the Athenian pretends that he and Cleinias are on the same side, Book 2 reveals a Cleinias who (like Polus) is unpersuaded that the tyrant is unhappy but concedes (like Polus) that tyrants behave shamefully. See *Gorg.* 527d–e, where, despite the fact that Socrates and Callicles are on opposite sides, Socrates still says "we." See, too, *Prot.* 361a–d.

8. See Saunders 1968, 423: "The Stranger may mean only 'That was one confusion; now here is another'. But *peri auta tauta* surely indicates a more intimate connection."

9. For other views see, e.g., Bury 1926; Stalley 1983; Saunders 1968. Bury sees no connection between the second contradiction and the first, mistranslating the phrase *peri auta tauta* to mean "in this respect." Stalley and Saunders do see a connection between the two contradictions and both attempt to explain it by suggesting that each can be resolved like the other, that is, by using the same strategy. Pangle (1980, 497–98) is to be credited with recognizing a more substantive

This chapter has three aims: (1) to explain the value of the Athenian's distinction between injustice and injury in resolving the contradiction in the many's view concerning the just and the beautiful; (2) to show that the practice of imposing harsher penalties for voluntary harmful acts and lighter ones or none at all for involuntary ones is compatible with, and even mandated by, the view that all injustice is committed unwillingly; and (3) to identify what it is about just punishment that the Athenian does, after all, find ugly.

The Distinction between Injustice and Injury

The Athenian's solution to the apparent contradiction in his view concerning punishment and the involuntariness of injustice involves the introduction of a new distinction, a distinction between injustice and injury (*blabē*),[10] intended to replace the many's distinction between voluntary and involuntary injustice.[11] As commentator after commentator has noted, however, despite the Athenian's apparent abandonment of the distinction between voluntary and involuntary injustice, the distinction between voluntary and involuntary bad

---

connection between the two contradictions, but even he fails to see how the *solution* to the second holds the key to the Athenian's view regarding the beauty of just suffering. Crombie (1962, I, 280) holds a view similar to Pangle's. For further discussion of these views, as well as analysis of some of the finer points of *Laws* 9, see Weiss 2003.

10. At 861b–c the Athenian appears troubled that his pronouncement that all injustice is involuntary will seem oracular, especially if he departs without having offered a supporting argument and proceeds to legislate in defiance of existing practice. The remedy he proposes comes in the form of making clear how, despite the involuntariness of all injustice, the distinction between voluntary and involuntary can nevertheless be preserved: whereas injustice is never voluntary, the infliction of harm is frequently involuntary but no less frequently voluntary (861e3–4, 861e8–862a1). At 861c–d, Cleinias gives the Athenian two choices—either retract the pronouncement that all injustice is involuntary or provide a new distinction. The Athenian feels constrained to reject the first choice because he believes the pronouncement to be true. He therefore chooses the second. The new distinction constitutes in itself the heretofore missing supporting argument for the pronouncement that all do injustice unwillingly. Note how the *hōs orthōs eirēken* of 861b7–c1 reappears in Cleinias's second choice: *hōs orthōs eirētai* (861d1). Indeed, with the new distinction in place, the Athenian will be able to legislate in a new way, for he will not have to regard unintended injury as injustice (862a). Furthermore, since the new distinction *justifies* the Athenian's institution of new legislative practices, he is absolved of the charge of having dogmatically "laid down the law" (*katanomothetēsei* [861c1]) in defiance of the old practices.

11. The new distinction that is to replace the old and mistaken one between voluntary and involuntary injustice is one that preserves them as distinct types (*duo te onta* [861c3]), but no longer as distinct types of *adikēmata*. They are now distinct types of *blabē*, the intentional ones

and harmful acts continues to be pivotal in his determination of the penalty to be levied for particular crimes. Why, then, does it matter whether one says that there is voluntary and involuntary injustice or that there is voluntary and involuntary harm or injury (*blabē*)?[12] The Athenian seems clearly to think it does matter, insisting that the distinction is more than merely verbal, more than a mere matter of names, *onomata* (864a8–b1).

The Athenian's insistence notwithstanding, many interpreters of the *Laws* think that the distinction is indeed either illegitimate or worthless. If, on the one hand, the notion that all injustice is involuntary is either exculpatory in some sense or at least renders all crimes equal (860e–861a), then it cannot be right to supplant it by a distinction between voluntary and involuntary injury that restores culpability and renders crimes decidedly unequal. And if, on the other hand, the notion that all injustice is involuntary neither excuses nor equalizes crimes and criminals, what exactly is to be gained by replacing voluntary injustice with voluntary injury?

Some scholars think that the Athenian simply relinquishes his notion of the involuntariness of injustice when it comes time to set forth actual punishments.[13] But it is hard to see why the Athenian would insist so firmly on the involuntariness of injustice, and even introduce a distinction between injustice and injury to shore it up, if he has no intention of sticking with it when it matters most. Moreover, the Athenian is quite adamant in his assertion that he means to be acting in consonance with his own statements when, despite his insistence that all injustices are involuntary, he not only persists in issuing penalties but is prepared to issue unequal ones (860e–861a). It seems he must have a reason for maintaining his commitment to the involuntariness of all in-

---

being *adikēmata*, the unintentional ones not being *adikēmata* at all. The matter of whether there is to be punishment at all will be determined henceforth exclusively by this distinction. The Athenian's new distinction between voluntary and involuntary is, then, "other" (*allēn*) than the standard one between voluntary and involuntary injustice. (There is no need for the emendation of *allēn* to *allēlōn* at 861c3 that Bury [1926] adopts [following Hermann]. Indeed, the emendation is rejected by England [1921], Ritter [1896], and Stallbaum [1859–60]. A. E. Taylor [1934] correctly translates: "other than supposed.")

12. See, e.g., Stalley 1983, 153–54.

13. Pangle 1980, 500: "It appears that in practice the Athenian must abandon his theorizing and give in to the naïve view of punishment rooted in human anger, which always tends to assign responsibility to the agent who inflicts hurt." Also Gulley 1962, 306: "for the purposes of his penal code Plato substantially abandons the Socratic thesis."

justice at the same time that he advocates distinguishing voluntary from involuntary injurious acts.

In order to clarify the meaning, purpose, and relevance of the Athenian's distinction between injustice and injury, the remainder of this section is devoted to (a) explaining what the Athenian means by the involuntariness of injustice; (b) clarifying the distinction between injustice and injury; and (c) showing how the distinction between injustice and injury both renders the Athenian's own statements internally consistent and provides him with the justification he needs for rejecting the many's proposition (2), "just sufferings are ugly."

The Involuntariness of Injustice

There can be no doubt that the Athenian equivocates on the terms "voluntary" and "involuntary" in *Laws* 9, both when he uses the terms *hekōn/akōn* and when he uses *boulomenos/mē boulomenos*. When he says that all injustice is involuntary, he uses the term in what might best be called its Socratic sense; on all other occasions, he uses the terms "voluntary" and "involuntary" in their ordinary sense.[14] When the Athenian proclaims "All commit injustice unwillingly" (*akontas adikein pantas* [860d9]), and derives it from the more basic maxim that "the bad are all bad unwillingly" (*hoi kakoi pantes* [*eis panta*] *eisin akontes kakoi* [860d1]),[15] the force of the "unwillingly" is that the act conflicts with something the agent deeply wants. The by-now familiar reasoning that underlies this dictum is as follows: no one wants to be wretched; having an unjust soul (which is the equivalent of being a bad man) is what in fact makes one wretched;[16] acting unjustly makes one's soul unjust;[17] hence, when one acts unjustly one acts unwillingly: one undermines one's own wish not to be wretched. When, by contrast, the Athenian speaks of the voluntariness or in-

---

14. Adkins 1960, 306.

15. See also 5.731c2–3: "the unjust man is not willingly unjust"; 734b4–6: "every unrestrained man must necessarily be living this way unwillingly; the whole mob of humanity lives with a lack of moderation because of their ignorance, weakness of will, or both."

16. See 2.660e: No matter how rich a person is, if he is unjust, he is wretched and lives a life of misery.

17. Acting unjustly is also, of course, what a bad man, or a man with an unjust soul, typically does.

voluntariness of harmful or beneficial acts—as opposed to the voluntariness or involuntariness of injustice—he reverts to the ordinary sense of voluntary and involuntary. In the ordinary sense, an act is voluntary as long as the agent is aware of the nature of what he is doing and/or acts in accordance with what he quite consciously wishes to do at the time. When a person commits an act that he wants to commit, even if what he wants to commit is something he knows is unjust, that person has acted willingly; indeed, he has committed an injustice willingly—in the ordinary sense of "willingly." Nevertheless, the injustice that he has committed willingly in the ordinary sense is an involuntary injustice in the Socratic sense: since in committing injustice—no matter how consciously, deliberately, and willfully—a person fails to achieve something he truly wants, namely, to live a genuinely good life and be a genuinely good man, he fails to act willingly. When the Athenian says that all injustice is involuntary, he means no more than that it puts the agent in a state that is objectively bad. A state of being that is objectively bad for one is a wretched state of being that one does not want to be in, no matter how much one wants and deliberately chooses the acts and things that put one in that state. Insofar as being unjust is in fact not good for anyone, no one's deliberate and intentional pursuit of injustice is voluntary—in the Socratic sense.

Injustice and Injury

A small but serious misunderstanding has found its way into the standard conception of the Athenian's distinction between injustice and injury as laid out at 861e6–862c4. According to this conception, injustice (as *adikia*) is taken to be a state of the soul, a state of character, that breeds a malicious intent and gives rise to the commission of unjust acts (*adikein*); and injury is thought of either as the bare act that causes harm (setting considerations of *mens rea* aside) or as the harm itself that is caused by the act. So, for example, if someone damages the property of another (breaks his fence, say, as in Saunders's example [1968, 423–24]), his action is unjust if and only if it springs from an evil intention expressive of the nasty disposition of his soul (he is jealous, perhaps, or spiteful); and the injury-element in the action is identified either as the damage itself (the broken fence) or as the act that causes damage (breaking the fence). So far, so good.

Where things begin to go awry, however, is when it is assumed that the Athenian divides injurious acts into but two categories, and that these are mutually exclusive and also jointly exhaustive. The first category of injurious acts is believed to contain unjust acts that emanate from a malignant soul and are maliciously intended to cause harm to others; the second is thought to contain just acts that emanate from a benign soul and are well intentioned, meaning to cause no harm to others. The fact is, however, that the Athenian identifies (if only implicitly) three categories of injurious (and the same three of beneficial) acts: (1) unintentional injurious (or beneficial) acts that are not unjust—and are not instances of justice, either; (2) injurious (or beneficial) acts that are wrongly committed and hence unjust; and (3) injurious (or beneficial) acts that are rightly done and hence just. (Note that in all three categories, the matter of whether there is injury or benefit is essentially irrelevant to the determination of the acts' justness or unjustness.) It is the third, largely overlooked, category of harmful acts, the one that contains acts that are positively just and not merely not unjust, that helps account for how the Athenian can later regard even harmful acts committed by people with well-ordered souls as "just and best for the whole of human life" (*dikaion . . . kai epi ton hapanta anthrōpōn bion ariston* [864a4–6])—high praise indeed.[18]

The Athenian begins by identifying acts of the first category: "If someone injures somebody in some way, not willingly, but unwillingly" (*mē boulomenos, all' akōn*), this is not a case of doing injustice unwillingly but rather a case of not doing injustice at all (862a3–7).[19] It would seem that the Athenian could easily complete the thought and say: "If someone benefits somebody in some way, not willingly, but unwillingly, this is not a case of doing justice unwillingly but a case of not doing justice at all." The Athenian then goes on to identify the second category: "when a benefit (*ōpheleian*) that is not correct (*ouk orthēn*) comes to pass,[20] the one responsible for the benefit *is* committing an injustice" (862a7–8). It would seem that here the Athenian could readily supplement his words with the following: "When a harm (*blabēn*) that is not correct comes to pass, the one responsible for the harm is committing an injustice."

18. The injury or harm (*blabē*) that is the subject of this discussion is bodily or material injury or harm that takes the form of pain or deprivation. This is the sort of injury that can, on occasion, be beneficial and just. Generally in Plato the term "harm" is withheld from suffering that is imposed justly and beneficially. In the *Gorgias,* for example, it is called "pain."

19. These are frequently referred to as "accidental." See, e.g., Mackenzie 1981, 201: "some acts, whether they benefit or injure, are done on purpose and others by accident."

20. At *Gorg.* 488a2, as here, "not rightly" (*mē orthōs*) has the sense of wrongdoing, of improper conduct.

In other words, it is when a person acts *wrongly* that, regardless of whether in doing so he confers benefit or harm, he is properly said to commit an injustice.[21] But the Athenian does not stop here. He goes on to identify yet a third category:

> If someone gives something to somebody else or, on the contrary, takes something away, this sort of thing should not be called simply just or unjust, but what the legislator should see is whether the person, in doing a benefit or injury to somebody else, employs a [just] disposition (*ēthei*) and a just way (*dikaiōi tropōi*). (862b3)[22]

Not only is it possible for an injurious act, then, to be unjust or not unjust, but it can be positively just. If it is to be positively just, however, it is not sufficient that it be unintentional; it must be done both from a just disposition and in a just way. Moreover, if, as the Athenian goes on to explain, what he means by an unjust benefit is that "someone makes someone else profit by doing him injustices" (*ean tis adikōn tina kerdainein poiēi* [862c6–7]), it is reasonable to assume that what he means by a just harm is that someone causes someone else to suffer harm by doing him justice. Harm, then, can result even when someone does right by another.

Let us turn now to the second text in which the distinction between injustice and injury is drawn—863e–864a—and where a similar misunderstand-

21. This interpretation of the second case is confirmed by what follows immediately in the text: "On the other hand, in the case of unjust injuries, and gains as well—when someone makes somebody gain by doing him an injustice" (862c).

22. This reading of the passage shields Plato from the charge that what he holds here (assuming that the Athenian speaks for him) is that it is only one's intention that matters, that, regardless of how heinous one's crime might be, so long as it stems from an innocent intention, it is just. This charge is leveled by Ritter (1896, 282–84) and Adkins (1960, 309). See also Levinson 1940, 678: "only in the Ninth book of the Laws (860 ff.) does Plato assert unequivocally that an ignorant and objectively wrong act, indeed 'a great and savage wrong,' may be a just act, if only it proceed from an agent acting under the control of reason and in light of his 'opinion of the best.'" On the reading I suggest, although the Athenian forgives accidents (since they are not unjust) and disapproves of wrong actions regardless of whether they result in harm or in benefit, he regards as positively just only those injuries (or benefits) committed by good people that are *done rightly*. Several translators take *dikaiōi tropōi* to mean "through a just character," but that the text has "not correct" (*ouk orthēn*) at 862a7 strongly suggests that "in a just way" is intended here. Also, if *tropos* is character, what does it add to *ēthos*, disposition?

ing prevails. Here is the passage. (The problematic expression *kan sphallētai ti,* to be discussed forthwith, is left untranslated.)

> Now at this point I would make clear for you what I say the just and the unjust are, without confusion. The tyranny in the soul of spiritedness, fear, pleasure, pain, jealousies, and desires, whether it does some injury or not, I proclaim to be in every way injustice. When, on the other hand, the opinion about what is best (however the city or certain individuals believe this to be) holds sway in souls and brings order to every man, then, *kan sphallētai ti,* what is done through this, and the part of each man that becomes obedient to such a rule, must be declared to be entirely just and best for the whole of human life—even though many are of the opinion that such injury constitutes involuntary injustice.

There is considerable scholarly disagreement over precisely how to understand this passage and, in particular, how to understand the words *kan sphallētai ti* at 864a4—whether as "even if it be somewhat mistaken" or as "even if some damage be done." On the former and apparently more widely favored translation,[23] the Athenian is thought to hold what has come to be known as the "good conscience" view,[24] seeing justice as a matter of conforming behavior to a belief concerning what is best—whether one's own belief or that of the city—even if that belief is mistaken; moreover, he is thought to hold that what determines whether an act is just is solely whether it is the work of a properly ordered soul. On the latter translation,[25] by contrast, the Athenian is thought to attribute the justness of an act to its conforming to an opinion, whether one's own or the city's, about what is best—even if the act results in untoward consequences.

23. Among those who take the clause in the sense of "even if it be somewhat mistaken" are Pangle (1980), Strauss (1975), Saunders (1968), Stallbaum (1859–60), Adkins (1960), and Rosenmeyer (1961).

24. Among its supporters is Adkins (1960, 308). O'Brien (1957) argues against the "good conscience" view, contending that in *Laws* 9, no less than elsewhere in Plato, wisdom is the source of justice and ignorance ultimately the source of injustice. For him, therefore, what emanates from a good but misguided conscience can only be *in*justice.

25. Among those who take the clause in the sense of "even if some damage be done" are England (1921, 403), O'Brien (1957, 85), Bury (1926), and A. E. Taylor (1934).

In order to choose between the two suggested translations of *kan sphallētai ti* (864a4), it is useful to consider the context in which the passage 863e–864a arises. Cleinias had asked (863a) that the Athenian clarify (*saphesteron*) how the difference between injustice and injury became confused (*diapepoikilētai*) with the difference between voluntary and involuntary. What Cleinias seeks, in other words, is a further elucidation of the distinction the Athenian had just drawn between injustice and injury at 861e–862c. The Athenian, by way of acceding to Cleinias's request, identifies three sources of misdeeds (*hamar-tēmata*)—pleasure, passion, and ignorance—in preparation for distinguishing clearly (*saphōs*) and without confusion (*ouden poikillōn*) between the just and unjust (863e5–6). By echoing the expressions for clarity and confusion that Cleinias used in his request for an elucidation of 861e–862c, the Athenian signals both (1) that it is by distinguishing between the just and unjust that he intends to sort out the confusion that infects the view that puzzles Cleinias, and (2) that his current distinction is intended to amplify the one he made earlier— at 861e–862c.

Having identified the three sources of misdeeds, the Athenian proceeds to define injustice as the tyranny in the soul of *thumos* (passion or anger), fear, pleasure, pain, jealousies, and desires, "whether it does some injury or not" (*ean te ti blaptēi kai ean mē* [863e8]). He then defines justice as the soul's being guided by the opinion of what is best—*kan sphallētai ti*. This distinction be- tween injustice and justice enables the Athenian to show how the difference between injustice and injury became confused with the difference between voluntary and involuntary: the many think that "such injury" (*tēn toiautēn blabēn* [864a7–8]) constitutes involuntary injustice. In other words, the many assimilate injury to injustice, and pronounce the injustice involuntary when it stems from a well-ordered soul. If, however, legislation is to proceed cor- rectly, these notions must be disentangled. It must be recognized that a re- sultant injury cannot turn a just act, that is, an act that emanates from the proper disposition of the soul, into an injustice, and that the proper disposi- tion of the soul is not what makes an injurious act that proceeds from it an in- voluntary one: such an act is simply "just . . . and best for the whole of human life" (*dikaion . . . kai epi ton hapanta anthrōpōn bion ariston* [864a4–6]).

When the phrase *kan sphallētai ti* is read in context, it is surely best read as "even if some damage be done" rather than "even if it be somewhat mis- taken"—for several reasons. First, insofar as this passage (863e–864a) recapit- ulates the earlier one at 861e–862b, it may be assumed to be making the same point: if the point made earlier was that an act is just even if it causes injury so long as it flows from a proper disposition of the soul and is done in the right way, so here the point must be that, regardless of any injury it might cause, an act is just so long as it issues from a rightly governed soul. Second, only on the "even if some damage be done" reading does the discussion of justice perfectly parallel the discussion of injustice: injustice is the tyranny of emotions and desires in the soul "whether it does some injury or not" (*eante ti blaptēi kai ean mē* [863e8]); justice is the soul's obeying an opinion about what is best "even if some damage be done" (*kan sphallētai ti* [864a4]). On this reading, moreover, the passage is seen to emphasize, as earlier, the strict irrelevance to both injustice and justice of the presence or absence of injury. Third, unless *kan sphallētai ti* refers to injury done, there is no discernible referent for *tēn toiautēn blabēn* ("such injury") at 864a7–8. Finally, unless it can be presumed that the opinion about what is best—the opinion to which the well-ordered soul conforms—is not a mistaken one, the Athenian's contention that everything done in obedience to that opinion constitutes not only what is just but also what is "best for the whole of human life" seems on its face rather implausible.[26]

The reading of *kan sphallētai ti* as "even if it be somewhat mistaken" is, by contrast, fraught with difficulties: (1) it introduces a new and different element into the definition of justice—incorrect opinion about what is best— one not found in 861e–862c; (2) it spoils the neat contrast between injustice and justice as opposite states of the soul to which the matter of injury is wholly irrelevant; (3) it fails to supply a referent for *tēn toiatēn blabēn;* and (4) it makes the untenable assertion that what is done in accordance with even a mistaken belief that rules the soul is not only not unjust but is actually "entirely just and best for the whole of human life."[27] Moreover, in view of the fact that the Athenian just established ignorance as the third cause of *hamartēmata* (863c), is it not unreasonable that he would now regard what is done in ignorance,

---

26. The main ground on which scholars reject the rendering of *kan sphallētai ti* as "even if some damage be done" is that the more common meaning of *sphallein* is "to stumble" or "to trip up." See *Gorg.* 461c–d and *Rep.* 2.361b. It is also used in the sense of making mistakes. See *Laws* 6.771e4 and *Theaet.* 196b2. Yet *sphallein* carries the meaning of doing damage at *Laws* 6.769c4, where *ean ti sphallētai to zōion hupo chronōn* means "if the painting should be damaged somewhat over time."

27. It is in order to avoid such a conclusion that Mackenzie (1981, 249) takes the error to be a mistake in the agent's "practical assessments" rather than a moral mistake. See also Görgemanns (1960, 139–40), who thinks the mistake is about means.

however well ordered the soul that does it, as both just and best for the whole of human life?[28]

The alternative, of course, to regarding the opinion to which the well-ordered soul conforms as possibly mistaken is to regard it as not mistaken. Are there grounds, however, to support this supposition?[29] We may wonder, too, why, if what the Athenian means by justice is the soul's being governed by a *true* opinion about what is best, he does not simply say so.

With regard to why the Athenian does not simply say that the just soul is one governed by *true* opinion, note that the Athenian's aim in this passage is, as he himself says, to contrast injustice with justice: injustice is the state in which the soul is tyrannized by desires and emotions, justice the state in which a belief concerning what is best holds sway. As the Athenian sees it, then, the distinction between injustice and justice has to do in the first instance with which element in the soul is in charge, not with whether the belief that is dominant in the just soul is or is not a true one.

With respect to the matter of the *grounds* for the claim that the belief to which the well-ordered soul conforms is not a mistaken one, it is fair to say that the *Laws* generally puts its trust in the collective wisdom of legislators and in the cultivated reason of an individual properly raised and properly educated, and therefore takes for granted that the opinion of a well-ordered soul, as well as that of a well-governed polis, is as close to true as can be reasonably expected.[30]

There are, it would seem, no compelling reasons to read *kan sphallētai ti* as "even if it be somewhat mistaken" and far better reasons to read it as "even if some damage be done." Indeed, the "even if it be somewhat mistaken" reading causes the argument to veer wildly off course: those scholars who endorse it feel constrained to maintain that, for the Athenian, a good but ignorant soul is not only never the source of injustice, but is actually the source of what is just and best for the whole of human life. They mistakenly suppose that

---

28. This, in part, is O'Brien's question (1957, 85).

29. O'Brien's attempt (1957, 85) to render *hē tou aristou doxa* not "the opinion as to what is best," but rather "the conviction that has the best for its object," besides being rather strained, also fails to yield the desired result: it does not guarantee that the conviction one has is not mistaken.

30. The *Laws* does not dwell on the worry expressed briefly at 875c–d that genuine and full-blown wisdom is not likely to be found anywhere and that law must serve, therefore, as a second-best substitute for it. See also 1.644c–d, 1.645c, 3.688b2–3, 3.689b, and 5.728a–b.

hamartēmata committed out of ignorance, unlike those committed out of tyranny in the soul, are certainly not unjust and hence fall under the legal heading of tort (*blabē*)—in the event that they do damage—as opposed to that of felony (*adikēma*). They cite in support of their view, first, the Athenian's use of the term *hamartēmata,* regarding it as broad enough and neutral enough to encompass both full-blown injustices and the most innocent of injuries,[31] and, second, the distinction the Athenian draws at 863d–e between pleasure and *thumos,* on the one hand, and ignorance, on the other, as sources of *hamartēmata.*

The term *hamartēma,* however, is not sharply distinguished from *adikēma* in the *Laws.* See 860e8–9, and earlier, 5.727b5–6. And even if *hamartēma* is a somewhat broader term than *adikēma,* one that can on occasion include offenses that are not strictly *adikēmata,* it is still the case that in our passage all the *hamartēmata* in question are also *adikēmata,* that is, culpable crimes. Moreover, even if it is characteristic of some *hamartēmata* that they are committed in ignorance, we may note that for Plato moral ignorance, that is, ignorance of what is right or what is best, is no excuse—not in the *Laws* and not anywhere else in Plato.[32] Ignorance is subject to reproach in the *Laws* no less than in the *Apology,*[33] and the *Laws* makes it quite clear that one who fails to hold himself responsible for his *hamartēmatōn* as for his *pleistōn kakōn kai megistōn,* "most and gravest evils" (5.727b4–6), dishonors his soul.

The *Timaeus* is often cited as evidence that Plato absolves men of blame for their injustices. But even the *Timaeus,* in which (1) madness (*mania*) and ignorance (*amathia*) are identified as diseases of the mind (86b) that cause men to commit injustice (86e), and (2) it is said to be inappropriate to reproach men (*ouk orthōs oneidizetai* [86d7]) for their lack of self-control (*akrateia*) with respect to pleasure, what is held to be inappropriate is not reproach simpliciter but rather reproach that proceeds on the presumption that these men are bad

---

31. See, e.g., Gould 1955, 127; Grube 1935, 228 ff.; Ritter 1896, 286.

32. Saunders (1968, 428–29) thinks that *Laws* 10.908b constitutes a refutation of the "good conscience" view because it advocates punishing the holding of mistaken beliefs about the gods, even when those who hold them have well-ordered and temperate souls. Yet the fact is that such people are liable to punishment not because their mistakes do not excuse their injustice, but because despite their justness their mistakes amount to impiety: they both subscribe to and are purveyors of false beliefs about the gods. For O'Brien's view, see note 24.

33. *Ap.* 29b1–2: *amathia eponeidistos* (most reproachful ignorance); *Laws* 3.689c: *kai hōs amathesin oneidisteon* (they are to be reproached as ignorant).

men willingly (*hōs hekontōn . . . tōn kakōn* [86d6–7]). The *Timaeus* does not excuse misconduct; it merely recognizes the unreasonableness of reproaching men for *becoming* bad—badness is not, after all, a state that anyone would willingly choose. That it would be unreasonable to reproach men for becoming bad hardly entails, however, that wrongdoing is not culpable on other grounds—specifically on the grounds that one has done nothing to eradicate one's madness or ignorance. The *Timaeus* indeed makes clear, though this is not its immediate concern, that people are required to make the effort to reverse the effects of their miseducation and to teach themselves to avoid vice and to attain *aretē*. But the *Timaeus* is a work that seeks to explain how the natural world came to be as it is, not to recommend ways of changing it. The program of instruction by which people might learn to avoid vice and attain *aretē* is, as the dialogue therefore explicitly states, a subject for another discussion (*tauta men oun dē tropos allos logōn* [87b8–9]). But ignorance is not, even in the *Timaeus,* an exculpatory condition.

Turning to the Athenian's distinction between ignorance, on the one hand, and pleasure and *thumos,* on the other, we must inquire into its motive. Does the Athenian mean to designate pleasure and *thumos* as sources of injustice but ignorance as a source of mere *blabē*? It seems unlikely. All three are sources of *hamartēmata* and none of them is benign.[34] Indeed, the way in which the Athenian characterizes ignorance makes at least one of its three forms particularly egregious (863c7): *megalōn kai amousōn hamartēmatōn* (great and monstrous instances of misdeeds).[35]

Furthermore, if the Athenian regards those *hamartēmata* whose source is ignorance as mere *blabai* and those whose source is pleasure or passion as in-

---

34. Cf. *Gorg.* 525d5–6, where the incurables are said to have "done misdeeds that are the greatest and most impious" (*megista kai anosiōtata hamartēmata hamartanousi*), an expression that is the equivalent of "committed the ultimate crimes" (*ta eschata adikēsōsi* [525c1]). See also *HMi.* 372d, where Socrates makes no distinction between those who "go wrong" (*hamartanontes*), on the one hand, and those who harm people (*blaptontes*), commit injustice (*adikountes*), lie (*pseudomenoi*), and deceive (*exapatōntes*). Moreover, all of these can be done willingly (*hekontes*). The *Hippias Minor* uses *hamartanein* to mean wrongdoing and the commission of injustice also at 375b7–c3, 375c5, d74d1–2, and 376b4–5. See chapter 1, note 22.

35. The three forms of ignorance are (1) the simple kind responsible for light faults and (2) the double kind—ignorance compounded by the false belief that one is wise—in which (2a) the ignorance is accompanied by strength and force, and (2b) the ignorance is accompanied by weakness (363c–d). Of these it is (2a) that is most serious. See 5.732a, where self-love is blamed for the supposition that our ignorance is wisdom.

justices, why is it that he (1) never affixes the term *blabai* to those misdeeds whose origin is ignorance, and (2) does not withhold punishment in those cases? The passage at 864b, where the Athenian discusses the third source of *hamartēmata,* would have been the most natural place for him to say that those *hamartēmata* whose source is ignorance are mere *blabai*. Yet, he says no such thing. And the most natural place for the Athenian to say that *hamartēmata* done in ignorance are not *adikēmata* but *blabai* that call for not punishment but compensation would have been at 864b–c, where he identifies five kinds of *hamartēmata,* the first two of which are attributable to pleasure and *thumos* and the last three to ignorance. Yet, again, he says no such thing. What he says instead is that two kinds of laws will be applied to *all five* kinds of *hamartēmata,* differentiating between those committed violently but openly, on the one hand, and those committed deviously and secretively, on the other (864c).

We may then confidently suppose that the Athenian's reason for setting ignorance apart from passion and pleasure is surely not that he regards the latter, but not the former, as sources of injustice.[36] His aim is a more modest one, namely, to explain to his audience in advance why ignorance will be excluded from the list he is about to present of things that tyrannize the soul. He makes the point at 863d that pleasure and *thumos* are distinct from ignorance in that in comparison with the former a person can be said to be "stronger" or "weaker," but not in comparison with the latter. Pleasure and *thumos* are forces. They are aggressive, combative, even violent (863b).[37] Ignorance, by contrast, is a kind of impotence. It cannot, therefore, be said to tyrannize the soul in the way that *thumos,* fear, pleasure, pain, jealousies, and desire do. That ignorance is not a force that overcomes one, however, hardly means that it cannot lead one to do wrong: ignorance, the Athenian assures us, no less than pleasure and passion, leads its victims in a direction opposite to their *boulēsis,*

36. The *Timaeus* does not distinguish between crimes whose source is passion and pleasure and those whose source is ignorance, finding the former but not the latter blameworthy. Nor does it call the former injustice and the latter *blabai*. On the contrary, the *Timaeus* attributes all injustice to ignorance and madness.

37. I see no reason to emend the text here to eliminate the violence of pleasure's trickery, as do A. E. Taylor (1934, 252, n1), England (1921), and, following England, Bury (1926). What the Athenian wishes to contrast is not the violence of *thumos* with the persuasion of *hēdonē,* but the uncalculating and open physical violence of *thumos* with the clever, calculating, secretive verbal force of persuasion. Coercion and persuasion do not in Plato always stand in opposition to one another. See, e.g., *Ap.* 35d2–3: "if I should persuade (*peithoimi*) and force (*biazoimēn*) you by begging."

to what they want. As a genuine cause of injustice, ignorance will need to be dealt with by law. Yet, since it cannot be said to tyrannize, it must be considered separately from the tyrannical causes: it is in fact taken up, just a bit later, at 864b6–7. Indeed, as we have just seen, the discussion of the third source of injustice concludes with the Athenian's stipulation that for all five classes of *hamartēmata*—those done from passion, those done from pleasure, and the three subclasses of those done from ignorance—the laws will adjust the level of harshness in their response in accordance with whether the acts are committed violently, deceitfully, or both. The laws' response to ignorant acts is, then, no different from their response to acts driven by pleasure or passion.

The passage in which the third souce of *hamartēmata* is finally discussed, 864b6–c2, is unfortunately most obscure. The text nevertheless leaves no doubt that this passage means to review the third source of *hamartēmata*, namely, ignorance (*agnoia*): (1) the *triton* (third) at 864b7 unmistakably echoes the *triton* at 863c1; (2) the division of the third form of *hamartēma* into three at 864b8–c1 recalls the earlier division of *agnoia*, first into simple and double ignorance and then the double ignorance into a more and a less egregious form at 863c–d; and (3) our passage is introduced at 864b1–2 with both a reminder that the three forms of *hamartēmata* have already been made clear (*dedēlōtai*)—thus preparing us for a repetition of what was said earlier—*and* an insistence that the first order of business is to bring them back to mind even more (*mallon*): now that *thumos* and fear (864b3) were enumerated as the first form (thereby recalling the earlier discussion of *thumos* at 863b2–4), and pleasure and desires (864b6) as the second (thereby recalling the earlier discussion of *hēdonē* at 863b6–9), what can the "third and distinct" (864b7) form of *hamartēmata* recall but the ignorance, *agnoia,* of 863c–d? (This third kind is "distinct," of course, in that, as we have seen, it does not tyrannize the soul.)

Yet despite the certainty that the passage 864b6–c2 recapitulates the third source of *hamartēmata* identified at 863c–d, namely, ignorance, it assigns neither the term *agnoia* nor even the term *amathia* to what it identifies as the third "form" of *hamartēma*. Instead, the manuscripts have: *elpidōn de kai doxēs tēs alēthous peri to ariston ephesis* (expectations and the striving for true opinion concerning what is best). On neither interpretation of the earlier passage just discussed (863a5–864a8) should the third source of *hamartēmata* be anything but ignorance. For if the Athenian defines justice (as I have argued he does) as having a well-ordered soul obedient to a belief that is *not* mistaken about what is best, one would expect the third source of *hamartēmata* to be not the striving for true opinion about what is best but the absence of true opinion or the presence of false opinion about what is best. But even if the Athenian thinks that justice is having a well-ordered soul obedient to any opinion, mistaken or not, about what is best, is it not still odd—indeed, is it not particularly odd— for him to identify the third source of *hamartēmata* as the striving for true opinion about what is best? Would not the striving for true opinion count for him as justice rather than as a source of *hamartēmata?*

Whereas some scholars labor to maintain the integrity of the text as it is,[38] many others have resorted to emending it—some quite radically.[39] One thing, however, seems clear: the third source of *hamartēmata* must turn out to be ignorance. And, as long as that is so, the recapitulation and amplification of the three sources of *hamartēmata* is now complete. Injustice comes from the tyranny in the soul of either *thumos* or pleasure, both of which hinder obedience to the opinion of what is best—whether it be the city's opinion or the individual's own opinion—or, alternatively, from ignorance, and especially from the kind of ignorance that convinces people that they are already wise and thus keeps them from seeking the truth about what is best.[40] Justice may be contrasted with injustice in all its forms: it consists in conforming one's conduct to the settled and seasoned opinion of a well-governed polis or a well-ordered soul.

The lesson of our passage 863e–864a is that when the soul is properly ordered and governed by an opinion regarding what is best, everything that it does is just and best for the whole of human life—even though most men characterize such things as involuntary injustice when injury (*blabē*) results. What the many see as involuntary injustice, the Athenian sees not simply as no injustice at all but as positively just—indeed, as best for the whole of human life. Accidental injury done by a good and well-intentioned person would hardly merit such praise.[41] Acts that the Athenian regards as just and best are

38. See O'Brien 1957, 87, n15; Saunders 1968, 433.

39. The more radical emendations are offered by Ast (1814) and Ritter (1896), followed by Bury (1926). More moderate emendations are proposed by England (1921), Diès (1956), Grou (1769), and H. Jackson, cited by Bury (1926).

40. See *Lysis* 218a–b, discussed in chapter 1, note 12.

41. Note that the involuntary and accidental crimes considered beginning at 864d are not called "just" and "best."

those that, stemming from a properly governed soul obedient to the well-formed opinion of polis or self concerning what is best, are themselves right and good even if they cause injury.

Much is at stake for the Athenian in sorting out the distinctions between injustice and injury, on the one hand, and voluntariness and involuntariness, on the other. For if those distinctions are confused with one another, the legislative practices that depend on them will be similarly confused. For the many (and for Cleinias as well), if there is injury there must be punishment, the nature and severity of which should reflect whether the injury was inflicted willingly or unwillingly. The Athenian, however, would use the criterion of justice/injustice to determine whether there should be punishment at all, and would determine the nature and severity of the punishment by other factors: the curability or incurability of the criminal (862e; 12.957e) and whether the criminal resorted to violence or deception (864c). For the Athenian, the committing of injustice, even if it brings benefit, merits punishment; but justice, even if it brings harm, merits praise.

The Athenian, then, in distinguishing between injustice and injury, seeks, first, to protect unintended injury from being called unjust; second, to fashion punishments so that they are imposed only on culpable agents and so that the degree of their severity turns on the presence or absence of deception and/or violence and on the curability or incurability of the criminal; third, to decry as unjust those acts that are wrong and spring from a corrupt disposition and bad character even if they bring benefit; and fourth, to extol as just and best those acts that are right and flow from a noble disposition and character even if they cause harm.

Just Sufferings Are Not Ugly

As we saw in the section immediately above, the Athenian's distinction between injustice and injury enables him to praise most highly—as both just and best—those acts that are done rightly and from a good character but that nevertheless bring harm in their wake. And it is hardly by chance that the Athenian makes this point. For insofar as the distinction between injustice and injury makes it possible to praise harmful acts that are right and well intentioned, it also provides the warrant for regarding just punishment—even when suffered—as beautiful. If harmful acts that are done rightly and proceed from a good character are just and best, then just *punishment,* though harmful, is just and best.[42] Given that all injustice is involuntary, that is, that those who willfully commit injustice bring on themselves a state of soul that is at odds with the good one they want, it follows that punishment, insofar as it either improves their bad state or puts an end to it (862e3–4: "it is not better for them to live longer"),[43] may be said to move them closer to or at least not further away from the good state they really do want.[44] That punishment benefits criminals in this way does not mean, of course, that it comes without harm. Indeed, harm, whether physical or social, is integral to punishment. But now that the Athenian has distinguished between injury and injustice, the case can readily be made that rightful punishment—punishment that is deserved because the perpetrator willfully chose his crime out of a bad disposition and character or out of wrong opinions about what is good—is just and best for the whole of human life, despite the harm it brings. As the Athenian says at 854d5–6: "For no judicial punishment that takes place according to law aims at what is bad" (*ou gar epi kakōi dikē gignetai oudemia genomenē kata nomon*).[45] The distinction between injustice and injury makes it possible for the harm to be kept separate from the just act of punishment, thereby leaving the latter all beautiful. Like the just person at 859d who is perfectly beautiful (*pankalos*) despite having an ugly body, so is just punishment perfectly beautiful despite the resultant harm to the criminal.[46] Insofar as there is no admixture of injustice in rightful punishment—it is fully just and only incorrectly

42. It also follows, of course, that dispensing justice as a favor, that is, acquitting someone ("benefiting someone") who is guilty, is unjust and bad for the whole of the criminal's life. See *Ap.* 35c. See also *Laws* 2.659a6–b2: "Nor, again, should lack of manliness and cowardice make him contradict what he knows, and pronounce a soft-spirited judgment, lying through the very same lips that just finished swearing an oath to gods" (trans. Pangle 1980).

43. See 12.957e, where death is a "cure" (*iama*) for those whose opinions are not otherwise curable but are fixed by fate.

44. Indeed, unless all injustice were involuntary, it could not be assumed that all punishment is beneficial or at least not harmful. The supposition that the wrongdoer himself could not want badness in his soul (see 5.731c–d) is what makes punishment—certainly when it cures the criminal of his *adikia* (862c, 12.957d–e)—something beneficial to him.

45. See also 5.730d: "Yet the great man in the city, the man who is to be proclaimed perfect and the bearer of victory in virtue, is the one who does what he can to assist the magistrates in inflicting punishment (*sunkolazōn*)."

46. Saunders (1968) misunderstands the Athenian's point at 859d–e insofar as he takes the Athenian to mean that just as a person may be beautiful in one respect and ugly in another, so can just punishment be beautiful in one respect, namely, from the moral perspective, and ugly in another, namely, from the perspective of the pain suffered. But what the Athenian in fact means is that in the same way that just people are, qua just, utterly beautiful (*pankaloi*), and the ugliness

thought of as unwillingly unjust—there is *no* element of ugliness in it.[47] Whether inflicted or suffered, just punishment is beautiful. The harm it brings can no more detract from the beauty of the just act than an ugly body can detract from the beauty of a just person.

Punishment

The notion that all injustice is involuntary in no way removes culpability or equalizes crimes—nor was it ever intended to do so. It is not because injustice is caused by uncontrolled passion or by false beliefs about what ultimately matters that it is called "involuntary";[48] crimes for which these are the causes are completely voluntary: they are deliberate and intentional. People can and should control their passions and expel their false beliefs, and if they fail to do so it is because they are not prepared to expend the requisite effort. At 5.727b and 5.731d the Athenian rails against those who excuse themselves and blame others when they fail to do as they ought, and identifies excessive self-love as the cause of wrongdoing (5.731e). At 5.728a–b it is said that a person must be willing "to use every means" to avoid what is *aischron* and *kakon* and "to use all his powers" in the practice of what is *agathon* and *kalon*. And at 5.728c–d (cf. 10.904c) the soul is said to be supremely suited for the avoidance of evil and the pursuit of what is best. Indeed, at 854a–b, he who is moved by a bad desire (*epithumia kakē* [854a6]) to engage in temple robbery is admonished to "guard against it" (*eulabeisthai* [854b5]) with all his strength.

Plato scholars too often succumb to the misapprehension that Plato ex-

---

of their bodies threatens not in the least their complete beauty, so acts that are just are perfectly beautiful, and this is so even when they cause pain.

47. See 5.728, where it is said that the *timōria* that one suffers (*pathos* [728c2]) by way of associating with and becoming like bad men while avoiding the company of good men cannot be considered a judicial punishment (*dikē*) because everything that is just—including punishment—is beautiful (*kalon gar to ge dikaion kai hē dikē* [5.728c2–3]). *Timōria* in Plato refers sometimes to the official punishment bestowed by a judge or judges (see, e.g., *Gorg.* 525b1–3), but not always (see, e.g., the *timōria* at *Ap.* 39c4, which denotes the unwelcome consequences that await those who condemned Socrates to death: "those who will refute you will be much harsher" than Socrates was [39d2]).

48. Some, like Görgemanns (1960), think crimes caused by *thumos* or pleasure are punishable because voluntary, but that crimes caused by ignorance are not subject to punishment because not voluntary. Moreover, ignorance, he thinks, leaves "unsullied" the character of the man who commits injustice. In the *Laws,* however, ignorance, no less than *thumos* or pleasure, needs to be combated and reversed.

cuses wrongdoers. Saunders (1968, 434), for example, thinks that, according to Plato, the wrongdoer, "because of the tyranny of the emotions etc. in his soul," emotions by which "he is unwillingly dominated," acts against his better judgment in going wrong; his unjust state is involuntary and he carries, therefore, no "individual responsibility." Consider also Bury 1926, 227: "as the slave of un-reason, the unjust man is never a free agent"; or Pangle 1980, 455: "Plato's Athenian—like his Socrates—contends that crime is due to ignorance rather than willful choice. . . . The unjust man is not responsible. . . . In questioning the moral responsibility of most men, philosophy threatens to subvert not only penal law but virtue and human dignity itself"; or Strauss 1975, 130–31: "This conclusion [that all crimes (unjust acts) are committed involuntarily] seems to be destructive of all penal law, which must attach greater penalties to voluntary than to involuntary crimes, not to say that involuntary crimes are not crimes at all."[49] Mackenzie (1981, 214) puts the point as follows: "those who pursue this evil do so involuntarily and so are not to be blamed, but pitied, since they are actually involved in the greatest misfortunes despite themselves."

Much of the confusion surrounding Plato's view of punishment derives from a failure on the part of his readers to appreciate the independence of pity from pardon.[50] Whereas the Athenian surely does think that those who are dominated by their emotions—indeed, those who pursue evil for any reason—are to be pitied, for they are wretched (see 5.731c7–8: "So the unjust man, like the man who possesses bad things, is pitiable [*eleeinos*] in every way"),[51] he nevertheless stops far short of absolving them of blame.[52] He re-

---

49. Note Strauss's caution here in saying "seems to be."

50. This is true of Aristotle, who at *EN* III.i.1111a1 regards an agent who is ignorant "of particulars"—though not one who is ignorant of the universal—as deserving of pity *and* pardon. Only such a person qualifies for Aristotle as an involuntary wrongdoer, since for Aristotle an involuntary wrongdoer is one who is neither wicked nor culpable. For the Athenian (and for Socrates), by contrast, the involuntary wrongdoer is the wicked and therefore blameworthy man who is not by any means to be pardoned. He is, however, to be pitied precisely because his wickedness makes him wretched. See Weiss 1985c, 319–22.

51. See *Gorg.* 469b, where the man who kills justly is said to be unenviable, but the man who kills unjustly is said to be wretched (*athlios*) and pitiable (*eleinos*) besides.

52. See *Ap.* 39d4, where Socrates says that he reproaches (*oneidizein*) those who claim to have acquired *aretē* but have not; see also the end of the *Apology* (41e1), where Socrates says of his accusers and of the jurors who voted for his conviction that "they are worthy of blame" (*axion memphesthai*) because their intention was to harm him.

quires of all people that they honor what is noble and just (854c1–2). Those who act unjustly and immoderately are, therefore, fully blameworthy, and those who celebrate and promote injustice and immoderation—no matter how firmly they may believe what they say—are dangerous and contemptible. The kind of involuntariness that is exculpatory is the kind, for example, that attaches to the crimes of madmen (864d), who are, because of their madness, held responsible only for damages. People who are dominated by their emotions, however, are not insane.⁵³ We may note that the Athenian regards crimes that are caused by impulsive, as opposed to long-simmering, anger as being closer to involuntary than to voluntary because anger of this kind erupts suddenly and is regretted immediately.⁵⁴ So, too, crimes caused by anger that arises in response to deliberate and unwarranted provocation. But crimes that arise from the tyranny in the soul of the emotions (anger, fear, pleasure, pain, jealousies, and desires) are voluntary. People are expected to prevent such emotional tyranny and are blameworthy when they succumb to it (863e–864a). Although one needs to learn to control all sorts of anger, one is less culpable when acting on anger that is spontaneous or provoked than when acting on well-entrenched anger that tyrannizes the soul. Even deliberate, premeditated retribution concerning which one is unrepentant is not quite as "voluntary" as acts that flow from corruption that has been permitted to take root in the soul.

All that is meant in the *Laws* by the involuntariness of injustice is that when a person is intentionally unjust and acts deliberately unjustly he renders himself and his life bad—a condition that no human beings can want for themselves. What is most certainly *not* meant by the involuntariness of injustice is that no one willfully chooses to act or live unjustly. Indeed, if no one willfully chose to act or live unjustly no one at all would be considered wicked or a "bad man." Yet it is precisely people who are unjust that punishment targets, people who deserve to be punished, people, that is, who choose to do wrong deliberately, whether because they have bad characters, do not control their passions, or think they are improving their lot when they are actually sabotaging

---

53. At *Timaeus* 86, as we have seen, unjust people are considered mad and their madness is regarded quite literally—and not merely metaphorically as in the *Gorgias* and the *Republic*—as a bodily disease. If, however, even in the *Timaeus* bad men are expected to abandon their evil ways and pursue *aretē*, it follows a fortiori that bad men in the *Laws,* men whose badness is not a form of madness, must do so.

54. The Athenian speaks at 863b of the "uncalculating violence," *alogistōi biāi,* of *thumos.*

their only chance for happiness.[55] Ignorance as well as the tyranny of pleasure or passion help account for how it is that people willingly (in the ordinary sense) make choices that are antithetical to their true interests. That people are ignorant or are tyrannized by pleasure or passion hardly makes their vicious acts less deliberate, nor, for that matter, does it excuse such acts. Punishments should not be imposed for accidental wrongdoings or for wrongdoings that arise because of mistakes about facts (for example, not knowing that the white granules in the sugar bowl are poison rather than sugar). Only when crimes are willful are punishments deserved; only when punishments are deserved are they just;[56] and only when they are just are they beautiful.[57] People who do wrong accidentally or by mistake have not harmed their souls and do

55. Mackenzie (1981, 145) introduces a distinction between responsible and culpable. She believes that Socratism exculpates criminals since the state of their soul that is the cause of their wrongdoing is not their fault; but it does not free them of responsibility for wrongdoing because they do wrong deliberately. As far as I can tell, there are no grounds in Plato for this distinction, nor are there grounds for the view that Socratism exculpates wrongdoing.

56. Platonic punishment, contrary to what is widely believed, is reserved for unjust action; it is not levied for the mere possession of an unjust soul. Even though punishment aims to benefit the criminal, it is the appropriate response only to vicious action. It is the "paying of the just penalty," that is, of what is deserved, for the commission of injustice. (See *Gorg.* 476a7–8: "Do you then call paying the just penalty [*to didonai dikēn*] and being justly punished for wrongdoing [*to kolazesthai dikaiōs adikounta*] the same thing?") Thus, when the Athenian speaks of incurables who are to be punished for the sake of others since they themselves are beyond help, there is no reason to think that he does not regard their punishment as first and foremost deserved. This is probably true of Socrates' myth in the *Gorgias* as well, where the incurables in Hades who are made to suffer in order to set an example for others are said to have "committed the ultimate crimes" (*ta eschata adikēsōsi* [525c1]). Indeed, the incurables are drawn for the most part from the ranks of tyrants, kings, potentates, and politicians who are said to be guilty of having "done wrong things that are the greatest and most impious" (*megista kai anosiōtata hamartēmata hamartanousi* [525d5–6]). The *Gorgias* makes it quite clear that punishment, though it counts among its purposes that the person punished serve as an example for others, must in the first instance be levied rightly (*orthōs* [525b1]), that is, justly. The sufferings to which souls are subjected are always to be "fitting" (*prosēkonta* [*Gorg.* 525a7, 536c1]). Plato provides ways other than punishment to help those who have unjust souls but have as yet committed no crime: reproach, refutation, and education. (In the case of incurables, the lex talionis principle may break down, insofar as the death sentence they receive is, according to the Athenian, "the least of evils" [854e7]: "union is in no way better for soul and body than dissolution" [828d4–5]. See also *Gorg.* 512a–b.)

57. Pangle (1980, 379) contends that the *Laws* introduces "an unprecedented penal code based on the premise that no one ever voluntarily does wrong," and in this way departs from the Athenian penal code of which Socrates disapproves in the *Apology*, since that code "assumes men can do wrong voluntarily and therefore punishes rather than educates the criminal" (378). In the *Apology*, however, Socrates is not generally critical of the Athenian penal code (except in certain

206 | Chapter Seven

not need to be put in a better state. It is people who do wrong on purpose who do harm their souls and who do need, therefore, to be put in a better state.[58] Indeed, one of the things that punishment accomplishes is the taming and putting to sleep of the bestial part of us (see *Rep.* 9.591b3). Since only voluntary injuries are injustices, and all injustices are involuntary, it follows, perhaps paradoxically, that only voluntary injuries are involuntary. Moreover, since only voluntary injuries put a person's soul in an undesirable—and therefore undesired—state, only voluntary injuries require punishment.[59] That the Athenian would levy the same penalty for theft (double the amount stolen) regardless of how much was stolen and from where (857b) is perfectly consistent with his view that punishment's aim is to improve the state of the criminal's soul.[60] And that he would vary the severity of the punishment in accordance with whether the crime involved violence, deception, or both (864) is similarly consonant with this penal aim.

The Ugliness of Punishment

If, according to the Athenian, just sufferings are not *aischra*—but decidedly *pankala*—is there nothing about punishment that the Athenian does regard as ugly? After all, Book 9 begins with the Athenian voicing his concern that pun-

---

of its details such as the provision for a one-day trial for capital cases), and finds it quite reasonable for the law to punish voluntary (i.e., deliberate) *hamartēmata*. Moreover, there is no departure in the *Laws* from the approval expressed by Socrates in the *Apology* at 26a6–7 of punishment for voluntary (in the ordinary sense) wrongdoing.

58. In 10.908, those who are impious, even if just, are subject to punishment. So, aside from the commission of injustice, the only other offense that incurs punishment is impiety, the holding and disseminating of false views about the gods. The aim of punishment, with respect to the impious as with respect to the unjust, is to improve the condition of those punished: in the case of the impious, improvement takes the form of ridding them of their false beliefs about the gods.

59. See *Laws* 862d: The Athenian's cure for injustice proceeds "toward making it so that whatever injustice, great or small, someone might commit, the law will teach and compel him in every way either never again to dare *willingly* to do such a thing or to do it much less." "Such a thing" can only refer to doing injustice, large or small, *adikēsēi mega ē smikron*. Since the Athenian uses "willingly" here in its ordinary sense of "deliberately"—and not in its Socratic sense—he slips just this once and speaks of doing injustice *hekonta* (862d3).

60. Judicial punishment "for the most part accomplishes one of two other aims: it makes the one who receives the judicial punishment either better or less wicked" (854d–e). Also: the "task of the noblest laws" is "to bring about hatred of injustice and desire, or lack of hatred, for the nature of the just" (862d–e).

ishing is ugly "in a certain sense" (*tina tropon* [853b4, 853c3]); something, then, about this practice must disturb him. The ugliness that the Athenian detects in punishment, as he says both at the beginning of Book 9 at 853b–c and again near its end at 880e, is that there has to be any at all, that even in a regime as excellent as the one he describes, the infliction of just sufferings is unavoidable. What the educational program in his polis should ideally accomplish is the eradication of voluntary injury.[61] It should teach people to want, consciously and actively, the concrete things that will make their lives good ones, good lives being something that everyone wants. In other words, it should teach men to see and seek as their good that which is really good and not some sham good. It should inculcate a love of justice and a hatred for injustice (862d7–e1). Moreover, it should properly educate the passions so that people are able to follow what they believe is best. To this polis's great shame, however, people *will* continue to do in it, out of ignorance or weakness, the voluntary injury to others that damages their own souls. Given the fact that people will still commit even heinous crimes, the polis cannot dispense with punishments—even most terrible ones. Punishments must try to compensate for what education fails to do, namely, make the people wise enough and strong enough to refrain from doing the things that make them wretched. Although for the Athenian, these punishments, despite the harms they bring, are, when just, certainly *kala,* it remains in his eyes an utter disgrace that no polis can do without them.

61. Cf. *Rep.* 3.405a–b, where Socrates argues that it is a sign of bad education that physicians and judges are needed at all.

8

CONCLUSION: SOCRATES RECONSIDERED

By reading the Socratic paradoxes against the backdrop of the pernicious sophistic views circulating in fifth-century Athens, I have sought to offer a new and more satisfying account of them. This new account of the paradoxes, however, yields a picture of Socrates uncomfortably at odds with the picture to which most Plato scholars subscribe.

Here is Socrates on the old and familiar account. Socrates intellectualizes virtue. His maxim "virtue is knowledge" is at the core of his philosophical thinking. He sees virtue as a craft that prevents wrongdoing by those who master it. The parts of virtue are all in some way manifestations of this single craft. No one who knows what is right does wrong; no one who does wrong knows what is right. Moreover, since people can do only what they believe is in their interest, and since all who do wrong fail to see that justice is in their interest, it follows that no one who does wrong could have done otherwise: all wrongdoing is error. The "old" Socrates is a psychological and ethical egoist: he thinks that all pursue what they regard as being in their own interest—and that this is just as it should be. He is also a eudaimonist: he believes that happiness is the end at which all human choices aim. This too, he thinks, is as it should be.

Here is Socrates on the new account. Socrates does not intellectualize virtue. His maxim "virtue is knowledge" means that those who choose justice choose wisely, as do those who choose temperance. Furthermore, justice and temperance require the courage to resist temptation and to overcome fear. Wisdom, justice, temperance, and courage come together, then, in the life rightly lived. What distinguishes good people, just people, from others, this "new" Socrates believes, is not that they have mastered a particular skill or specialized branch of knowledge but that they wish to harm no one. It is these people who do not intentionally do wrong; other people, however, do. Bad people, unjust people, deliberately choose injustice, either because their passions or appetites lead them astray or because they think injustice is to their advantage. Yet the new Socrates regards neither of these grounds as exculpatory. For, he maintains, people can (and should) overcome their desires and fears and do what is good and right. And they can (and should) act even in opposition to what they believe is in their interest if what they believe is in their interest is unjust. The new Socrates is thus neither egoist nor eudaimonist: he believes neither that one must and should always seek one's own advantage nor that one must and should always aim at one's own happiness. Since he holds that those who choose injustice could have done otherwise, he considers them to be fully to blame and not subject to pardon. But although he thinks such men are not to be pardoned, he nevertheless thinks they are to be pitied. For the deliberately unjust are the wretched ones who fail to do what they want. They deprive themselves of the happiness that all people want, a happiness that comes only through justice.

What most troubles this new Socrates is the failure of the older generation to provide the younger with proper moral training. The very Socrates who believes it to be desirable, even essential, for young people—indeed for all people—to question their moral beliefs, also recognizes the danger of their doing so when their souls are disordered and undisciplined. He wonders, too, how young people can turn out well if they not only are not taught in their childhood to care about the important things but are also seduced, when they are a bit older, by sophists eager to substitute their short course in how to get ahead for whatever moral instruction young people do get. Whereas the messages children get from their parents may be mixed—parents are likely to praise justice and temperance while plainly admiring and envying the powerful and wealthy—the message they get from sophists is chillingly uniform: it encourages the unabashed pursuit of the competitive edge.[1] What Socrates is most acutely, and most painfully, aware of is that unless people's desires are redirected away from self-serving

1. As Plato portrays the sophists, what the more prudent among them say in public or to Socrates in Platonic dialogues is not what they say to the young whom they teach or hope to

pleasures and power and toward self-restraint and concern for the good of others, they will harbor false moral beliefs and will act badly. Since Socrates thinks that people, like all other animals, are best when tame, when gentle (*Gorg.* 516c; cf. *Ap.* 20a–b and *Rep.* 9.591b), he condemns the sophists who, by enflaming passions and turning intellect into passion's slave, make people worse.

Many of the protagonists in the dialogues we have explored are flawed in their characters or in their beliefs. The dialogues in which they are featured track their consequent inevitable defeat at Socrates' hand. In the *Protagoras,* Protagoras plummets from a supremely confident teacher of virtue to a reluctant and cowed peddler of the utilitarian craft of pleasure- and pain-calculation. Protagoras's tragic flaw is dishonesty born of cowardice. Wanting more than anything to be safe, he disingenuously represents the verbal skills he teaches as the kind of conventional virtue that parents, relatives, and other associates teach young people. The truth is, of course, that Protagoras entices young people away from the traditional sources of moral education available to them, and teaches them instead the skills they need to make a name for themselves on the political scene.

Gorgias's flaw is that he abdicates responsibility for the bad uses to which his students put the agonistic skill he teaches. As he sees it, the skill he teaches is a good one, even the best one, insofar as it provides the greatest benefit there is: freedom and dominance. That it is typically wielded in courts of law and in other venues in which matters of justice arise, by men who neither know about nor care about what is truly right, is not his concern. He regards himself as no more at fault than boxing or wrestling instructors whose pupils use their skills to harm their friends and relatives. Yet boxing and wrestling instructors do not teach justice or anything that resembles or could be mistaken for justice. Nor do they whisk young people away from the influence of family and friends to show them how to substitute slick speech for genuine justice and temperance. Polus and Callicles are indeed Gorgias's responsibility, for it is no accident that these two men latch on to him. They do so because of what his rhetorical *technē* promises: for Polus, the power to do whatever one pleases without paying the penalty; for Callicles, the power to avoid being a victim and to satisfy ever-growing desires.

Meno, too, is a pupil of Gorgias's. Although he regards justice, temper-

---

teach. Their message to their young clients is unequivocal: they promise them worldly success in the form of power and wealth—not the virtues of temperance and justice.

ance, and piety as virtues, he fails to see any connection between them—the so-called parts of virtue—and real virtue. For him, real virtue is the virtue of a man, a virtue that has only to do with ruling others, with "doing good to friends and harm to enemies, and taking care lest one suffer any such thing" (*Meno* 71e). Yet when just this one virtue counts as genuine, how can women, children, old men, and slaves be virtuous? In the final analysis, they cannot. As Meno sees it, the virtuous are those who aspire to, and are able to attain, the "finer" things in life—political power and gold and silver.

The well-known and well-paid sophist Hippias openly endorses the traditional conception of goodness, praising the truthful Achilles as Homer's favorite and denouncing the wily Odysseus. Yet Hippias associates with wiliness the positive traits of intelligence, prudence, ability, and wisdom, leaving nothing for the truthful, simple man but foolishness, imprudence, and impotence. Is it, however, the truthfulness and simplicity of the well-intentioned but bungling Achilles that professional teachers of virtue teach, or is it the wily cleverness of Odysseus?

The gulf that divides the virtue-as-skill that sophists teach from the ordinary virtue that all people must acquire if they are to be good and live well cannot be bridged—not by the pretensions of Protagoras to teach ordinary virtue, not by the protestations of Gorgias that his craft is in itself harmless, not by the niceties and nods to convention of Meno and Hippias. As Socrates sees it, what people need if they are to flourish is better character, better souls. He bemoans the fact that those who would profess to improve young men are more likely to screen their students for ability to pay than for prior moral cultivation. Indeed, from Socrates' perspective, what sophists do by encouraging self-promotion and self-advancement is actually undermine any chance their students might have of becoming better.

But Socrates must surely also lament that *he* can do so little to improve young men. By the time they come into contact with him it is too late—too late for him to provide essential moral nurture, too late for him to inculcate in the very young a love for justice and a distaste for injustice, respect for the temperate and disdain for the licentious, and an appreciation for the goods of the soul over and above the goods of the body. By the time Socrates talks to people their characters are already fairly well formed.[2]

---

2. This is true even of Socrates' younger interlocutors—Lysis, Charmides, and Hippocrates. As a rule, however, the younger interlocutors seem less sure of themselves, and Socrates speaks

What Socrates cannot do, then, is make people good; he cannot eradicate from them either the desire to harm others or the lack of discipline that impels them to harm themselves. Socrates is well aware that it is not only false beliefs that pose intractable obstacles to goodness; unruly appetites and passions do so as well. Those who have disordered souls do not, and perhaps cannot, find appealing that which is truly good: justice. The only thing that can appeal to such people is what is bad: the indulging of unrestrained appetite through intemperance or the amassing of power and wealth through injustice. And this is so even if they become convinced—whether by being told or through argument—that it is justice that is truly beneficial to them, for lessons learned late are largely ineffective in undoing years of improper or inadequate early moral training.[3] This is not to say that adults cannot or need not get their appetites and passions in check. They must; for there is no other path to a good life. But getting passions and appetites in check is not something that Socrates can do for people—certainly not by the time he comes to converse with them.

Since Socrates talks not to children but to younger and older men, he can do only what is second-best: wield his elenchus. It is through refutation that he examines and exhorts and reproaches and tries to persuade people to care about the right things and not about the wrong.[4] Refutation is the only way in which he can hope to change people's thinking about what the important things are and perhaps even to improve their souls. Elenchus is painful: it confers shame; it is a form of punishment. Like all just punishment, its aim is to benefit the one punished. That is why at the end of the *Apology* Socrates implores his condemners to "punish and pain" (*timōrēsasthe . . . lupountes* [*Ap.* 41e2–3]) his sons as he, Socrates, pained his condemners: Socrates regards

far more gently and less confrontationally to them. He is most forthcoming with the young Glaucon and Adeimantus since what they seek from him is a defense of justice.

3. Socrates seems to have anticipated the following point made by Aristotle (*EN* X.ix. 1179b23–29): "Argument (*logos*) and teaching (*didachē*) are not uniformly effective unless one's soul has been cultivated through proper habits (*tois ethesi*) to take pleasure in the right things and to dislike the right things. Unless one's life is not the sort that is governed by passion, force—not argument—is needed." See *Rep.* 7.518e–519b, where Socrates observes that all the virtues except prudence come by habituation and practice, and that a nature corrupted by excess pleasure will use its wisdom for evil.

4. See Weiss 2005, where I argue that the examination, exhortation, reproach, persuasion, and counsel that Socrates speaks of in the *Apology* as what he goes around doing are not distinct from his practice of *elenchein,* refutation.

such treatment as "doing *dikaia*," that is, as just treatment (42a1).[5] And, for Socrates, to be treated justly is to be benefited.

Elenctic examination does not, however, qualify as teaching. Socrates is in no position to teach. He is neither a moral expert who is within his rights to persuade or coerce people for their own good (see *Gorg.* 517b), nor a parent to his interlocutors, able to train them, as if they were his children, to desire what is right and noble and good and to despise what is wrong and ugly and bad. All he can do is show his partners in conversation that they cannot sustain their own views and therefore are not entitled to hold them or promulgate them. Through defeating them in argument he has the barest hope of affecting their character—of humbling them or even making them more gentle.[6] Elenchus is shame therapy and, like punishment and medical treatment that are similarly therapeutic, arrives on the scene only after the damage has been done. As such it is necessarily second-best to proper moral nurture and education in the formative years. Like gymnastics and good legislation, solid early moral training is prophylactic; it is the all-important ounce of prevention. But the moral training of children is not a task that falls to Socrates. He is sent by the god to fix what is broken; he is the gadfly whose task is to awaken the already too sluggish Athenian horse.

5. Note that what Socrates asks his condemners to do to his sons he asks them to do when the children grow up (*epeidan hēbēsōsi* [*Ap.* 41e2]). What Socrates does he also does only to grown-ups. Elenchus is not something to practice on children. It is what one does when it is too late to mold character in a more direct way.

6. Is this not what happens to Thrasymachus?

WORKS CITED

Adam, J., and A. M. Adam. 1905. *Platonis Protagoras.* Cambridge: Cambridge University Press.

Adkins, A. W. H. 1960. *Merit and Responsibility.* Oxford: Oxford University Press.

———. 1973. "*Aretē, techne,* Democracy and Sophists: *Protagoras* 316b–328d." *Journal of Hellenic Studies* 93:3–12.

Allen, Reginald E. 1984. *Dialogues of Plato.* Vol. I. New Haven: Yale University Press.

———. 1991. *Greek Philosophy: Thales to Aristotle.* 3d ed. New York: Free Press.

Apelt, Otto. 1912. *Platonische Aufsätze.* Leipzig: B. G. Teubner.

Ast, D. Fridericus. 1814. *Platonis Leges et Epinomis.* Leipzig: Weidmann.

Austin, J. L. 1961. "A Plea for Excuses." In *Philosophical Papers,* ed. G. J. Warnock and J. O. Urmson, 123–52. Oxford: Clarendon Press.

Benardete, Seth. 1991. *The Rhetoric of Morality and Philosophy: Plato's "Gorgias" and "Phaedrus."* Chicago: University of Chicago Press.

Benson, Hugh H. 2000. *Socratic Wisdom.* New York: Oxford University Press.

Bloom, Allan, trans. 1968. *The Republic.* New York: Basic Books.

Bluck, R. S. 1961. *Plato's "Meno."* Cambridge: Cambridge University Press.

Blundell, Mary Whitlock. 1992. "Character and Meaning in Plato's *Hippias Minor.*" *Oxford Studies in Ancient Philosophy.* Supp. vol.: 131–72.

Bobonich, Christopher. 1994. "Akrasia and Agency in Plato's *Laws* and *Republic.*" *Archiv für Geschichte der Philosophie* 76:3–36.

Brickhouse, Thomas C., and Nicholas D. Smith. 1994. *Plato's Socrates.* New York: Oxford University Press.

———. 2000. *The Philosophy of Socrates.* Boulder: Westview Press.

Brisson, Luc. 1998. *Plato the Myth Maker.* Trans. Gerard Naddaf. Chicago: University of Chicago Press.

Burnet, John. 1902. *Platonis Opera.* Vol. II. Oxford: Oxford University Press.

———. 1903. *Platonis Opera.* Vol. III. Oxford: Oxford University Press.

———. 1907. *Platonis Opera.* Vol. V. Oxford: Oxford University Press.

———. 1924. *Platonis Opera.* Vol. I. Oxford: Oxford University Press.

Bury, R. G. 1926. *Plato, Laws.* London: Loeb.

Carone, Gabriela Roxana. 2001. "*Akrasia* in the *Republic:* Does Plato Change His Mind?" *Oxford Studies in Ancient Philosophy* 20:107–48.

Cooper, John. 1984. "Plato's Theory of Human Motivation." *History of Philosophy Quarterly* 1: 31–49. Rpt. Cooper. 1999. *Reason and Emotion.* Princeton: Princeton University Press, chap. 4, 118–37. Rpt. Ellen Wagner, ed. 2001. *Plato's Psychology.* Lanham, Md.: Lexington Books, chap. 4, 91–114.

Cornford, Francis MacDonald. 1927. *Cambridge Ancient History.* Ed. J. B. Bury, S. A. Cook, and F. E. Adcock. Vol. VI, chap. 11. New York: Macmillan.

———, trans. 1945. *The Republic of Plato.* New York: Oxford University Press.

Coventry, Lucinda. 1990. "The Role of the Interlocutor in Plato's Dialogues: Theory and Practice." In *Characterization and Individuality in Greek Literature,* ed. Christopher Pelling, 174–96. Oxford: Clarendon Press.

Crombie, I. M. 1962. *An Examination of Plato's Doctrines.* Vol. I. London: Routledge and Kegan Paul.

Cushman, Robert. 1958. *Therapeia: Plato's Conception of Philosophy.* Chapel Hill: University of North Carolina Press.

Davidson, Donald. 1980. "How Is Weakness of the Will Possible?" In *Essays on Actions and Events,* ed. Donald Davidson, 21–42. Oxford: Oxford University Press.

Davis, Michael. 1988. *Ancient Tragedy and the Origins of Modern Science.* Carbondale: Southern Illinois University Press.

Devereux, Daniel T. 1995. "Socrates' Kantian Conception of Virtue." *Journal of the History of Philosophy* 33:381–408.

Diès, Auguste, Louis Gernet, and Édouard des Places, eds. 1956. *Plato, Les Lois: Livres VII–X.* Vol. 12, bk. 1, of *Oeuvres complètes,* ed. and trans. Maurice Croiset et al. Paris: Budé.

Dilman, Ilham. 1979. *Morality and the Inner Life: A Study in Plato's Gorgias.* New York: Harper and Row.

Dodds, E. R. 1959. *Plato: Gorgias.* Oxford: Clarendon Press.

Dyson, M. 1976. "Knowledge and Hedonism in Plato's *Protagoras.*" *Journal of Hellenic Studies* 96: 32–45.

England, E. B. 1921. *The Laws of Plato.* 2 vols. Manchester: University of Manchester Press.

Euben, Peter. 1990. *The Tragedy of Political Theory: The Road Not Taken.* Princeton: Princeton University Press.

Ferrari, G. R. F. 1990. "*Akrasia* as Neurosis in Plato's *Protagoras.*" *Proceedings of the Boston Area Colloquium in Ancient Philosophy* 6:115–40.

———, ed. 2000. *Plato: The Republic.* Trans. Tom Griffith. Cambridge: Cambridge University Press.

—————. 2003. *City and Soul in Plato's Republic*. Sankt Augustin: Academia Verlag.

Flew, Antony. 1973. *Crime or Disease?* London: Macmillan.

Frede, Dorothea. 1986. "The Impossiblity of Perfection: Socrates' Criticism of Simonides' Poem in the *Protagoras*." *Review of Metaphysics* 39:729–53.

Frede, Michael. 1992. "Introduction." In *Plato: Protagoras*, trans. Stanley Lombardo and Karen Bell. Indianapolis: Hackett.

Friedländer, Paul. 1964. *Plato*. Trans. H. Meyerhoff. Vol II. Princeton: Princeton University Press.

Fussi, Alessandra. 1996. "Callicles' Examples of *nomos tēs phuseōs* in Plato's *Gorgias*." *Graduate Faculty Philosophy Journal* 19:119–49.

Gallop, David. 1964. "The Socratic Paradox in the *Protagoras*." *Phronesis* 6:117–29.

Gentzler, Jyl. 1995. "The Sophistic Cross-Examination of Callicles in the *Gorgias*." *Ancient Philosophy* 15:17–43.

Goldman, Harvey S. 2004. "Reexamining the 'Examined Life' in Plato's *Apology of Socrates*." *Philosophical Forum* 35:1–34.

Gomperz, Theodor. 1905. *Greek Thinkers*. Trans. Laurie Magnus. 4 vols. London: Murray.

Goodell, T. D. 1921. "Plato's Hedonism." *American Journal of Philology* 42:25–39.

Görgemanns, H. 1960. *Beiträge zur Interpretation von Platons Nomoi*. Munich: Beck.

Gosling, J. C. B. 1973. *Plato*. London: Routledge and Kegan Paul.

Gosling, J. C. B., and C. C. W. Taylor. 1982. *The Greeks on Pleasure*. Oxford: Clarendon Press.

Gould, J. P. A. 1955. *The Development of Plato's Ethics*. Cambridge: Cambridge University Press.

Grote, George. 1875. *Plato and the Other Companions of Sokrates*. 3 vols. 3d ed. London: Murray.

Grou, Jean. 1769. *Loix de Platon*. Amsterdam: M.-M. Ray.

Grube, G. M. A. 1935. *Plato's Thought*. London: Methuen. Rpt. 1958. Boston: Beacon Press.

—————, trans. 1992. *Plato: Republic*. Revised by C. D. C. Reeve. Indianapolis: Hackett.

Gulley, Norman. 1962. "Review of Winfried Knock: *Die Strafbestimmungen in Platons Nomoi*. *Klassische-Philologische Studien* 23. Weisbaden: Harrassowitz, 1960)." *Classical Review* 12:306.

—————. 1965. "The Interpretation of 'No one does wrong willingly' in Plato's Dialogues." *Phronesis* 10:82–96.

—————. 1968. *The Philosophy of Socrates*. London: Macmillan.

—————. 1971. "Socrates' Thesis at *Protagoras* 358b–c." *Phoenix* 25:118–23.

Guthrie, W. K. C., trans. 1956. *Plato: Protagoras and Meno*. Baltimore: Penguin.

—————. 1975. *A History of Greek Philosophy*. 5 vols. Cambridge: Cambridge University Press.

Hackforth, R. 1968. "The Hedonism in Plato's *Protagoras*." *Classical Quarterly* 22:38–42.

Hall, Robert William. 1963. *Plato and the Individual*. The Hague: Martinus Nijhoff.

—————. 1971. "Techne and Morality in the *Gorgias*." In *Essays in Ancient Greek Philosophy*, ed. J. Anton and G. Kustas, 202–18. Albany: State University of New York Press.

Hamilton, Edith, and Huntington Cairns, eds. 1961. *The Collected Dialogues of Plato*. Princeton: Princeton University Press.

Heinaman, Robert. 2002. "Plato's Division of Goods in the *Republic*." *Phronesis* 47:309–35.

Hoerber, R. G. 1962. "Plato's Lesser Hippias." *Phronesis* 7:121–31.

Irwin, Terence. 1977. *Plato's Moral Theory*. Oxford: Clarendon Press.

—————, trans. 1979. *Plato: Gorgias*. Oxford: Clarendon Press.

————. 1986. "Coercion and Objectivity in Plato's Dialectic." *Revue internationale de philoso-phie* 40:49–74.

————. 1995. *Plato's Ethics.* New York: Oxford University Press.

Johnson, Curtis H. 1989. "Socrates' Encounter with Polus in Plato's *Gorgias.*" *Phoenix* 43:196–216.

Jowett, Benjamin. 1892. *The Dialogues of Plato.* 3d ed. 5 vols. Oxford: Oxford University Press.

Kahn, Charles. 1983. "Drama and Dialectic in Plato's *Gorgias.*" *Oxford Studies in Ancient Philosophy* 1:97–121.

————. 1992. "Vlastos's Socrates." *Phronesis* 37:233–58.

————. 1996. *Plato and the Socratic Dialogue.* Cambridge: Cambridge University Press.

Klein, Jacob. 1965. *A Commentary on Plato's "Meno."* Chicago: University of Chicago Press.

Klosko, George. 1986. *The Development of Plato's Political Theory.* New York: Methuen.

Kraut, Richard. 1984. *Socrates and the State.* Princeton: Princeton University Press.

————, ed. 1992. *The Cambridge Companion to Plato.* Cambridge: Cambridge University Press.

Leake, James, trans. 1987. *Lesser Hippias.* In *The Roots of Political Philosophy: Ten Forgotten Socratic Dialogues,* ed. Thomas L. Pangle, 281–306. Ithaca: Cornell University Press.

Levinson, R. B. 1940. "Moral Obligation in Platonic Ethics." *Journal of Philosophy* 37:677-78.

Mackenzie, Mary Margaret. 1981. *Plato on Punishment.* Berkeley: University of California Press.

Manuwald, B. 1975. "*Lust und Tapferkeit: Zum gedankilichen Verhaltnis zweier Abschnitte in Platon 'Protagoras.'*" *Phroneisis* 20:22–50.

McGibbon, D. 1964. "Plato's Final Definition of Justice." *Proceedings of the African Classical Association* 7:19–24.

McKim, Richard. 1988. "Shame and Truth in Plato's *Gorgias.*" In *Platonic Writings/Platonic Readings,* ed. Charles Griswold, 34–48. New York: Routledge.

McTighe, Kevin. 1984. "Socrates on Desire for the Good and the Involuntariness of Wrongdoing: *Gorgias* 466a–468e." *Phronesis* 29:193–236.

Morrison, J. S. 1942. "Meno of Tharsalus, Polycrates and Ismenias." *Classical Quarterly* 36:57–78.

Mulhern, J. J. 1968. "*Tropos* and *Polytropia* in Plato's *Hippias Minor.*" *Phoenix* 22:283–88.

Murphy, N. R. 1951. *The Interpretation of Plato's Republic.* Oxford: Oxford University Press.

Nakhnikian, G. 1973. "The First Socratic Paradox." *Journal of the History of Philosophy* 11:1–17.

Nehamas, Alexander. 1998. *The Art of Living.* Berkeley: University of California Press.

Nichols Jr., James H., trans. 1998. *Plato: Gorgias.* Ithaca: Cornell University Press.

Nietzsche, Friedrich. 1992. *Basic Writings of Nietzsche.* Trans. Walter Kaufmann. New York: Random House.

Nussbaum, Martha. 1986. *The Fragility of Goodness.* Cambridge: Cambridge University Press.

O'Brien, Michael. 1957. "Plato and 'Good Conscience': *Laws* 863E5–864B7." *Transactions of the American Philological Association* 88:81–87.

————. 1967. *The Socratic Paradoxes and the Greek Mind.* Chapel Hill: University of North Carolina Press.

Pangle, Thomas L., trans. 1980. *The Laws of Plato.* Chicago: University of Chicago Press.

Parry, Richard. 1996. *Plato's Craft of Justice.* Albany: State University of New York Press.

Penner, Terry. 1971. "Thought and Desire in Plato." In *Plato,* vol. II, ed. Gregory Vlastos, 96–118. New York: Doubleday.

————. 1973. "Socrates on Virtue and Motivation." In *Exegesis and Argument,* ed. E. N. Lee, A. P. D. Mourelatos, and R. M. Rorty, 133–51. Assen: Van Gorcum.

————. 1990. "Plato and Davidson: Parts of the Soul and Weakness of Will." In *Canadian Philosophers,* ed. David Copp. *Canadian Journal of Philosophy.* Supp. vol. 16:35–74.

————. 1991. "Desire and Power in Socrates: The Argument of *Gorgias* 466A–468E that Orators and Tyrants Have No Power in the City." *Apeiron* 24:147–202.

————. 1992. "Socrates and the Early Dialogues." In *Cambridge Companion to Plato,* ed. Richard Kraut, 121–69. Cambridge: Cambridge University Press.

————. 1997. "Socrates on the Strength of Knowledge: *Protagoras* 351B–357E." *Archiv für Geschichte der Philosophie* 79:17–49.

Penner, Terry, and C. J. Rowe. 1994. "Desire and Power in Socrates: The Argument of *Gorgias* 466A–468E that Orators and Tyrants Have No Power in the City." *Apeiron* 24:147–202.

Pohlenz, Max. 1913. *Aus Platos Werdezeit.* Berlin, Weidemann,

Randall, John Herman. 1970. *Plato: Dramatist of the Life of Reason.* New York: Columbia University Press.

Reeve, C. D. C. 1988. *Philosopher-Kings: The Argument of Plato's Republic.* Princeton: Princeton University Press.

————. 1992. "Introduction." In *Plato: Republic,* trans. G. M. A. Grube, rev. C. D. C. Reeve. Indianapolis: Hackett.

Ritter, Constantin. 1896. *Platos Gesetze: Kommentar zum griechischen Text.* Leipzig: B. G. Teubner.

————. 1933. *The Essence of Plato's Philosophy.* Trans. Adam Alles. London: George Allen and Unwin.

Rosenmeyer, T. G. 1961. "Review of Paul Rabbow, *Paidagogia.* Göttingen 1960." *Gnomon* 33: 1–6.

Rudebusch, George. 1989. "Plato, Hedonism, and Ethical Protagoreanism." In *Essays in Ancient Greek Philosophy III: Plato,* ed. John P. Anton and Anthony Preus, 27–40. Albany: State University of New York Press.

————. 1999. *Socrates, Pleasure, and Value.* New York: Oxford University Press.

Ryle, Gilbert. 1976. "Many Things Are Odd about Our *Meno.*" *Paideia* 5:1–9.

Santas, Gerasimos. 1964. "The Socratic Paradoxes." *Philosophical Review* 73:147–64.

————. 1971. "Plato's *Protagoras* and Explanations of Weakness." In *The Philosophy of Socrates,* ed. Gregory Vlastos, 264–98. Garden City, N.Y.: Doubleday.

————. 1979. *Socrates: Philosophy in Plato's Early Dialogues.* Boston: Routledge and Kegan Paul.

Saunders, Trevor. 1968. "The Socratic Paradoxes in Plato's *Laws.*" *Hermes* 96:421–34.

————. 1987. *Plato: Early Socratic Dialogues.* Harmondsworth: Penguin.

Schmid, W. T. 1985. "The Socratic Conception of Courage." *History of Philosophy Quarterly* 2:113–30.

Schmidt, H. 1874. *Beiträge zur Erklärung Platons Dialogen.* Wittenberg: R. Herrosé.

Segvic, Heda. 2000. "No One Errs Willingly: The Meaning of Socratic Intellectualism." *Oxford Studies in Ancient Philosophy* 18:1–45.

Sesonske, Alexander. 1963. "Hedonism in the *Protagoras.*" *Journal of the History of Philosophy* 1: 73–79.

Sharples, R. W., trans. 1985. *Plato: "Meno."* Wiltshire, UK: Aris and Phillips.

Shields, Christopher. 2001. "Simple Souls." In *Plato's Psychology*, ed. Ellen Wagner, 137–56. Lanham, Md.: Lexington Books.

Shorey, Paul. 1909. *"Phusis, Melete, Episteme." Transactions of the American Philological Association* 40:185–201.

———. 1928. "Review of Bury. *Plato with an English Translation. The Laws* (1926)." *Classical Philology* 23:403–5.

———. 1933. *What Plato Said.* Chicago: University of Chicago Press.

Siewert, Charles. 2001. "Plato's Division of Reason and Appetite." *History of Philosophy Quarterly* 18:329–52.

Sprague, Rosamond Kent. 1962. *Plato's Use of Fallacy.* London: Routledge.

Stallbaum, G. 1859–60. *Platonis Leges et Epinomis.* Gotha: F. Hennings.

Stalley, R. F. 1983. *An Introduction to Plato's "Laws."* Indianapolis: Hackett.

Stewart, Donald Ogden. 1922. *Perfect Behavior.* New York: George H. Doran.

Stewart, J. A. 1960. *The Myths of Plato.* Carbondale: Southern Illinois University Press.

Stocks, J. L. 1913. "The Argument of Plato, *Prot.* 351A–356C." *Classical Quarterly* 7:100–4.

Stokes, Michael. 1963. Review of Bluck, *Plato's "Meno." Archiv für Geschichte der Philosophie* 45: 292–99.

———. 1986. *Plato's Socratic Conversations.* Baltimore: Johns Hopkins University Press.

Strauss, Leo. 1975. *The Argument and the Action of Plato's "Laws."* Chicago: University of Chicago Press.

———. 1989. "The Problem of Socrates." In *The Rebirth of Classical Political Rationalism*, ed. Thomas L. Pangle. Chicago: University of Chicago Press.

Sullivan, J. P. 1961. "The Hedonism in Plato's *Protagoras." Phronesis* 6:9–28.

Taylor, A. E., trans. 1934. *The Laws of Plato.* London: J. M. Dent.

———. 1937. *Plato: The Man and His Work.* London: Methuen.

Taylor, C. C. W., trans. 1991. Rev. ed. *Plato: Protagoras.* Oxford: Clarendon Press.

Tennku, J. 1956. "The Evaluation of Pleasure in Plato's Ethics." *Acta Philosophica Fennica* 11: 23–56.

Thompson, E. Seymer, ed. 1901. *The "Meno" of Plato.* London: Macmillan.

Villa, Dana. 2001. *Socratic Citizenship.* Princeton: Princeton University Press.

Vlastos, Gregory. 1967. "Was Polus Refuted?" *American Journal of Philology* 88:454–60.

———. 1969. "Socrates on Acrasia." *Phoenix* 23:71–88.

———. 1971. *Plato.* Vol. II. New York: Doubleday.

———. 1983. "The Socratic Elenchus." *Oxford Studies in Ancient Philosophy* 1:27–58.

———. 1985a. "Happiness and Virtue in Socrates' Moral Theory." *Topoi* 4:3–32.

———. 1985b. "Socrates' Disavowal of Knowledge." *Philosophical Quarterly* 35:1–31.

———. 1988. "Socrates." *Proceedings of the British Academy* 74:89–111.

———. 1991. *Socrates: Ironist and Moral Philosopher.* Cambridge: Cambridge University Press.

Wagner, Ellen, ed. 2001. *Plato's Psychology.* Lanham, Md.: Lexington Books.

Walsh, James J. 1963. *Aristotle's Conception of Moral Weakness.* New York: Columbia University Press.

Waterfield, Robin. 1987. "Introduction to the *Hippias Minor.*" In *Early Socratic Dialogues*, ed. Trevor Saunders, 267–71. New York: Penguin Books.

Watson, Gary. 1977. "Skepticism about Weakness of Will." *Philosophical Review* 86: 316–39.

Weingartner, Rudolph. 1973. *The Unity of the Platonic Dialogue.* New York: Bobbs-Merrill.

Weiss, Roslyn. 1992a. "*Ho Agathos* as *Ho Dunatos* in Plato's *Hippias Minor.*" In *Essays on the Philosophy of Socrates,* ed. Hugh H. Benson, 242–62. New York: Oxford University Press. Rpt. 1981. *Classical Quarterly* 31: 287–304.

———. 1992b. "Killing, Confiscating, and Banishing at *Gorgias* 466–468." *Ancient Philosophy* 12 (1992): 299–315.

———. 1985a. "Socrates and Protagoras on Justice and Holiness." *Phoenix* 39: 335–41.

———. 1985b. "Courage, Confidence, and Wisdom in the *Protagoras.*" *Ancient Philosophy* 5: 11–24.

———. 1985c. "Ignorance, Involuntariness, and Innocence: A Reply to McTighe." *Phronesis* 30: 14–22.

———. 1998. *Socrates Dissatisfied: An Analysis of Plato's "Crito."* New York: Oxford University Press.

———. 2000. "When Winning Is Everything: Socratic Elenchus and Euthydemian Eristic." In *Plato: Euthydemus, Lysis, Charmides,* ed. T. M. Robinson and Luc Brisson, 68–75. Sankt Augustin: Academia Verlag.

———. 2001. *Virtue in the Cave: Moral Inquiry in Plato's "Meno."* New York: Oxford University Press.

———. 2003. "Oh, Brother!: The Fraternity of Rhetoric and Philosophy in Plato's *Gorgias.*" *Interpretation* 30: 195–206.

———. 2005. "Socrates: Seeker or Preacher?" In *The Blackwell Companion to Socrates,* ed. Sara Rappe and Rachana Kamtekar. Oxford: Blackwell.

West, Thomas G., and Grace Starry West, trans. 1984. *Four Texts on Socrates: Plato's "Euthyphro," "Apology," and "Crito" and Aristophanes' "Clouds."* Ithaca: Cornell University Press.

White, F. C. 1990. "The Good in Plato's *Gorgias.*" *Phronesis* 35: 117–27.

Wolz, H. G. 1967. "Hedonism in the *Protagoras.*" *Journal of the History of Philosophy* 1: 205–17.

Woolf, Raphael. 2002. "Consistency and Akrasia in Plato's *Protagoras.*" *Phronesis* 47: 224–52.

Zembaty, Jane. 1989. "Socrates' Perplexity in Plato's *Hippias Minor.*" In *Essays in Ancient Greek Philosophy,* ed. J. P. Anton and A. Preus, 3: 51–69. New York: State University of New York Press.

Zeyl, Donald. 1980. "Socrates on Hedonism: *Protagoras* 351b–358d." *Phronesis* 25: 25–69.

INDEX